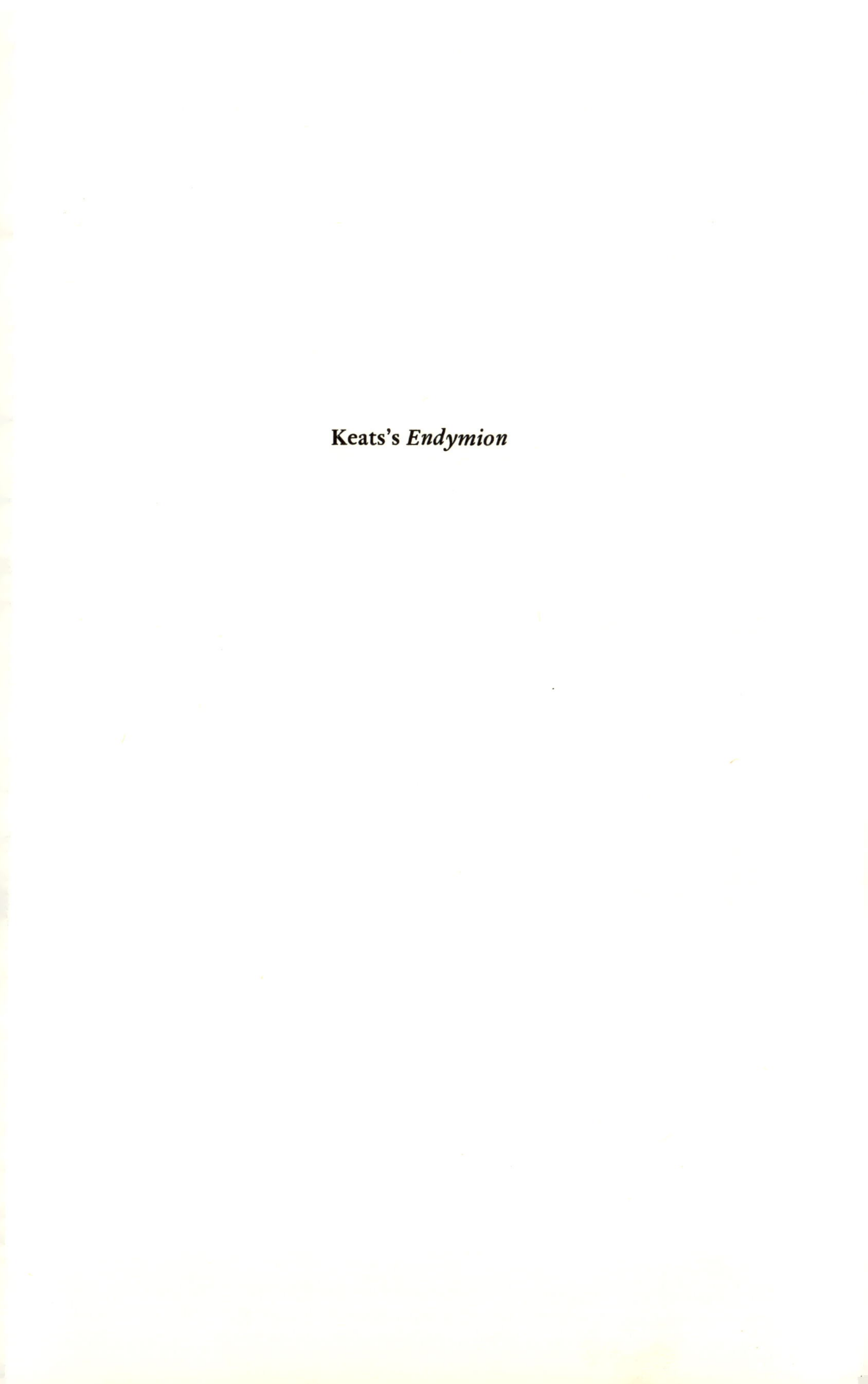

Keats's *Endymion*

Keats's *Endymion*:

A Critical Edition

edited by

Stephen T. Steinhoff

The Whitston Publishing Company
Troy, New York
1987

Library of Congress Catalog Card Number 82-50410

ISBN 0-87875-236-6

Printed in the United States of America

CONTENTS

PREFACE

Endymion may well be the least read of Keats's major poems. Nor is it difficult to see why this seemingly diffuse, mawkish and formless work has put off all but the most devoted readers. And yet as the only poem of epic intent Keats managed to complete, it is an essential text for comprehending the full extent of his poetic vision. As Harold Bloom remarks, it "exposes the complete anatomy of a great mythical structure and is our fullest revelation of the reach and power of Keats's poetic mind."[1] Since no editor to date has attempted to articulate that anatomy, I have here provided a cross-section of the major criticism on *Endymion,* with particular emphasis on readings that clarify its mythical structure. I have also included the more traditional type of annotation, aiming to place the poem in the context of its literary relatives and the body of Keats's work. For this I am indebted to previous annotated editions, especially Ernest de Selincourt's *The Poems of John Keats,* Douglas Bush's *Selected Poems and Letters of John Keats,* and Miriam Allott's *The Poems of John Keats.*[2]

I wish to thank Professor Jack Stillinger for permission to use his definitive text of *Endymion.*[3] Readers interested in the textual variants—which I have cited only when an important critical point is at issue—are referred to his excellent textual edition for authoritative discussions. I would also like to acknowledge a debt of gratitude to Professors John E. Grant and Oliver Steele of the University of Iowa, without whose advice and encouragement this edition would not have been completed. Needless to say, whatever inspiration they provided, the errors in taste and judgment I must acknowledge as my own.

ABBREVIATIONS

Abbreviations in both the Introduction and the notes are minimal. The most important form used in the notes is the superscript to indicate multiple works by a given author—a method adopted by Carey and Fowler in their edition of Milton. Page references are omitted when unnecessary, as in dictionaries or in the textual notes of previous Keats editions. The bibliography at the end of this edition provides complete bibliographical information for all references cited.

D	draft (Woodhouse's record of the now lost draft text of Books II-IV)
FC	The extant holograph fair copy
F.Q.	Spenser's *The Fairie Queene*
Letters	Hyder Rollins, ed., *The Letters of John Keats* (Cambridge, 1958), 2 vols.
Met.	Ovid's *Metamorphoses*
P.L.	Milton's *Paradise Lost*

INTRODUCTION

Biographical Background

Keats began *Endymion* in April, 1817. He had wanted to write a metrical romance for some time, and with the publication of Hunt's *The Story of Rimini* in 1816 came an irrepressible desire for emulation. Keats's deep interest in the relation between sleep and poetry naturally led him to the fable of Endymion, which he had toyed with in *I Stood Tip-toe.* Though barren of circumstance, this story of a dreamy, indolent youth beloved of Phoebe, who sleeps (or dies) into immortal life, could provide Keats with an ideal vehicle for a personal allegory.[4] Now "with Child of glorious great intent," he was ready, or at least determined, to spin a long romance out of it:

> . . . it will be a test, a trial of my Powers of Imagination and chiefly of my invention which is a rare thing indeed—by which I must make 4000 Lines of one bare circumstance and fill them with Poetry; and when I consider that this is a great task, and that when done it will take me but a dozen paces towards the Temple of Fame—it makes me say—God forbid that I should be without such a task. I have heard Hunt say and may be asked—why endeavour after a long Poem? To which I should answer—Do not the Lovers of Poetry like to have a little Region to wander in where they may pick and choose, and in which the images are so numerous that many are forgotten and found new in a second Reading. . . ? (*Letters* I, 169-70)

Conceived with the urgency of a vocational crisis, Keats's heroic task, then, was to be a kind of initiation rite into poethood, a search for evidence of election. It would be a "test" of his poetic powers and of the truth of his dream of poetic fame, where the test was as difficult as the dream was lofty. To make this Herculean labor even more difficult Keats added an unrealistic timetable, whereby he was to finish the poem by autumn.[5] He thus limited his writing time to nature's growing season, as though out of a hope that inspires magic he could identify his powers of "invention"—his "breathless" attempt to fill "4000 Lines" with "Poetry"—with the gradual ripening process of organic growth. Out of this paradoxical intention, somewhat akin to a mother willing her own labor, *Endymion* was born.

Anxious to get his muse moving, Keats withdrew to the Isle of Wight to begin writing. But instead of experiencing the creative outburst he had hoped for, he was overcome with a paralyzing anxiety: "From want of regular rest, I have been rather narvus—and the passage in Lear—'Do you not hear the Sea?'—has haunted me intensely" (*Letters* I, 132). Keats had hoped Shakespear would be the "good Genius" presiding over his task. Eventually he would be a "Comfort," but initially the ghost of the mighty bard appears to have appealed too dramatically to his sense of "how great a thing" poetry is. Now he was momentarily overwhelmed by Shakespeare's immense sea, separating is dream of fame from its realization, and "The Cliff of Poetry towers above me."[6] Turning to "marble with too much conceiving," with doubts about his poetic calling, and homesick for London and his brothers, Keats left the Isle after a week and returned to Margate.

But his restlessness did not subside there. In a letter to his publisher written a month after he began the poem, Keats complains of "the effects of a Mental Debauch—lowness of Spirits—anxiety to go on without the Power to do so. . . ."[7] He proceeds to blame the lack of trees at Margate for his own aridity—evidently without the trees the leaves could not come naturally. Having now gotten only "a little way in the 1st Book," he packed up after a "brief treeless affair," determined to "get some trees" at Canterbury, where the "Remembrance of Chaucer will set me forward like a Billiard-Ball." Whether or not Chaucer's natural geniality was of any help in establishing continuity, by mid-June Keats was back in Hampstead writing rapidly, and by August had finished the second book.

At this time Keats's Wordsworthian friend, Benjamin Bailey, invited him to Oxford, where there are "plenty of Trees thank God" (*Letters* I, 149). While there he divided his time reading Milton and Wordsworth, and writing, with the regularity of evensong, fifty lines a day. By now, however, he was beginning to have doubts about the poem, for he had conceived from his study of Milton an even greater romance:

> My Ideas with respect to it I assure you are very low—and I would write the subject thoroughly again, but I am tired of it and think the time would be better spent in writing a new Romance which I have in my eye for next summer . . . all the good I expect from my employment this summer is the fruit of experience which I hope to gather in my next poem. (*Letters* I, 168)

Keats returned to Hampstead in early October to begin the fourth and final book, but by the end of the month had completed only three hundred lines. Evidently the ghost of his "new Romance" was leaving him diffident about the old one. Needing a change, he left for Burford Bridge, where on November 28—the trees now barren of leaves—he finished the poem. He spent the winter hastily revising, at which time he added his "favorite Speculation," the controversial "fellowship with essence" passage. And at the end of April, 1818, *Endymion* was published.

A Survey of the Criticism

When *Endymion* appeared in April, 1818, there were eight reviews: three were favorable (written by personal friends) and three, hostile.[8] Lockhart's review in *Blackwood's* was a continuation of that journal's absurdly malicious campaign against Leigh Hunt and the "Cockney School," and so was too personal to be dangerous. But Croker's review in the Tory *Quarterly*, with its large circulation, killed off any hope of the poem's success. The faults exposed by the reviewers included indecent and affected diction or "Cockneyisms," forced and meaningless rhyme, irregular meter (reflecting an uncouth disregard of eighteenth century technical gains), and general incoherence. Some of the faults are real, but most reflect either the reviewer's neo-classic bias against, or ignorance of, the Renaissance prosody and diction Keats adopted in *Endymion*.

Keats's social and political affiliations with Hunt, moreover, practically precluded any chance of a disinterested reception of

Endymion. Politically, the poem had to suffer the broadsides of the powerful Tory *Quarterly.* But it also had to endure rough weather of a more insidious socio-sexual nature. Neo-classic taste, with its inbred gentility, obviously considered any expression of sexual or sensual emotions by the "shabby genteel" as vulgar and indecent. Its revulsion to Keats's sensuality—a reaction Matthews appropriately calls "sexual apartheid"—fostered the myth of Keats as an effeminate adolescent indulging in onanistic fantasies.[9] Unfortunately, this revulsion was not confined to highbrow reviewers. Byron responded to *Endymion* and the 1817 volume with such notorious outbursts as "Johnny Keats's p_ss a bed poetry," while later in the century Swinburne found Endymion's "liquorish endearments" "nauseous and pitiful."[10] Though granting a certain sentimental indulgence in the verse, the exaggerated nature of the responses suggests that the critics, in itching to destroy Keats's Bower of Bliss, have tapped something disquieting in themselves. But Ricks's recent analysis of the prurient element in neo-classic taste, coupled with symbolic interpretations of Keats's erotic diction, makes this kind of response to *Endymion* no longer defensible.[11]

A fault more difficult to defend is the poem's apparent lack of coherence. Arnold's criticism will serve here as a nineteenth century touchstone: "although undoubtedly there blows through it the breath of genius," he remarks, it "is yet as a whole so utterly incoherent, as not strictly to merit the name of a poem at all."[12] Its story, one had to concede, was lost in ornament, such that the nineteenth century reader from Shelley on wished Keats had torn it up into beautiful fragments. But such a reader, if he cared for anything other than regional beauties, expected a coherent story on a literal level. With the almost unique exception of Ruskin, the allegorical tradition of interpretation was dead, and besides, Keats was a poet of sensations, not reflections. It was not until Frances Owen's study in 1880 that critics began to view *Endymion* as a sustained allegory.[13] The allegorical approach did not solve all the poem's structural problems, but it was, despite its theoretical rigidity, a necessary counterweight to the touchstone or "beautiful fragment" approach of the tradition of taste.

A number of influential allegorical interpretations followed in the wake of Owen's pioneer work, dominating Keats criticism over the first half of the twentieth century. Colvin's remarkable critical biography, de Selincourt's edition of the poetry, critical works by Bridges, Murray, and Thorpe, and Finney's explicitly Neoplatonic source study are the most notable.[14] Although differing in terminology and emphasis—Colvin, for instance, believes the poem is less an "obvious and deliberately thought out allegory" than a "passionately tentative parable," and Bridges prefers to call it "legend" rather than "allegory"—all agree that Endymion is the poet or human soul in quest of ideal beauty (Cynthia) attained through an understanding and appreciation of sensuous beauty or the "Mystery" (the Indian Maid or Cynthia in dusky disguise).[15] With the exception of Amy Lowell, who emphatically denies any allegory in Keats, this critical tradition went virtually unquestioned until Newell Ford's rebuttal in his two essays of 1947 and monograph of 1951.[16]

In reviewing the traditional allegorical readings, Ford finds that their validity rests on the "fellowship with essence" passage in the first book of *Endymion.* He subjects this passage to detailed analysis and concludes that " 'fellowship with essence' appears to have no reference to the transcendental, and can be approximately translated as fellow-feeling or empathic fusion with a concrete, particular, mundane aesthetic object. . . ."[17] In his own reading, Ford continues to keep both feet on the ground. In emphasizing the prefigurative theme of the poem, he replaces the spatial and Platonic concepts of the allegorists with temporal, typological ones. Here he relies heavily on Keats's famous letter to Bailey of November 22, 1817, where Keats speaks of Adam's dream as prefiguring "truth," and of "happiness on earth repeated in a finer tone" hereafter (*Letters* I, 185). Ford interprets "truth" and the repetition of "happiness" as a post-mortal elysium of "everlasting eroticism," insisting that this, rather than ideal beauty, is the goal of Endymion's quest.[18]

Critics since Ford—with the exception of Pettet, who carries Ford's anti-allegorical position to the brink of anti-intellectualism —have either ignored the controversy or found a golden mean.[19] Bate, for instance, while refuting the anti-allegory arguments, believes the allegorical intention is diluted and, in fact, difficult to see at all apart from biographical considerations.[20] Hence he prefers to call the poem "allegory manque," the expression of the personal and moral urgency of Keats's youthful idealism rather than of any doctrinal Platonism. Bate, incidently, attributes a hidden difficulty in the controversy "to the growing stock reaction to the word 'allegory' since the rise of symbolism and the resurrection of Coleridge's distinction between 'allegory' and 'symbol'."[21]

Begining with Wigod's article of 1953, a new meaning is given to the "allegory" of *Endymion.*[22] Viewing the poem as a continuation of Keats's preoccupation with the nature of poetry in his earlier verse, Wigod calls it a "Romantic, hence personal allegory," an allegorical representation not of Neoplatonic essence but of Keats's own imaginative experience.[23] Following Wigod's suggestion, Allen and Sperry, in related articles, also read *Endymion* in the context of the earlier verse, where they see Keats's conflicting attitudes toward the "truth" or permanence of imaginative experience beginning to emerge.[24] In view of this, they feel Keats was attracted to the myth of Endymion not as a mere love story but as a close analogue to visionary experience, providing the means of dramatizing his fundamental conviction of "the truth of the imagination." The erotic diction that Byron thought onanistic and Swinburne "nauseous and pitiful" becomes infused in their readings with allegorical significance, expressing "not so much the physical passion of real lovers as the communion of the poet with the vital springs of his imaginative life."[25]

Dickstein, in a long chapter on *Endymion,* also views the poem as a "personal allegory," where the erotic element becomes largely an extended metaphor for imaginative transcendence.[26] Yet, while he links the poem with the "infant bowers" of the earlier verse, he also sees its affinities with the "double ironic perspective" of the mature Keats—a perspective that "asserts the claims of the imagination and at the same time registers skepticism about those claims."[27] *Endymion* for him, then, is situated in the tumultuous "space of life between" two poles of health and stability (childhood and maturity, early and late verse), which Keats refers to in his Preface. But unlike many of the earlier critics, Dickstein manages here to balance psychological and allegorical interpretations. While, like Ford and Pettet, he can view the poem as an expression of Keats's adolescent erotic longings, he also sees its ability to "transmute those longings into a larger quest for" the two poles of "selfhood": a static state of self-transcendent perfection and an evolutionary state of growth and development, corresponding to Cynthia and the Indian Maid respectively.[28]

Unfortunately, Dickstein's perceptive commentary is largely confined to the first book of the poem. This is not true, however, of Walter Evert's comprehensive, if somewhat diffuse, study —one of the few serious attempts to organize the entire poem by means of its recurring mythic imagery.[29] Evert regards *Endymion* as the culmination of the "Apollonian aesthetic" that informs Keats's earlier poetry, Apollo's light or "essence" being here reflected in Endymion's love, the moon-goddess Cynthia. Evert's position differs both from Ford's and from that of the traditional allegorist in its claim "that the pursuit of love, in the poem, is intended to signify . . . the romance equivalent of the imagination's search for 'light,' in the sense it had been habitually understood in Keats's mythologized poetic."[30] In this view, "light" or "essence" is "neither the transcendental object of the allegorists nor Ford's natural or aesthetic object, but the *feeling* of transcendence engendered by the natural object, which leads us to a fellowship of our essence with its own."[31]

By shifting the emphasis from "object" to empathic response or "feeling," Evert opens the door for what Patterson, in a recent study, calls the daemonic element in *Endymion.*[32] In his view, the daemonic quest, unlike the tranquilizing, ennobling Neoplatonic quest for "essence," is an intense, emotional striving for ecstatic joy. This quest "usurps and superimposes itself upon the quest for the ideal," as Endymion repeatedly turns Cynthia into a daemonic agent rather than a representative of Neoplatonic essence.[33] Patterson believes that this accounts for the puzzling quality of the poem that has eluded allegorical and erotic interpretations alike.

Critics who still speak of Keats's Platonism now think in terms of a temperamental rather than doctrinal type. Trilling, for instance, remarks that "Keats is Platonic, but his Platonism is not doctrinal or systematic: it was by the natural impulse of his temperament that his mind moved up the ladder of love. . . . But the movement is of a special kind . . . it is his characteristic mode of thought all through his life to begin with sense and to move thence to what he calls 'abstraction,' but never to leave sense behind. Sense cannot be left behind for of itself it generates the idea and remains continuous with it."[34] And Frye, while viewing *Endymion* as a poetic cosmos of four levels, makes it clear that the levels "are not a Platonic ladder, as Platonism is generally understood. It would be inconsistent with everything we know of Keats to assume we ascend from the body into a higher world of the soul abandoning the sexual basis of Eros, a basis which is also the matrix of one's love and compassion for society."[35]

Like the line of criticism beginning with Wigod, this view of Keats's Platonism offers a means of bridging the traditional allegorical and erotic schools of interpretation. But much critical work still needs to be done if what is essential in the two schools is to interpenetrate, enabling the reader to view the poem as both a puberty rite or adolescent crisis and the story of the universal process of imaginative creation. This goal would necessitate some knowledge of romance conventions and their psychological significance, without which the critic is unlikely to free himself from a fixed and exclusive set of concepts (Neoplatonic, Freudian, Jungian, or whatever) foreign to the poem, or from the tendency to judge the poem by mimetic standards. Fortunately, some work has been done toward this end by such leading romance theorists as Northrop Frye and Harold Bloom.[36] Bringing to the poem a profound understanding of romance conventions and Romantic, particularly Blakean myth-making, they are able to avoid the confusing terminology and distracting issues that have sprung up from the critical controversy, and to organize the poem without resorting to constructs foreign to it. Although Evert had made a strong case for the poem's coherence, it is only with these critics, especially Frye, that the ghost of Arnold has been finally laid to rest. But I shall defer further discussion of Frye and Bloom until the final two sections of the Introduction, where they help compose both a literary context for, and a possible reading of, *Endymion.*

Meter and Diction

Endymion is written almost entirely in the heroic couplet. Keats rebelled with Hunt against the "rocking-horse" rhythm of the eighteenth century epigrammatic, closed couplet, finding more freedom of pause and movement in the mellifluous, open couplet of Elizabethan and Jacobean verse. According to Bate, Keats in *Endymion* broke the couplet more radically than his Jacobean model, William Browne, or, for that matter, his contemporary model, Leigh Hunt.[37] His general procedure was to reverse the neoclassic couplet structure by placing a pause at the end of the first line and running on the second without break into the next couplet. Colvin nicely describes this metrical principle as letting "sentences, prolonged and articulated as freely and naturally as in prose, wind their way in and out among the rimes, the full pause often splitting a couplet by falling at the end of the first line, and oftener still breaking up a single line in the middle or at any point of its course."[38]

A thing of beauty is a joy for ever:/
Its loveliness increases;/it will never
Pass into nothingness;/but still will keep
A bower quiet for us, and a sleep
Full of sweet dreams, and health, and quiet breathing./
Therefore, on every morrow, are we wreathing
A flowery band to bind us to the earth,/
Spite of despondence, of the inhuman dearth
Of noble natures, of the gloomy days,/
Of all the unhealthy and o'er-darkened ways
Made for our searching:/yes, in spite of all,/
Some shape of beauty moves away the pall
From our dark spirits./Such the sun, the moon,/
Trees old, and young sprouting a shady boon
For simple sheep. . . . (I.1-15)

Here and throughout *Endymion* Keats achieves the speed and variety of line necessary for a long narrative by means of varied pause and enjambment, and such forms of stress failure as pyrrhic (1-3) and elided trisyllabic (1,5,10) feet, vowel-gaping (1,7,8,10), and feminine caesure (2,3,8-11). Moreover, the medial stress failure here works by a kind of imitative harmony to express the sinking into "despondence" or "nothingness" (the lines sag under a slightly oppressive melancholy), which is counteracted ("but. . .") by a strongly accented iambic rhythm, affirming ("yes. . .") and reaffirming ("Such. . .") a more positive, hopeful movement. The result is a "breathing" (rising and falling) rhythm, expressing the dialectic of hope and despondency, joy and sorrow, central to the poem. Although this excessive use of stress failure, especially the feminine caesura in the second half-line, produces a rhythm too languid for neoclassic tastes, it helped Keats to establish a colloquial four-stress line, the pervading thythm and the native strength of English poetry which the neoclassic couplet largely abandoned:[39]

A thing of beauty is a joy for ever:
Its loveliness increases; it will never
Pass into nothingness; but still will keep. . . .

In choosing to write a romance "epic" in open couplets, Keats naturally turned to "the native strength" of Chapman's *Odyssey* and Browne's pastoral romance, *Britannia's Pastorals.* He found in Chapman's use of enjambment and varied pause (as well as vowel-gaping and trisyllabic feet) a means of increasing the narrative flow. In contrast to the epigrammatic couplet of Pope's Homer, which breaks up the narrative into a series of rhetorical antitheses, the heroic couplet of Chapman's *Odyssey* is capable of producing a cumulative rhythm or paragraph effect—what might be termed the open couplet form of the blank verse paragraph. Keats could then add variety to this cumulative rhythm by experimenting with Browne's varied use of caesura, particularly the feminine caesura in the second half-line.

Unfortunately, the free use of the couplet sometimes led to a looseness of rhyme in Chapman and to what Saintsbury calls in Browne a "flaccidity and prolixity," a "loss of strictness and clearly marked sequence in narrative and in composition generally."[40] While Keats did not always escape the laxity of his models, Saintsbury feels that he did learn the secret of writing the open couplet perfectly. This entailed using a touchstone line to break up or hold back the torrent of the poem's rhythm, "How tiptoe Night holds back her dark-grey hood" (I.831), and more importantly, using "a due astringency of strong pause or weighty word" to neutralize the looseness of the rhyme, producing, in effect, "blank verse rhymed"[41]:

> Forth from a rugged arch, in the dusk below,
> Came mother Cybele! alone—alone—
> In sombre chariot; dark foldings thrown
> About her majesty, and front death-pale,
> With turrets crown'd. Four maned lions hale
> The sluggish wheels; solemn their toothed maws,
> Their surly eyes brow-hidden, heavy paws
> Uplifted drowsily, and nervy tails
> Cowering their tawny brushes. Silent sails
> This shadowy queen athwart, and faints away
> In another gloomy arch. (II.639-49)

Keats achieves a weighty impressiveness here primarily through the strong pause of the grave sixth syllable caesura, a characteristic of the Miltonic blank verse he will use in *Hyperion.* But he does not write uniformly on this level in *Endymion,* nor, given the poem's studied lightness, would it be appropriate for him to do so. In fact, when writing in a mode unsuited for him, such as satire, Keats loses his flexible control of tone and movement, spending the poise and power here in a didacticism that jars loose the rhyme:

> There are who lord it o'er their fellow-men
> With most prevailing tinsel: who unpen
> Their baaing vanities, to browse away
> The comfortable green and juicy hay
> From human pastures; or, O torturing fact!
> Who, through an idiot blink, will see unpack'd
> Fire-branded foxes to sear up and singe
> Our gold and ripe-ear'd hopes. (III.1-8)

Thus, although it seems Keats could do anything he wanted with the open couplet, sometimes his experimental freedom or (as here) didactic intentions lead to a laxity in meter and diction. Pointing to Chapman's *Iliad* as Keats's great forerunner in this lax use of words for their rhyme's sake, Colvin thinks the habit is connected with Keats's "general disposition to treat language as though it were as free and fluid in his own day as it had been two hundred years earlier."[42] He also feels that this "disposition" to use language as if it still had an Elizabethan flexibility makes Keats somewhat

> reckless in turning verbs into nouns (a "complain," an "exclaim," etc.), and nouns into verbs (to "throe," to "passion," etc.); in using at his convenience active verbs as passive and passive verbs as active; and in not only reviving archaic participial forms ("dight," "pight," "raft," etc.), but in giving currency to participles of the class Coleridge denounced as demoralizing to the ear, and as hybirds equivocally generated of noun substantives ("emblem'd," "gordian'," etc.). . . .[43]

Keats, with an eye on Chatterton, apparently thought that archaic diction could be the basis of a more concrete and specific style. But for this he turns almost exclusively to Shakespeare and the Elizabethans. Frye speaks of Keats's desire for a concrete, "completely flexible style, a style with the dramatic versatility of Shakespeare's," and feels that "the uncertainties of taste in *Endymion,* such as the clanging rimes," are part of his "attempt to develop a style without levels which can encompass the sublime and the familiar at once."[44] Thus Keats begins to experiment with the familiar concreteness of Shakespearean idiom to anchor images of possible sublimity:

> or ye, whose precious charge
> Nibble their fill at ocean's very marge,
> Whose mellow reeds are touch'd with sounds forlorn
> By the dim echoes of old Triton's horn. (I.203-6)

Here both archaic ("marge") and familiar ("nibble") diction secures the mythic ambience to the shore of concrete particularity. Even more typical is Keat's use of Elizabethan colloquial idiom in light, familiar counterpoint to the sublime or impressive, as in the "snorting" of "Apollo's snorting four," or in the simile,

> like dying rolls
> Of abrupt thunder, when Ionain shoals
> Of dolphins bob their noses thorugh the brine. (I.309-11)

where the colloquial "bob" playfully undercuts both the fixed grandeur of the epic simile and the mythic significance of the dolphin as a vehicular transport to eternity. Such a style continually reminds divinity of its natural origins: Venus is "ooze-born" and Neptune "drips" with brine. By such means, then, Keats achieves, if not a Shakespearean flexibility, at least the relaxed tone of a story being told, avoiding the uniform hieratic style of the Miltonic sublime on the one hand and the laxity and bathos of common speech on the other.

Unfortunately, as critics have noted, Keats is not always so successful in balancing the sublime and the familiar. Having reacted with Hunt against the fixed decorum of eighteenth century diction, he has a tendency to use an idiom (often Huntian) too close to common speech.[45] Although attempting in *Endymion* to wean himself from Hunt's familiar idiom (or "cockneyisms") by drawing heavily on the Elizabethans, Keats still occasionally lapses into a Huntian chatty briskness and sentimentality of phrase:

> Here is wine,
> Alive with sparkles—never, I aver,
> Since Ariadne was a vintager. . . . (II.441-3)

> His poor temples beat
> to the very tune of love—how sweet, sweet, sweet.
> (II.764-5)

Yet not only are such lapses less common than a cursory reading of the poem might suggest, they can often be defended on the grounds of dramatic decorum.[46] The above lines, for instance, are spoken by a putti-like Cupid, whom one expects to tweet such sweet nothings.

Overall, the poetic style of *Endymion* is, like Hunt's, light and rapid. While more flexible, it is less concrete and specific than the weightier uniform style of *Hyperion* and the odes. Bate finds that in *Endymion* Keats, like Hunt, has a tendency to "use diction relatively soft in phonetic texture, often lacking in strong consonants, and frequently Latin in origin:

> Full in the middle of this pleasantness
> There stood a marble altar, with a tress
> Of flowers budded newly; and the dew
> Had taken fairy phantasies to strew. . . ."[47]

In contrast to the slow, absorbing movement of the odes, here the greater frequency of Latinity and polysyllabic words tends both to increase the speed of the line and to lighten it. Bate also notes that *Endymion* is more adjectival than the later poetry, that its adjectives are more frequently addressed to the eye, and that the fleeting y-ending adjective, replaced by the more solid past participle in the later verse, is particularly prominent.[48] Though Bate counts 163 instances of this type (29% of all the adjectives) in the first book of the poem, I can find only 83, and of these less than a third are the "bowery," "surgy," "shrilly" kind, while only one ("spangly") is coined.[49] Since Keats revised more into the poem and even returned to them late in his career in *Lamia,* it seems unfair to view them, as does Bate, merely as signs of his immaturity or lack of imaginative control. Besides, the y-ending adjective is uniquely appropriate for evoking the fragile and fleeting, crystalline beauty of Endymion's moon-lit dream-world, the threshold realm Blake calls a "little lovely Moony night." In Shakespeare's most "mature" play, Prospero conjures up a fragile masque with the conspicuous use of "dusky," "turfy," "spongy," "bosky," and the like. It seems, then, that we ought to defer judgement on the diction of the poem until matters of literary genre and convention are taken into account. Only by discovering relevant literary contexts other than Keats's "mature" verse can we arrive at an informed appraisal of *Endymion.*

Literary Contexts: Sources and Genres

Comparing the finished *Endymion* with the projected *Hyperion,* Keats says "the Hero of the written tale being mortal is led on, like Buonapart, by circumstance; whereas the Apollo in Hyperion being a fore-seeing God will shape his actions like one" (*Letters* I, 207). In *Hyperion* it is "knowledge enormous" that makes Apollo a "fore-seeing God," and in *Endymion* Keats pursues, through an immersion in sensation, the knowledge that will return as Apollo's prophetic power, realizing that without this he could never be anything more than a pastoral poet of indolent sensation led on by "circumstance." Looking back on *Endymion* when beginning *Hyperion,* Keats speaks with the confidence of newly acquired poetic power in justifying his headlong pursuit of knowledge:

> I have written independently without Judgment—I may write independently and with judgment hereafter.—The Genius of Poetry must work out its own salvation in a man: It cannot be matured by law and precept, but by sensation and watchfulness in itself—That which is creative must create itself—In Endymion, I leaped headlong into the Sea, and thereby became better acquainted with the Soundings, the quicksands, and the rocks, than if I had stayed upon the green shore, and piped a silly pipe, and took tea and comfortable advice. (*Letters* I, 374)

For the "Genius of Poetry" to work out its own salvation in Keats, it would have to create or resurrect itself out of the vast sea of the poetic past. In other words, for Keats to realize his genius, he would have to absorb the "knowledge enormous" of his major precursors, exploring "all forms and substances/ Straight homeward to their symbol-essences" (III.699-700). Although in practice Keats borrowed as much as he stole (or absorbed)—to use Eliot's distinction—he rarely borrowed without a purpose. And yet he wished to be open, even experimental, and not exclude knowledge or sensation on the basis of "law and precept": the "immortal drink" of "the mighty dead" was to be a "comfort" drunk with "full-throated ease."

Only after finishing *Endymion* does Keats seriously examine the perplexity he feels (betrayed in the change of tone and intention in the final book of the poem) in trying to recreate the poetic past in a belated age. Puzzling over the relationship of his contemporaries to the great poets of the past, Keats, in his letters, comes to see his age as one of subjective genius capable at most of a certain "circumscribed grandeur" as opposed to the "golden age" Renaissance with its impartial genius for creating vast poetic provinces. Thus Wordsworth's "self-consciousness" and "egotistical sublime" are opposed to Shakespeare's "disinterestedness" and "Negative Capability" (*Letters* I, 223-5; 386-7).[50] Wordsworth "martyrs himself to the human heart, the main region of his song" and thus sacrifices the impartial sympathy and amplitude of Shakespeare and possibly even the "true epic passions" of Milton (*Letters* I, 278-9). Yet Keats learned from the "rocks" and "quicksands" of *Endymion* that "it is easier to think what Poetry should be than to write it" (*Letters* I, 238). However much he loved the wide prospect of high romance, he was, like Wordsworth, a martyr to an age that left romance behind in "the grand march of intellect." If the enlightened age brought any compensation, it was that it humanized Milton's dark religious "superstitions" and thus enabled Wordsworth to gain an insight into the human heart "deeper than Milton's" (*Letters* I, 281-2). In short, Keats felt the Wordsworthian need to humanize romance, but feared that leaving old romance behind meant being exiled from great poetry.

Keats's problem of developing a poetic mode that satisfies his personal needs without sacrificing the fiction of romance is anticipated by Wordsworth himself. In *The Excursion* he has the Wanderer prescribe the gentle superstitions of Greek myth ("a creed outworn") as a naive cure for the despondency of the Solitary. The Solitary, Wordsworth's own isolated selfhood, is the typical post-Enlightenment poet stricken with a "meddling intellect" that reduces nature to an inanimate clod.

> Once more to distant ages of the world
> Let us revert, and place before our thoughts
> The face which rural solitude might wear
> To the unenlightened swains of pagan Greece.
> —In that fair clime, the lonely herdsman,
> On the soft grass through half a summer's day,
> With music lulled his indolent repose:
> And, in some fit of weariness, if he,
> When his own breath was silent, chanced to hear

A distant strain, far sweeter than the sounds
Which his poor skill could make, his fancy fetched,
Even from the blazing chariot of the sun,
A beardless Youth, who touched a golden lute,
And filled the illumined groves with ravishment.
(IV.847-60)

Other swains see with this kind of spiritual repetition Diana in her chase, "fleet Oreads," "Zephyrs fanning . . . their wings," and "Pan himself,/The simple shepherd's awe-inspiring God!"

What is most striking about this "pretty piece of paganism" is that it is closer to Elizabethan pastoral and Keats than to Wordsworth himself, who generally is not interested in absorbing nature into the human, picturesque mode of Greek myth. Keats, like Hazlitt, was no doubt impressed with it, *The Excursion* for him being one of the "three things to rejoice at in this Age" (*Letters* I, 203). But is this golden surmise much more than the "sounds forlorn" of an irrecoverable past—"the dim echoes of old Triton's horn" (*Endymion* I.205-6)? If so, how is it to be recreated to serve the poetic needs of the present age? For the poet of "the egotistical sublime" (the Solitary rather than the Wanderer) this would involve internalizing (and thus circumscribing) the archaic fictions of the past by looking

Into our Minds, into the Mind of Man—
My haunt, and the main region of my song.
—Beauty—a living Presence of the earth,
Surpassing the most fair ideal Forms
Which craft of delicate Spirits hath composed
From earth's materials—waits upon my steps;
Pitches her tents before me as I move,
An hourly neighbour. Paradise and groves
Elysian, Fortunate Fields—like those of old
Sought in the Atlantic Main—why should they be
A history only of departed things,
Or a mere fiction of what never was?
For the discerning intellect of Man,
When wedded to this goodly universe
In love and holy passion, shall find these
A simple produce of the common day.
(Prospectus to *The Excursion*)

Here Wordsworth offers the belated poet or Solitary the opportunity of waking into his dream like a new Adam in Paradise, but only at the cost of humanizing and naturalizing its "fair ideal Forms." In our first glimpse of a solitary and self-absorbed Endymion, he is alienated from his antique home "like one who dream'd/Of idleness in groves Elysian" (I.176-7). Paralyzed by the remoteness of his dream, he is unable, despite his sister's appeals, to root its elusive ideal form (a mere fiction?) in "the common day" (cf.IV.820). By contrast, the shepherds of his pastoral home, Keats's "unenlightened swains," are instinctively capable of "wedding this goodly universe," celebrating their sacremental union with nature by chanting in "love and holy passion" a hymn to Pan. Wordsworth, according to Frye, is "the decisive influence" in making the hymn possible, but it is less the Wordsworth of the "unenlightened swains" than the poet of the egotistical sublime with his personal yet primitive sense of "huge and mighty forms."[51] It is these "forms"—the fallen pagan gods surviving in nature as latent numinous powers—that establish the numinous ground necessary for Keats's belated recreation of the Elizabethan pastoral tradition, just as the gentle superstitions of his archaic shepherds are rooted in the numinous presence of a huge and mighty Pan. For in the grand march of the hymn, Pan evolves from the woodland deity or "shepherd's god" of Elizabethan pastoral (with a suggestion of the Christ as Good Shepherd of the Renaissance allegorical tradition) into a Wordsworthian naturalized form of these—a numinous power or "leaven" that gives "this dull and clodded earth . . . a touch ethereal—a new birth" (see I.298n.). As the "Dread opener of the mysterious doors/Leading to universal knowledge" (I.287-8), and "the unimaginable lodge/For solitary thinkings" (I.293-4), Pan comes to represent the threshold of an immortal realm, evoking, in Wordsworth's phrase, "an obscure sense of possible sublimity." At this point in the hymn, however, we are no longer hearing unenlightened swains hoping to enter the pagan or Christian fiction of Pan's "Elysium," but a Wordsworthian Keats, whose humanized elysium or "unimaginable lodge" is within the Mind of Man, into which one can pass unalarmed by the "dread voice" (*Lycidas*) of Christian "superstition."

In essence, then, Wordsworth endows Keats with a displaced or Romantic version of the Edenic myth. Unlike the traditional superstitious account, this, is, according to Frye, not a vision of "innocence forever lost under a curse, but an innocence which is present in the mind and is a potentially creative power."[52] In *Tintern Abbey,* Wordsworth speaks of this vision of innocence existing in the quiet of the mind as an awareness of Nature's "beauteous forms"—an awareness that remains in the memory as "sensations sweet," which are not only the seed of "tranquil restoration" in the poet's darker hours, but "Of aspect more sublime," the "blessed mood" that lightens the "burden of the mystery" and leads to a more intensely experienced kind of reality where the "eye made quiet" by the "deep power of joy" and harmony can "see into the life of things." Similary, in the proem to *Endymion,* "A thing of beauty" is not merely a perpetual solace or "cheering light" that "moves away the pall/ From our dark spirits," but a heightened sense of "joy" that, in keeping "A bower quiet for us," enables us to see a sublime fountain of "essences" connecting the landscape with the quiet of the sky: "An endless fountain of immortal dark/Pouring unto us from the heaven's brink."

Accompanying this aesthetic version of the Edenic myth is a Romantic version of the "fall" from innocence, which, unlike the traditional moral account, is epistemological—the "fall" into self-consciousness or man's present subject-object relation with nature. This is essentially the poet's alienation from a time of innocent or unconscious intercourse with nature, when she was "Apparelled in celestial light/The glory and the freshness of a dream" (*Intimations Ode*). Alienated by his self-consciousness from his boyhood "golden age," Endymion turns to dream as a subconscious form of intercourse with nature, finding that in "dreaming beyond self" he can experience the glory of nature's "celestial light." But, as in Wordsworth, the experience is momentary, and he repeatedly falls into a more painful self-consciousness in the "journey homeward to habitual self" (II.276). He thus seems doomed to repeat the recurring Wordsworthian crisis of the fall, the perplexity of loss in "Whither has fled the visionary gleam/Where is it now, the glory and the dream?" (see *Endymion* I.970-1n.). This recurring fall and restoration accounts for the dialectic of joy and despondency, hope and doubt, *Endymion* shares with the typical Wordsworthian lyric.

Unlike Keats's dream of nature, which is fostered (as we'll see) by the romance of Shakespeare, Spenser, and Milton, Wordsworth's, according to Hartman, "does not lead to formal Romance, but is an early, developmental step in converting the solipsistic into the sympathetic imagination. It entices the brooding soul out of itself, toward nature first, then toward humanity."[53] Although ambivalent about this Wordsworthian compromise of "ideal Forms," Keats attempts to adopt it as a natural cure for Endymion's solipsism. He entices his hero into the dark passages leading from the "Chamber of Maiden Thought" into the "burden of the Mystery" (*Letters* I, 281) in order to gain "the universal knowledge" necessary to lighten that burden. This descent, in the second and third books, teaches Endymion the tragic consequences of solipsistic alienation from man and nature. In the final book, he seeks to reconcile the Wordsworthian truth derived from his descent with the ideal beauty of his dreams, but unable to keep the burden of the Indian Maid's "still sad music" aloft, he sinks to earth and renounces his dream quest. Endymion now appears ready to accept fully the Wordsworthian compensation for lost vision in the "natural piety" and "primal sympathy" of Peona and the Indian Maid. But these moral truths still seem out of tune with his highly erotic nature. Though they are real pleasures, Endymion feels "there are higher ones I may not see,/If impiously an earthly realm I take" (IV.853-5). Hence, at the climax of the poem, Keats drops his Wordsworthian solution to the problem of solipsism and reverts to high romance. The Indian Maid becomes identified with, or transformed into, her ideal form, Phoebe, and Endymion is "ensky'd" by a "self-destroying" love or "Negative Capability" that transfigures rather than transcends his Wordsworthian rapport with man and nature. Whether or not this is an inevitable solution, Keats appears genuinely unwilling to renounce romance for Wordsworth's "common day" in "an age too late." Reluctant to relinquish even one delight, he will have his Phoebe and his Indian Maid too.

Unlike Wordsworth, whose influence is ambivalent and problematic, Shakespeare was to be a "Comfort" for Keats, a "good Genius" presiding over his task, and hence an idealized influence on *Endymion.* As his letters indicate, Keats was drinking deep of Shakespeare when he began the poem—haunted at the Isle of Wight by Edgar's sea—and continued to drink heavily (with the exception of a sober month at Oxford with Milton and Wordsworth) throughout the period of composition, so that by the time he had finished the poem he could say he understood "Shakespeare to his very depths" (*Letters* I, 239). As a result, nearly every play, many of the sonnets, and *Venus and Adonis* have gone into the making of *Endymion.* Much of the influence is, to be sure, the mere borrowing of image and idiom from Shakespeare's infinitely rich language. But much, too, has a deeper structural significance, reflecting Keats's profound understanding of the romance contours of Shakespeare's world.

Keats sought in Shakespeare's "perpetual and golden dream" an impersonal form of romance that would lend permanence or "truth" to Endymion's dreams, creating by means of Negative Capability a world of universal or archetypal significance out of the personal and solipsistic. He found this form or power in the "green world" of Shakespeare's comedies—a world, according to Frye, associated with "sleep, dream, magic, fairies, sexual desire, and a more direct contact with a physical nature unspoiled by human perversity."[54] The victory of this world over fate or reality at the comic conclusion of the play indicates for Frye "that desire and love are not merely impotent expressions of a 'pleasure principle' feebly struggling against reality, as in Freud, but mighty powers capable of subduing reality to themselves."[55] In Keats, the "green world" is the pastoral realm of the Latmians—the home from which Endymion descends into reality and to which he returns in order to subdue reality at the comic climax of the poem. As the seed-bed of desire, it can be viewed as the potentially creative power in Endymion's dreams—that which is capable of giving substance to his ardent hope in their permanence or "truth."

The Tempest and *A Midsummer Night's Dream* become for Keats inexhaustible sources of the "green world."[56] The elemental spirits and haunting airs of *The Tempest* create a magical dream-like atmosphere recreated in the "airy voices" of *Endymion.* Ariel becomes the daemonic spirit of Endymion's dreams. Negatively capable of penetrating water, air, and land (cf. I,ii,252-6), he is able to lead Endymion through Diana's sublunary elements. But since dream enchantment is too often an elusive tease, promising more than it fulfills, Ariel becomes a will-of-the-wisp or cheating fancy, enticing Endymion, who is shipwrecked on the shore of nature, deeper into the furze and briars of her labyrinthine ways (see II.277-80n.). Prospero, in turn, is the poet as magician, whose "knowledge enormous" makes him the human counterpart to the divine agents of providence or foreseeing gods in the other romances: Diana in *Pericles,* Apollo in *The Winter's Tale,* and Jove in *Cymbeline.* Such knowledge gives him the magical power to wake the dead (cf. V,i,48-9), as he frees spirit from its material prison in reality (Ariel from the pine) in order to redeem a drowned society. This becomes the basis of the miraculous "sea-change" in the third book of *Endymion,* where Glaucus and Endymion have to learn Prospero's magic, the art of releasing the "symbol-essences" in the prisons of subject and object alike, in order to resurrect a society of lovers drowned in a tempest. One aspect of this redemption or rebirth is the renewal of a "green world" of natural fertility and innocence, representing the future brave new world of the lovers, and symbolized by the "skyey masque" Prospero conjures up in honor of the approaching marriage of Miranda and Ferdinand. Keats uses the masque to create a pastoral threshold on "ocean's very marge" in the first book, as well as to recreate it, in the air, so to speak, in the masques celebrating the marriage of Glaucus and Scylla (following their rebirth from the sea) at the end of the third book and that of Endymion and Phoebe in the fourth (IV.563-611).

The sea in *The Tempest* is the "World as Elemental space," Antonio's political sovereignty over society as opposed to Prospero's magical sovereignty over the elements—a distinction Keats makes in the opening of the third book. Wishing to explore this dark reality—contained in *The Tempest*'s "dark backward and abysm of time"—Keats turned to the tragic depths of *King Lear.* In the third book, Endymion learns from Glaucus, who had "No housing from the storm and tempest mad" (III.522), that the poet's magical powers of redemption develop only through a purgatorial ripening in a sea of sorrow. But the god-like ease of the comic redemption there is not ultimately redemptive for Endymion himself, who must prove Glaucus's purgatorial knowledge on his own pulses. He begins to experience this "better way" by seeing "feelingly" the "extremes of passion, joy and grief" (*Lear* V,ii,197-8) in the Song of the Indian Maid and the Cave of Quietude of the final book. By losing his personal will or "identity" (IV.477) in the mystery of things, becoming, that is, negatively "capable of being in uncertainties, Mysteries, doubts," Endymion is able to enter a sea of "woe-hurricanes" in the Cave of Quietude. There he discovers, like Lear in prison, that all disagreeables evaporate in the intensity of a state "where anguish does not sting nor pleasure pall" (IV.526). He emerges from the Cave detached from fortune's "gilded butterflies," now able to accept fate to the extent of deferring his "self-destroying" impulses—his "breathless" attempts to transcend nature—until his imaginative powers have become "for earth too ripe": "Men must endure/Their going hence, even as their coming hither;/Ripeness is all" (*Lear* V,ii,9-11). Having put out his eyes in a Prospero-like renunciation of the "nothing" (IV.637) of dream enchantment, Endymion is left to wander in a barren dream "with the slow move of time" (IV.922), like a tragic scapegoat figure whose "kingdom [is] at its death" (IV.940). Yet out of the ashes of his renunciation and the acceptance of "heaven's will" comes the "full golden" fruit of redemption, though a redemption curiously more subdued and individualized than the comic one of Glaucus.

The verbal echoes of *Lear* in *Endymion* may be misleading, however, since tragedy has to suffer a sea-change in romance. As Frye points out, "the sinister and tragic in Keats are seen within the conventions of romance, which means that they are often seen as incomplete forms of beauty."[57] Tears of tragic sorrow become the luxurious pearls of Phoebe's saving grace. Mystery is the picture of mystery, its aesthetic equivalent. And yet the darker mood of imminent tragedy in the fourth book suggests that Keats was drifting toward Shakespeare's Song of Experience—he will soon sit down to read *Lear* once again. In fact, Keats is so absorbed in the luxury of sorrow here that he almost forgets he is writing a romance and must adhere to "the old tale" (IV.780) that "enskys" Endymion.

But romance wins out in the end, and we come much closer to the heart of *Endymion* as such in *A Midsummer Night's Dream*—a play even more important than *The Tempest* for an understanding of "desire and love" as "mighty powers" in Endymion's erotic dreams. Knight considers the play the "nearest of kin in literature to *Endymion,*" and mentions as common to both "India in close association with fairy land and fairies" (the latter being symbols of dream and sleep), "the moon as a ruling symbol," and "changeable love-loyalties."[58] Keats, perhaps with some irony, connects Endymion's dream-visions with Bottom's bottomless dream (see I.574-8n.). Bottom, the most romantic and fantastic of the mechanics, has a dream under a fairy spell, in which the Fairy Queen makes love to him, promising through her love to "purge thy mortal grossness so/That thou shalt like an airy spirit go . . ." (III,i,163-4). Bottom's oxymoronic attempt to express his "most rare vision" suggests not only the unfathomable nature of dream, but its connection

with the creative faculty as well. In fact, Bottom plans to have Quince make a ballad of it to serve as a comic epilogue to the tragedy of Pyramus and Thisbee. Unfortunately, like the comic epilogue to *Romeo and Juliet,* also prefigured in dream (V,i,5-9), it succumbs to the reality principle, its performance thus left to the imagination of the spectator.

The comic climax of *A Midsummer Night's Dream* represents the victory of its fairy "green world" over reality. This involves casting out all possessive humours or irrational laws, such as Titania's possessive refusal to relinquish to Oberon the progeny of a "mortal" Indian maid, or Egeus's refusal to hand over his daughter Helena to Lysander—a refusal enforced by the irrational Athenian law of Theseus as reality principle. Once these are cast out with the help of Cupid's potion, Oberon and Titania are reunited and the "changeable love-loyalties" of the courtly lovers (who till now have wandered in a dark labyrinth of thwarted desire) are stabilized. The contrary forces of chastity and eros are then reconciled in the marriage solemnities under the moon's "silver bow." Similary, Endymion's changing "love-loyalties" and Cynthia's chaste and erotic personae are reconciled once Cynthia relinquishes her divinity to Endymion in the mortal form of an Indian maid and overcomes an irrational sexual taboo created by her own chaste possessiveness. Their "airy" or "spiritualiz'd" marriage can then take place under Cynthia's "lucent bow" (IV.988). The comic conclusion, the fulfillment of desire in both works, is a vindication of the supreme illusion of the lover's "shaping fantasies." As Hippolyta, the best critic in the play, says, the lovers's dreams "More witnesseth than fancy's images/And grows to something of great constancy" (V,i,25-6). Hence what the lover, like the poet and the lunatic, sees is, or becomes, truth, though it be the spiritual in the sensuous, Cynthia in the Indian Maid, "Helen's beauty in a brow of Egypt."

Shakespeare's "green world" is reborn in Milton's pastoral poetry, including the Eden of *Paradise Lost,* where Adam has his prefigurative dream. This poetry naturally merges with the more erotic Shakespearean comedies in developing the dominant drama in *Endymion* of allegro and penseroso moods: joy and frustration, enchantment and disenchantment, earliness and belatedness, escape and annihilation. Endymion, like the young poet of *L'Allegro,* is enchanted by "such sights as youthful poets dream/On summer eves by haunted stream." The moods of his

dream enchantment range from the "heart-easing Mirth" (the Mirth born of Bacchus and Venus in *L'Allegro*) of the celebratory shepherds, which is distilled in the wine of happy communion Hebe pours for Endymion in Jove's Elysium (IV.437), to its parody in the "pleasing poison" of Circe's sensual and essentially solipsistic "bliss," that of Comus born of Bacchus and Circe in *Comus.* But these allegro moods prove ephemeral, repeatedly dispelled by Endymion's return to "habitual self," an habitual melancholy that forces him, in the final book, to choose an ascetic penseroso retreat from the world. The final expression of allegro and penseroso moods for Keats, however, can only be in their union at the point of greatest intensity of both, a union developed contrapuntally in the Song of the Indian Maid (IV.146-290). Here the Indian Maid's luxurious melancholy gives rise to Bacchus's joy, where Bacchus represents the wine or energy distilled from the grapes of sorrow, a more exuberant type of joy springing, like the dolphin, from the Indian Maid's Circean sea of experience. This redemptive joy harrows Melancholy and its false gods (see IV.265-7n.) in a Dionysian analogy to Christ's dispersal of the dark deities in the *Nativity Ode.*

The influence of *Paradise Lost* is less pervasive than that of the pastoral poetry, becoming prominent only late in *Endymion,* and then generally grounded in Wordsworthian post-visionary sentiment. Keats's reading of Milton and Wordsworth while working on the third book of *Endymion* may account for this belated influence. At any rate, the Glaucus of that book has attributes of both Wordsworth's Solitary figures and Milton's Satan, while the belated invocation opening the fourth book is in a Miltonic mode chastened and subdued by Wordsworthian echoes (see IV.1-29 and notes). Furthermore, the Wordsworthian Indian Maid of the fourth book evokes what Keats, in his annotations to Milton, calls "the sublime pathetic," a humanizing loss in the "mortal" or post-visionary limitations of the fallen angels: "In Demons, fallen Angels, and monsters [Keats comments] the delicacies of passion living in and from their immortality is the most softening and dissolving Nature."[59] He sees this quality, somewhat akin to Wordsworth's "still sad music of humanity," in Milton's "more mild" angels, who, by retreating to a "silent valley," are capable of transport in the midst of loss, of suspending all Hell with the harmony of their "partial" song (*P. L.* II, 546-55). Similarly, the Indian Maid, having lost the paradise of her "dear native land"—"when . . . myriads bade/Adieu to

Ganges and their pleasant fields" (IV.31-3)—expresses "delicacies of passion" in her tender love for Hyacinthus in his "green prison" (IV.66f.), out of which love comes a song capable of suspending Endymion's solipsistic hell. But her song is "partial" —a contrapuntal "roundelay" of joy and sorrow—and the transport it brings, in Endymion's attempt to regain Jove's heaven with her, is partial as well, ending in his melancholy fall through Chaos and the Cave of Quietude back to nature's "green prison" (see IV.441-3n.). No longer now the prospective Adam hoping to wake into his dream, Endymion becomes, like Milton's retrospective angels and the Indian Maid, powerless to change worlds. He is forced, then, to take consolation in what is left behind, acknowledging not only the power of heaven to bring desolation, but also the capacity of loss to humanize through "the delicacies of passion" evoked by "the still sad music" of the Indian Maid.

Keats's natural preference for the pagan luxury and pathos of Milton's "old wine" over the Christian allegory of the new holds for *Lycidas* as well as for *Paradise Lost.* Brisman, commenting on the echoes of *Lycidas* in *Endymion* (see II.505-6n.), notes that Keats translates Milton's tension between "inspiration (spiritual energy) and nature (relatively inert object of the energizing)" into a natural rhythm and continuity, suggesting "inspiration renewed as faithfully as the plants and seasons."[60] Although *Endymion,* like *Lycidas,* attempts a problematic transition from pastoral to prophetic mode, from Pan as "the shepherd's god" to Pan as "Dread opener of the mysterious doors/Leading to universal knowledge" (I.288-9), there is none of the spiritual tension of Christian high seriousness to break its pastoral continuity, no "dread voice" to shrink its Spenserian streams. Unlike Milton, Keats apparently found the Alpheus-Arethusa myth of *Lycidas* sufficient to express such a transition, to bring about yet once more the renewal of the natural cycle. He has Endymion, then, follow in sympathy (cf. II.927f.) these sexually-thwarted river-gods to "the bottom of the monstrous world," the underwater world of sexual stasis and degeneration of the third book. There, though they disappear, the myth tells of their ongoing continuity beneath the sea. Hence in a prophetic moment at the end of the book, where dead lovers are resurrected from the sea, the river-gods, now Spenser's Thames and Medway, reappear in a joyful wedding of waters (see III.994-1004), their sexual conflict ending, not in

degenerated immobility, but in a naturally regenerated stream of poetic images. With the renewed energy Endymion acquires from his descent into the sea, he is able to imitate the regenerative course of the rivers. Resolving his sexual conflict in a marriage that fulfills desire, he is "ensky'd," becoming, like Lycidas (but without the aid of Christian intervention), both a protective genius of the pastoral shore and a saint or immortal in heaven.

The primary source of *Endymion*'s natural continuity is Spenser, who is Keats's, as well as Milton's, "Original." In fact, Keats's boyhood "romping" through the magical realms of Fairie is said to have resulted in his poetic conversion. From then on "poesy" and "Spenser" became interchangeable, and Spenser's sweet-slipping style second nature. Keats in *Endymion* does not, however, merely recreate the melting harmony of Spenser's sweet-flowing style. Having a deep affinity with the picturesque and voluptuous side of Spenser, Keats recaptures more faithfully than any other "modern" poet the "gorgeous pageantry" of Spenser's antique world (see III.994-1004n.). Although he could only hope to emulate Spenser's wealth of invention, Keats has a Spenserian instinct for mythological grammar, which enables him to animate his natural landscape with the nymphs, satyrs, and other natural gods and genii of pagan myth. Here, like Spenser, Keats creates a pictorial surface by using archaic diction and by drawing attention to the archaic conventionality of his poetic material, as in the allusive echoing (often elegiac) of precursors: echoes of the poetic past (including antiquated poetic forms and rhetorical figures) sound on the shores of *Endymion* like "the dim echoes of old Triton's horn" (see I.205-6n.).

Spenser's "Fairie," which Keats associates with Shakespeare's fairy "green world," is an antique world extending backward to Eden and the Golden Age. In the Faerie perspective, idealized forms or forces of good and evil are separated out of the ordinary world. Keats, however, drops Spenser's moral allegory, so that the forces of good and evil become primarily aesthetic forms of light and dark enchantment. Hence while caves and bowers, concealing dainty nymphs, dusky enchantresses, and "glistering" gold, are sources of evil temptation in Spenser, they become rich sources of aesthetic luxury in Keats. As Frye suggests, Keats, like Spenser, closes off the quiet bowers of his romance world, referring to the latter only obliquely: either allegorically, as in the historical allegory of the satirical

inductions to the second and third books, or symbolically, as in the sexual world presided over by Venus in the second book and represented by the "satyrs" of Circe and Bacchus of the third and fourth books respectively.[61] As in *The Fairie Queene,* each book of *Endymion* tends to be organized around an epiphanic center or "temple" that is surrounded by a series of maze-happenings.[62] (I later discuss how the second and third books of *Endymion* are organized around Spenser's Garden of Adonis and Bower of Bliss respectively.) Like Spenser's fairy knights, Endymion is led through a series of labyrinthine trials or circumstances that culminate in natural epiphanies. Just as the Spenserian quest depicts the trials of the mind by horror and enchantment, Endymion's is the search for truth or finality in dream that generates enchantment at every turn. The finality of this topmost world is represented, as in Spenser, by Cynthia, though in Keats, Cynthia and her dark double (the Indian Maid or Mutabilitie) are ultimately identified rather than separated by Nature's "doome." Spenser's fairy knights are yoked in Keats's imagination with Shakespeare's fairies (especially Puck and Ariel) and at times Milton's pagan genii and even Satan to provide the "breathless" daemonic force for Endymion's "elfin journey." They represent the creative and compulsive power of romance by means of which Keats hoped to overcome the stasis of self-consciousness, the legacy of Wordsworth and a belated age.

Endymion, as Frye remarks, is "a revival not only of Spenser but of the Elizabethan Ovidian mythological poem," of which Lodge's *Glaucus and Scilla,* Shakespeare's *Venus and Adonis,* Drayton's *Endimion and Phoebe,* and Marlowe's *Hero and Leander* are examples.[63] Whatever the extent of their influence —and here generic affinity is as important an issue—three of the poems elaborate myths that are structurally significant for *Endymion.*[64] All represent, like *Endymion,* an aesthetic and pagan, rather than moral and Christian, development of Ovid. Written in a "sweet" style surfeit with "honey-words," they satisfy Keats's insatiable appetite for sweets: "every sense/Filling with spiritual sweets to plentitude/As bees gorge full their cells" (III.38-40). With the exception of Drayton, whose chaste Neoplatonic style would have appealed to Keats's youthful idealism, these poems are highly erotic—Shakespeare and Marlowe quite frankly so. Steeped in the conventions of the "love-complaint," they furnished Keats with such forms as the catalogue of anatomical parts (cf. I.612-9), as well as the fanciful amatory rhetoric necessary to break the dumb enchantment of his love-sick hero.

Like *Endymion,* the mythological poem is a youthful attempt at sustained writing (800-1200 lines) on "one bare circumstance." With little concern for strict metrical regularity or narrative economy, the poet wanders where he pleases, through lush gardens copiously planted with mythological allusions blossoming into luxurious pictorial detail. Hence it provided Keats with "a little Region to wander in," where he could test his powers of "invention" free of the inhibiting restraints of the formal French gardens of Augustan verse. Readers who do not find *Endymion* to their taste are probably objecting to features it shares with its rather wanton Elizabethan cousin, which, possessing neither a dense texture nor a high-seriousness, "simply tells the most heart-easing things."

Despite the similarities, however, *Endymion* is a more ambitious enterprise than the Elizabethan mythological poem. Both its size (four times that of the typical mythological poem) and theme (the Jobean trial by enchantment) relate it to what Milton calls the "brief" epic. According to Frye, *Endymion* is in Blakean terms "a brief epic concerned with the poet's mind as a youthful Orc in the state of Beulah."[65] What this means will hopefully become clearer as we go along. For now it need only be said that *Endymion,* viewed as a brief epic, tones down the epic grandeur of the traditional epic while limiting its theme to "one bare circumstance," however diffusely elaborated. At the same time it adopts a number of epic conventions. The poem begins in *medias res*: its chronological beginning is narrated by Endymion from Peona's bower, much as Ulysses narrates the beginning of his adventures from the garden of Alcinoos. There is a Miltonic invocation to the Muse (if somewhat belated) at the beginning of the fourth book; a descent underground in search of oracular knowledge of the future; and a climactic Apollonian epiphany, though in a minor key in keeping with the tone of the brief epic.

Two major examples of the brief epic in English literature are Milton's *Paradise Regained* and Blake's *Milton.* Despite their use of Biblical myth and their radical renunciation of the classical tradition, the two have structural similarities with *Endymion* worth pointing out. In Blake and Milton, the success of the hero's quest depends on his renouncing, in a kind of Jobean trial, Satanic charm or the Selfhood. In Blake, the feminine aspect of this charm is Rahab and Tirzah, who try to tempt Milton (Blake's poet-hero) into a false paradise; in Milton, it is the temptresses who, having sprung from the head of Satan, serve up a banquet to Christ's senses. Similarly, Endymion's success depends on his ability to renounce, explicitly in the person of Glaucus, though implicitly throughout, Circean charm. This includes the renunciation of all willful or assertive action, such as the pagan forms of heroism Keats renounces in the name of pagan eros; Milton renounces in the name of Christian agape; and Blake renounces in the name of Spiritual Warfare or "Mentat Fight." In each poem, the hero descends into the Satanic or Circean element: the sea in Keats, which Blake calls the "Sea of Time and Space," and the labyrinthine desert in Milton. Endymion descends to redeem himself and Glaucus by internalizing Circe's scroll just as Milton descends to redeem himself and Blake in *Milton* by internalizing Urizenic law. Each protagonist seeks his female emanation, all that he has come to create and love, though in Milton the only female is the mother, Christ renouncing Athene, the virgin mother of Athens, in order to return to his true virgin mother, the redeemed Eve. Blake, recreating Milton's vision, has Milton descend to redeem his emanation Ololon, who until now has remained as elusive as Endymion's dream goddess. But Ololon, because now sought within Milton, is also seeking him, and after throwing off her virginity or female will, the veil of elusive mystery, descends to him as a redeeming "Moony Ark" on the "Sea of Time and Space." He, in turn, casts off Satan, the cloak of purity and dogmatic willfulness, in an act of "Self Annihilation," and they are wed. Similarly, the moon-goddess Cynthia seeks Endymion as he seeks her. When she finally renounces her chastity (see IV.752-7n., 989-90n.), which Keats, like Blake, associates with the Lady in Comus carrying Athene's Gorgon shield, Endymion casts off the last rags of his identity, and their marriage of "self-destroying love" is consummated, a marriage prefigured by the redemption of the drowned lovers from the sea.

The climax of the three poems is quiet. Like *The Fairie Queene,* they end close to home, but with the sense of a greater vision or quest soon to follow. In Keats, this is *Hyperion;* in Blake, *Jerusalem;* and for Milton's Christ, his Messianic Mission proper, Milton himself having already completed *his* diffuse epic. In Blake's terms, the youthful Orc in Beulah has succeeded in his initial, rather personal quest of reversing the Fall or internalizing the lost innocence of Eden. He can now go about his Father's business in attempting a more mature and heightened form of imaginative consolidation in the hope of shaping his actions like "a fore-seeing God."

Frye in the *Anatomy of Criticism* calls *Endymion* the most exhaustive treatment of the second phase of romance, the innocent youth of the hero, in English literature.[66] In traditional quest romance the hero turns his back on society and rides off into a forest—the threshold symbol of a dream world—following some visionary gleam through a series of trials or adventures. Similarly, Endymion turns his back on the society of Pan and withdraws into a series of dream bowers, following his vision of Cynthia. But as Frye remarks, the fictional romance becomes internalized in the Romantic period, so that

> the thematic poet becomes what the fictional hero was in the age of romance, an extraordinary person who lives in a higher and more imaginative order of experience than nature. He creates his own world, a world which reproduces many of the characteristics of fictional romance. . . . The encyclopedic tendency of this period is toward the construction of mythological epics in which the myths represent psychological or subjective states of mind.[67]

Unlike Spenserian romance, for instance, the romance of the Romantic period involves the poet in a more direct, psychological relationship with the hero and his antagonists. In fact, the latter are merely the poet's imagination and its blocking agents respectively. Hence, while Spenser's impersonal quest for a redeemed nature produces a variety of evil adversaries, Keats's quest for his own mature powers limits his adversaries to himself or his own confusions and despairings. This accounts for the multiple mirror-image characters in *Endymion*, a certain underdetermination of language and over-determination of meaning. Keats may have wanted the romance of "the old Poets, and Robin Hood" (*Letters* I, 225), but what he created was a "personal allegory" or "internalized romance."

Bloom develops Frye's concept of "internalized romance"

into a tradition of the Solitary, which extends from the Red Crosse Knight and Colin Clout of Spenser's *The Faire Queene,* through Milton's *Il Penseroso* and the Satan of *Paradise Lost,* Wordsworth's Solitary of *The Excursion,* Coleridge's *Ancient Mariner,* and Shelley's *Alastor,* down to Yeats's *Wandering of Oisin* and Wallace Stevens's parodistic treatment of the theme in *The Comedian As The Letter C.*[68] Although consideration of the entire tradition is beyond the scope of this Introduction, it bears pursuing as a fascinating and fruitful context in which to view *Endymion.* Keats uses his precursors in this tradition not only to develop an elegiac or penseroso mood, but to help clarify the implications of solitude—the poet-hero's isolation from man and nature—for the imagination. Wordsworth and Shelley are especially important for the internalized theme of *Endymion,* since, according to Bloom, *The Excursion* and *Alastor* "both emphasize the destructiveness of an inward-turning and stagnant solitude."[69] In fact, *Endymion* can be viewed as Keats's answer to both Wordsworth's Solitary and Shelley's poet-hero, since Keats wants his hero to learn the lessons of both, and thereby escape their tragic fates.

Wordsworth's Solitary of *The Excursion* is a prisoner of the post-visionary state of death-in-life, forced to accept the killing truth of the Wanderer

> That 'tis a thing impossible to frame
> Conceptions equal to the soul's desires;
> And the most difficult of tasks to keep
> Heights which the soul is competent to gain. (IV.136-9)

Unable either to recapture his lost "heights" or to bind himself to man and nature, the Solitary lives "shut out from all the world" (II.332) in an "Urn-like" hollow in the mountains. Keats represents the Solitary in the sea-shepherd Glaucus, who lives a "cold pastoral" solitude in a spectral realm of pure subjectivity. The similarity between Glaucus's story and Endymion's own—"We are twin brothers in this destiny" (III.713)—suggests that Glaucus is the disillusioned or post-visionary result of a tendency in Endymion himself—a tendency clearly seen in the dream-visionary of the first book who views the natural and human world as a barrier to his "higher hopes" (I.691). But Keats seems determined to make Endymion into a kind of pagan Wordsworthian Wanderer, whose imagination, because bound to "primal sympathy" and "natural piety," can help to redeem Glaucus and the lovers confined in the crystal prison of solipsism. Wordsworth's Wanderer counsels knowledge of man and nature as a means of acquiring the tranquility necessary for correcting the despondency of the Solitary:

> Happy is he who lives to understand,
> Not human nature only, but explores
> All natures,—to the end that he may find
> The law that governs each. . . . (IV.332-5)

Similarly, the ashes of Glaucus's death-in-life state fertilize a new birth once Endymion (with Glaucus's aid) "explores all forms and substances/Straight homeward to their symbol-essences" (III.699-700). Although this is a more radically imaginative solution than the Wanderer's, the emphasis in both is on "universal knowledge" through sympathetic identification, what Keats calls "a widening speculation, to ease the Burden of the Mystery" (*Letters* I, 277).

Shelly, too, wants his poet-hero to avoid the fate of Wordsworth's Solitary, but he is unwilling to temper his imaginative desire with the "wisdom" of the Wanderer. His "Poet," Bloom remarks, has "too much intensity to cease his drive toward a glorious extinction."[70] Unlike Endymion, who renounces the ideal love of an elusive dream goddess for the Indian Maid, "a natural love, a human sympathy, that will yet satisfy the imagination," Shelley's Poet spurns human love (the "Arab maiden") in pursuing the creative form of his desire, the ideal love or "veiled maid" (151) of his dreams.[71] This love of his own shadow commits him to a state of isolation. Cut off from others and his own true imagination, "He eagerly pursues/Beyond the realm of dream that fleeting shade" (205-6), lost "In the wide pathless desert of dim sleep" (210). Led on "By love, or dream, or god or mightier Death" (428), he is himself pursued, like Actaeon, by the "Spirit of Solitude"—what Bloom calls "the avenging daemon . . . a baffled residue of the self, determined to be compensated for by the loss of natural assurance. . . ."[72]

Endymion in the first book has all the fragility of Shelley's dreamer, and is equally prone to the avenging daemon of "habitual self." But Keats sends him down into the roots of experience (in the opposite direction from his dream goddess) to broaden and lighten his vision through the love of nature and humanity. As Bloom remarks, Keats "does not surrender his sense of existential contraries. The reality of earth and the strength of the natural impulse toward adhering to it will both save Keats's hero and give him an ideal in a form that flesh can touch."[73] If the object of the internalized quest is, as Bloom claims, "to widen consciousness as well as intensify it," then *Alastor* achieves the intensity, but only by narrowing consciousness to an acute preoccupation with the self, while *Endymion* attempts a "widening speculation" (in counteracting solipsism), but only by adhering to the labyrinth of nature—a realm where "nothing narrows to an intensity, and ever passionate impulse widens out to a diffuseness. . . ."[74]

Endymion escapes (narrowly) the precipitant self-destruction of Shelley's Poet and the death-in-life of Wordsworth's Solitary, completing his quest by renouncing it, and thus without betraying either imaginative desire or the "natural assurance" of the self. The inevitability of such a completion, which paradoxically accepts and rejects the labyrinth of nature, is perhaps not wholly convincing. Even with the Renaissance behind him, there is little reason to believe Keats felt confident in his romance solution to the problem of solitude posed by two representative poets of his age.

The final and most elusive literary context to be considered is the earthly paradise tradition, some aspects of which I have already touched upon in Shakespeare's "green world." Here the seminal influence on *Endymion* is Spenser's Gardens of Adonis and Bower of Bliss. But, as Frye suggests, Blake's recreation of this tradition in the state he calls Beulah may serve not only as an instructive analogy, but also as a means of determining how Keats made use of Spenser:

> The student of Blake, reading Keats's *Endymion*, may see in the pattern of its symbols, the moon, love, silver, water, sleep, night, dew, "eternal spring," triple rhythms, and its drowsy, relaxed and rather feminine charm, a vision of the state of existence which Blake calls Beulah. He will be able to see how the themes of the elusive virgin, the young shepherd poet, the kingdom under the ocean, the "fabric crystalline" presided over by Circe, the escape from a watery world by exploring the "symbol-essences"

> of all forms and substances, and so on, fit together. He will be able to see the relation of the world of *Endymion* to Spenser's Gardens of Adonis and Bower of Bliss, and so understand how Keats interpreted and made use of Spenser.[75]

Blake's Beulah, like the traditional earthly paradise, is a moon-lit garden of unorganized innocence–both a pastoral playground and a seed bed of sleeping love. Here, like Adonis in the lap of Venus or Endymion in his dream bower, the imagination reposes in delicious indolence–the state of passive receptivity in which the poetic process or visionary quest begins. The imagination is in its in-fancy here and hence dependent on a nourishing body outside itself, like "the endless fountain of immortal drink" (I.23) fertilizing Keats's poetic nursery. We notice that as Venus's "stately Mount" is "in the middest" (*F.Q.* III,vi,43) of Spenser's "Fruitfull soyle of old" so Pan's altar on Mount Latmos is "Full in the middle of this pleasantness" (I.89). Pan, like Venus, is both a parental source of fertility and a protective influence closing off the garden from the "gloomy shades" of death and chaos. In a ritualistic foreshortening of time, the "completions" of "the fresh budding Year" (I.259-60) are sacrificed on Pan's green altar, creating a circle or *templum* of "continuall spring, and harvest" (*F.Q.* III,vi,42) that shuts out wintry death.[76] As Beulah represents the unconscious innocence of ritual and belief, the Latmian shepherds believe in, without fully comprehending, the paternal beneficence of Pan and the higher order of happiness or "Elysium" of "eternal spring" he represents. They are content to worship the mystery of Pan as "dread opener to the mysterious doors/Leading to universal knowledge" (I.288-9) rather than (as will be the burden of Endymion's quest) to enter those "doors." In other words, the imagination here rests in the cool light of a contemplative belief in its higher powers rather than actively realizing them.

In Blake's *The Crystal Cabinet,* Beulah is described as a "little lovely Moony Night" of mirror reflections. The reflections are the spatial illusions woven by a "threefold" maiden or moon-goddess–"threefold" implying the three dimensions of time and space as well as Blake's three states of existence within the natural cycle. Similarly, Endymion's looking-glass world is presided over by a moon-goddess or *diva triformis* of "silvery enchantment" and "crystal mocking." As the silvery moon, itself a reflection of the creative Apollonian sun, she sits in the crystalline sky above and is reflected in the "silver lakes" and "floods of crystal" below.[77] Endymion first dreams of this goddess near a "silvery" flood shaped like a "crescent moon" (I.544). and later sees her reflected in the "crystal eye" (I.871) of a well. Yet since she is a narcissistic reflection of his own melting desire, the liquid charm of a dream image, she remains elusive, coming and going, alternately virgin and wanton, like the ebb and flow of the water cycle she governs. Moreover, as a spatial and temporal mirror of a reflection and recurrence, this cycle can easily consolidate into a crystal sublunary prison—the "fabric crystalline" (III.427) in which Circe (the Hecate of the *diva triformis*) confines the lovers drowned in the "Sea of Time and Space." In Blake's terms, this is Beulah reverting to the solipsism of Ulro, exemplified in the young man in *The Crystal Cabinet,* who having failed to grasp the "inmost Form" of his crystal world of mirror reflections, is left in a state of dumb passivity, a "weeping babe" in the "wild." Thus, in *Endymion,* the Circean charm and dumb enchantment of Glaucus's "specious heaven" congeals into a "real hell" (III.476) of mute and swaddled impotence. For if the imagination sleeps too long in Beulah (as in Spenser's false paradises), it dies, and a separate spatial world or fixed Circean "female will" takes the place of the fluid enchantment of the elusive dream goddess. Wonder becomes vacuity, and the female or spatial forms that once enticed the imagination now possess and imprison it.

Like the traditional earthly paradise, the setting of the first book of *Endymion* is a temperate region located on a mountain beneath the moon. Fragile yet animate, it evokes the spring and dawn of childhood innocence, with all its intimate wonder—a place where "cold springs . . . run/To warm their chilliest bubbles in the grass" (I.102-3). Here the ephemeral beauty of spring creates a charmed circle, or *temenos,* held together, according to Frye, "by the charm of chastity or purity, which sexual experience would instantly destroy."[78] Like the chaste and fragile world of Blake's *The Book of Thel*—a crystal or chrysalis world only potentially alive—here nothing takes on definite existence as evanescent moods or spirits "melt out" their "essence fine/ Into the winds" (I.99-100). Unable to strike roots in this looking-glass world of dissolving forms or images, Endymion descends into the mysterious labyrinth of sexual generation, at the heart of which lies the Garden of Adonis.

Keats apparently places the Garden of Adonis underground in sexual generation because, as in Spenser, it is the seed-bed of sexual love that generates the cycle of nature. The covert location also contributes to a sense of mysterious enclosure—a still center hidden from mutability and death—which Keats found in Spenser. Spenser's Adonis is hidden by Venus in an enclosed garden of oriental luxury:

> There yet, some say, in secret he does ly,
> Lapped in flowers and pretious spycery,
> By her hid from the world, and from the skill
> Of Stygian Gods, which doe her love enuy;
> But she her selfe, when eure that she will
> Possesseth him, and of his sweetness takes her fill.
>
> (*F.Q.* III,vi,46)

Similarly, Keats's Adonis is enclosed by Venus, who "strove to bind/Him all in all under her doting self" (II.459-60), in a luxurious "myrtle wall'd" bower, lapped in flowers. The flowers seem to be part of Venus's "balmy power" (or embalming power), by means of which she has healed Adonis's wound and "Medicin'd death to a lengthened drowsiness" (II.484), as he sleeps through the winter and revives when Venus returns on a summer breeze.[79] Endymion arrives in time to help wake Adonis from his charmed sleep. The resulting reunion and erotic ascent of Venus and Adonis prefigures, and is possibly the condition for, Endymion's own sexual awakening immediately afterwards. Here the elusive virgin of the first book renounces her chastity, thereby transforming Endymion's dream-bower into a Spenserian garden of fertile love, where "Frankly each paramour his leman knowes" (*F.Q.* III,vi,41). This sexual experience, though more possessive than his elusive dreams, gives Endymion the roots in experience that he lacked before. He also learns from it one of the essential features of Spenser's Gardens of Adonis and Blake's Beulah, which is that the spiritual and the sexual underlie each other equally. Spenser's forms, sometimes interpreted as Neoplatonic, are also (like Keats's Venus) "ooze-born"—"uncouth forms" spawned from the muddy banks of the Nile (cf. *F.Q.* III,vi,8 & 35). Spenser's Adonis, "the Father of all formes," both rises from Chaos as the fertile seed and descends from heaven as the life-giving power of the sun. Endymion now knows that the sexual "essence" of love, as much as the spiritual, is a gate opening into a golden age of Hesperidean fulfillment:

Now I have tasted her sweet soul to the core
All other depths are shallow: essences,
Once spiritual, are like muddy lees,
Meant but to fertilize my earthly root,
And make my branches lift a golden fruit
Into the bloom of heaven. . . . (II.904-9)

But as Spenser discovers that the forms and substances of his garden of love are rooted in a "huge Chaos" (*F.Q.* III,vii,36), Endymion must descend further, following the "slippery" course of sexual bliss into a sea of chaos. The sea represents the degenerative phase of the natural cycle presided over by Circe—the wintry world of the boar, which Adonis (when under Venus's "balmy power") sleeps through as a passive prisoner of female experience or matter. Here Circe, a "terrible mother," consolidates the possessive and destructive aspects of sexual love inherent in Venus, the more beneficent mother of the generative phase. Like Spenser's Acrasis, she reigns in a "twilight bower" as "arbitrary queen of sense" (III.459), spreading out a net of illusory beauty to catch the unwary lover or poet. Entangled in the chain of her "charming syllables" (III.444), Glaucus (another Adonis figure) is reduced to a state of helpless dependency, "a child of suckling time . . . cradled . . . in roses" (III.456-7), and left "dead-drifting" in a watery prison. Circe's tyranny of the senses here recalls the siren or echo song of Spenser's Bower of Bliss and the terrifying image of Acrasia sucking her male victim's "spright" "through his humid eyes" (*F.Q.* II,xii,73). Like Acrasia, Circe is a black magician, whose magnetic attraction or "fatal power" pulls forms down the "precipitious path" (III.489) of being in a metamorphosis of descent, reducing human spirit to dumb animal pathos. Since her "sable charm" masks an inhuman chaotic force, her "twilight bower" or "dark lair of night" (III.560) is surrounded, like the Bower of Bliss, by waters of regression and "whirlpools" of decay and degeneration full of "monsters" of uncontrolled energy. But unlike Spenser's, Keats's watery bower is an epistemological, not an "immoral allegory." In this respect, it resembles Blake's "Sea of Time and Space" (cf. *Milton* 34.24-31), the deluge that overwhelms the Golden Age of Atlantis and the sleeping Albion in the process explained earlier of Beulah reverting to Ulro.

Within the frozen purgatory of Circe's "fabric crystalline" star-crossed lovers are preserved in an embalmed state of suspended animation. Like the seeds or "uncouth forms" in Spenser's Gardens of Adonis, they are ranked "in silent rows" (III.635) for a thousand years. Endymion descends into this world afraid of being torn "piece-meal" (III.263), the traditional *sparagmos* fate of the seasonal god or Adonis in the underworld. But a magical scroll is torn up by him instead, which fertilizes the seeds that they may "lift a golden fruit/Into the bloom of heaven." This act consummates Glaucus's task of exploring "all forms and substances/Straight homeward to their symbol-essences" (III.699-700), and thus revives the lovers by freeing their symbol-essences from the prison-world of subject and object. "The Sea of Time and Space" thereby recedes, as the Circean force of natural and historical necessity is transformed into the living form of Neptune's mythic Atlantis. Now "ripe from hue-golden swoons" (III.861), the lovers joyfully ascend through Neptune's "golden age," obeying, like Adonis in the second book, "the south summer's call" (III.815). Similarly, Spenser's ripened forms—those that have remained in the garden "some thousand years" after completing their natural cycle—are "clad with other hew" by "Old Genius" (*F.Q.* III,vi,33) and set free through the gate in the garden's golden wall. As in Keats, this gate opens into a mythic home of "everlasting joy" (*F.Q.* III,vi,49), where reunited lovers, now free of material form and substance, can interknit, like Venus and Adonis, or Cupid and Psyche, as pure mythic powers or essences of love. Only after exploring all forms and substances in the Gardens of Adonis does Spenser achieve this consummate vision of symbol-essences, where, as Berger remarks, "nature has become culture, dream has become poetry, force has been caught up in mobile form."[81]

At the threshold of Neptune's "golden gate," like the upper gate of Spenser's Gardens of Adonis, the imaginative seed can either blossom into eternal "essence," or fall back into the sublunary realm of mutability. Endymion, having failed to be uplifted with Adonis to "starry eminence" in the second book, and having failed, after rising out of chaos, to remain with Glaucus in Neptune's "golden globe" in the third, falls in the fourth book from Jove's "golden world" back into the autumn of the natural cycle, where his "kingdom's at its death." But he enters nature through the Cave of Quietude, which does for him what the cave imprisoning the boar of Time-Death does for Spenser. It allows him to experience the ache of mortality to its depths, thus enabling him to contain it within his garden rather than futilely attempting to wall it out. This experience provides him with the "balmy power" necessary for healing the wounds of self- and time-consciousness. By generating forms ripe with the consciousness of time and death, he can triumph over them, lifting the "full golden" Phoebe out of the dusky depths of the Indian Maid. As Spenser's Adonis is "eterne in mutabilitie" by means of perpetually dying or disappearing into the forms he generates (as the seed disappears into its golden fruit), so Endymion at last wins an immortality by dying into the "full golden" "inmost Form" of his crystalline dream.

An Interpretation

From the discussion thus far a general framework of interpretation can be constructed on the concept of *Endymion* as transitional. In terms of literary tradition, the poem bridges the "naive" fictional romance of Spenser and the Elizabethans, and the "sentimental" internalized romance of Wordsworth and the Romantics. In terms of Keats's own poetic development, it comes between the boyhood bowers of the early verse and the autumnal ripeness of the mature odes, between the early pastoral mode and the late prophetic mode of the Hyperion poems.[82] And autobiographically, it expresses the tumultuous "space of life between" the healthy imagination of the boy and the "mature imagination" of the man, which Keats refers to in his Preface to *Endymion.*

Picking up on this last statement, we can begin by viewing the development within the poem itself as that of an adolescent crisis—adolescence being a stage of growth characterized by self-consciousness, high idealism, and erotic dream. But to avoid collapsing literary into Freudian romance here, the personal or biographical must be given an universal or mythic dimension. Viewing the two as complementary, Hartman speaks of Apollo's adolescent crisis in *Hyperion* in terms that characterize Endymion's own:

> Apollo's crisis, for example, is clearly that of adolescence. He has left the "chamber of Maiden-Thought" and hovers darkling between ephebe state and god-head. He is at once too young and too old: the middle state is what is

> obscure, and to emerge from it as a decisive, individuated being may require something equivalent to infanticide or parricide.[83]

Endymion's attempt to develop a mature or permanent vision involves leaving behind the childhood innocence of Pan and Peona, and descending into the obscure mysteries of experience, where he hovers, vacillating between self-conscious stasis and premature flights toward god-head. Only after renouncing the paternal Pan, all the maternal, Sphinx-like muses, and his own selfhood or identity, can he emerge from this middle state as an "ensky'd" god. The imaginative stages involved here, as Hartman notes, are the Romantic equivalent of the Christian drama of Eden, Fall, and Redemption, the terms now being Nature, Self-Consciousness, and Imagination, or in Blake, Innocence, Experience, and Organized Innocence.[84] For Endymion, the stages are idealized dream, "the return to habitual self," and the "truth" of imaginative vision in which he beholds "awake his very dream." Whatever terms are adopted, the final state (like Pan's Elysium where lost sheep are found again) redeems by recreating or internalizing the unconscious innocence of the original state.

We are now talking about *Endymion* as a poem recording the growth of the poet's mind, though "mind" should be taken as universal as well as personal, since Keats's use of myth and archetype lend an impersonal and universalizing quality to the autobiographical. As an adolescent or vocational crisis, the poem expresses the dramatic struggle between Keats's genius or, universalized, the genius of *the* ephebe, with "The Genius of Poetry." If the puberty rite weans the adolescent from the mother and reconciles him with the father, Endymion's rite involves renouncing the maternal bowers of natural beauty and sensuous delight in order to identify with the father or precursor, who represents "The Genius of Poetry." This is ideally and ultimately accomplished by espousing "Jove's daughter," thereby being "reckon'd of his house" of immortal precursors. In the interpretation of the poem which follows I hope to make this reductive framework of inter-relationships more concrete.

When Keats began *Endymion,* "the high Idea . . . of poetical fame" towered above him" (*Letters* I, 169). The poem was to be a "test" of the truth of that "Idea," the means in part of achieving it. We notice that Endymion's dreams, however diffusely erotic, are prefigurative of the high truth of some future achievement, raising in him "A hope beyond the shadow of a dream" (I.857). His "hope" is to be included in the fellowship of "the mighty dead" (I.21), the immortal poets who reside in the Western Isle of Apollo's golden setting.

Apollo's elysium is part of a long line of western paradises, including the Isles of the Blessed, Atlantis, and the Garden of the Hesperides with its "golden fruit," and is essentially identical in Keats's poetic geography with the other paradises in the poem: Pan's "Elysium" of "eternal spring" in the first book, Neptune's golden Atlantis—"A firmament reflected in a sea" (I.300)—in the third, and Jove's "golden world" in the fourth. The natural setting of Endymion's dreams consists of Cynthia, the virgin queen of the moon and "golden age" muse, rising in the evening from Apollo's western elysium as "a fair vestal, throned in the west." Endymion believes that his "immortal," "self-destroying" love of Cynthia transcends any "poor endeavour after fame" (cf. I.846-9) apparently because, as Phoebus tells the "uncouth swain" of *Lycidas,* fame resides with "all-judging Jove" and not with any mortal "rumour" in the poet's lifetime. If he can only realize his dream as the higher aim, he will be able to marry Cynthia, the reflection of Apollo's golden light or essence, and thereby "interassimulate" (to borrow the portmanteau word Keats uses for his ideal society) with the essence of the "mighty dead." The clearest expression of this association of poetic ambition and prefigurative dream comes in the fourth book;

> There came a dream, shewing how a young man
> Ere a lean bat could plump its wintery skin,
> Would at high Jove's empyreal footstool win
> An immortality, and how espouse
> Jove's daughter, and be reckon'd of his house.
>
> (IV.376-80)

But connecting the ambition of the poet with the wish-fulfillment of dream poses certain problems. When we first see Endymion, he is in a "fixed trance" (I.403), paralyzed by the elusive charm of his dream—a charm, like Medusa's, that would turn him into "senseless stone" (II.200) if not renounced. Since his dream is in part about a great achievement in the future, it is accompanied, as Frye notes, by the paralyzing "anxieties that go with the dislocation of time."[85] Dream, then, is at best an ambivalent ally in Endymion's quest. On the one hand, it is preferable to nature, which is more reductive and thus generally viewed by Endymion as a blocking agent. For the dreamer, like the poet, encloses his world rather than standing outside it. On the other hand, while furnishing the poet with a transient intuition of immortality, it fails to provide the means of developing or realizing that intuition, repressing or blocking desire with an endlessly teasing enchantment that never fulfills.[86] Since its "crystal-smooth" surfaces cannot offer the resistance necessary for the spirit to develop, the poet's mind (Endymion complains) cannot grow and mature: "Where soil is men grow,/Whether to weeds or flowers; but for me,/There is no depth to strike in" (II.159-61).

In order to strike roots in a more substantial reality, then, Endymion must descend underground. In a letter to Reynolds, Keats explains this gradual descent from the light enchantment of dream into the obscure corridors of experience (which radiate a kind of dark enchantment of "gleaming melancholy" of their own) in terms of a "large Mansion" of many chambers:

> . . . we no sooner get into the second chamber, which I shall call the Chamber of Maiden-Thought, than we become intoxicated with the atmosphere, we see nothing but pleasant wonders, and think of delaying there for ever in delight: However among the effects this breathing is father of is that tremendous one of sharpening one's vision into the [heart] and nature of Man—of convincing ones nerves that the World is full of Misery and Heartbreak, Pain, Sickness and oppression—whereby the Chamber of Maiden-Thought becomes gradually darken'd and at the same time on all sides of it many doors are set open—but of dark—all leading to dark passages—We see not the ballance of good and evil. We are in a Mist—We are now in that state—We feel the "burden of the Mystery. . . ." (*Letters* I, 281)

This transition is prefigured in the Hymn to Pan. Here Pan is initially addressed as a pastoral deity, a beneficent protector of the vulnerable realm of innocence. But as the tone of the hymn gradually darkens he becomes the "Dread opener of the mysterious doors/Leading to universal knowledge" (I.288-9). While the Latmians (like the "marble men" on the Grecian urn) are content with a static sacremental relation to Pan, Endymion—driven by a guilty sense of a responsibility not yet assumed—descends through these "doors." But they are opened for him, not by Pan, but by Diana as *diva triformis,* "the completed form of all completeness." Since she controls all of nature from the moon to the moon-drawn sea, she represents "universal knowledge" returning as power over the natural elements, the power of internalizing their spatial and temporal dimensions as "symbol-essences." Thus Keats's Homer, though blind to the external world, can see the paradises within of Pan, Neptune, and Jove (the mythic or eternal dimensions of the elements) because he sees with the power of Diana's "triple sight":

> There is a triple sight in blindness keen;
> Such seeing hadst thou, as it once befel
> To Diana, Queen of Earth, and Heaven, and Hell.
>
> (*To Homer*)

The Actaeon fate of Shelley's Alastor-Poet had shown Keats that Diana could not be approached directly. Hence Endymion renounces his direct pursuit of the virgin dream-goddess of the first book and descends into the Mystery of experience to gain knowledge of Diana's three-fold identity through her elements. In the second book, he gains a physical and sexual knowledge of her as Queen of Earth. In the watery chaos of the third book, the consolidation of Mystery, he learns of her dark destructive phase as Queen of Hell. And in the fourth book, he gains a painful knowledge of the Indian Maid, a darker and more fully developed form of the human and sexual love of the Queen of Earth. Once Endymion accepts the Indian Maid in full, she waxes into Phoebe, the Queen of Heaven. As Phoebe contains all the phases of Diana, Endymion's union with her represents the union of his "triple-soul" with the "inmost Form" of his threefold vision.

Since knowledge for Keats can only be acquired by "convincing one's nerves" through an agonizing receptivity to sensation, Endymion must prove "the burden of the Mystery" on his pulses. Descending through the purgatorial world of "Elemental space" in the second book, he experiences "The silent mysteries of the earth" (II.214) in all their tangled wonder and horror. Here surfaces are opaque and roll away, and beauty is barren because divorced from the warm familiarity of the garden above. Space and time take the form of indeterminate or labyrinthine extension, for Endymion is descending into "the dark backward and abysm of time," where a spatial abyss separates subject and object. Here the influence of "the mighty dead," a still present fountain of light in the garden-world above, becomes self-enclosed in a remote past, congealing into hard, opaque prisms of light, like those of an "orbed diamond" (II.245). As Blake's Thel must enter experience by being planted in her own "grave-plot," Endymion is entering nature's cold tomb—the "gleaming melancholy" of nonliving matter in the mineral monuments or sediment of the past.

But his descent is also a plummeting into the "oozy bed" of sexual generation, the energy that keeps the natural cycle revolving. Endymion's sexual awakening by the Queen of Earth here, though the death of his childhood innocence, is a necessary step in his maturation. It dispels the charm of his dream-goddess—the muse of his naive idealizations. For he now realizes that her charm is based on sexual sublimation, that his idealizations have their roots in a sexual nature:

> Now I have tasted her sweet soul to the core
> All other depths are shallow: essences,
> Once spiritual, are like muddy lees,
> Meant but to fertilize my earthly root,
> And make my branches lift a golden fruit
> Into the bloom of heaven. . . . (II.904-9)

And yet if sexual union were the ultimate consummation, Endymion's quest would now be completed. We notice that Endymion's sexual experience brings about a desire for a still more complete union which it cannot satisfy: the excessive liquid diction ("slippery blisses," "twinkling eyes," "milky sovereignties," etc.) expresses his unfulfilled desire to "interknit" (cf. I.812) with Diana more completely than a physical embrace allows. Diana, who is essentially the Indian Maid here, complains of a taboo on sexuality (II.789f.)—later described as the "gorgon wrath" (IV.754) of Minerva's chastity—which prevents her from fully intermingling or interknitting with Endymion's essence, a union that would raise him to "starry eminence." Later in the book, Arethusa complains of her sexual experience in Alpheus's "deceitful stream" (II.970), which Frye regards as a chorus to Endymion's own, since in both cases sexual union is "as much a frustration and upsetting of a balance as it is a satisfaction."[87] Thus Endymion learns that there is a residual virginity or opacity in physical sexuality. The "little curtain of flesh, on the bed of our desire" that drove Thel back to her garden prevents the complete intermingling of essences, though it is nonetheless, as the fertile incarnation of love, the necessary means of lifting "a golden fruit" into the heaven of final fulfillment.

Endymion's sympathy toward the frustrated lovers, Alpheus and Arethusa, leads him to "the bottom of the monstrous world." Here the latent frustration in sexual intercourse is consolidated, for everything that blocks wish-fulfillment is concentrated in this realm of dense matter and thwarted desire. Finding it impossible "To interknit/Ones senses with so dense a breathing stuff" (III.380-1), the subject abandons the object of his desire and turns inward, suspended in a "crystal-smooth" prison of pure subjectivity. Circe, the destructive muse who vamps rather than nurtures, reigns over this submarine realm as Hecate or Queen of Hell, consolidating the demonic Mystery inherent in the crystal charm of Endymion's dream-goddess. Like the "forlorn" country of "La Belle Dame," hers is the scene, in Trilling's words, "of erotic pleasure which leads to devastation, of an erotic fulfillment which implies castration."[88] Hence the lovers who have drowned in her crystalline abyss are necessarily estranged.

Since this is the wintery sea of death and chaos, it is the end of the seasonal and water cycles, and perhaps the end of the historical-cultural cycle as well. Here Glaucus, a victim of Circe's false enchantment, has fallen from youthful innocence into aged impotence. Scylla, the object of his innocent desire, has been imprisoned in Circe's abyss of space and time as a visible but remote statue or monument, leaving Glaucus to drift in the death-in-life state of solipsism. Viewed as the Genius of the Past, Glaucus represents the "universal knowledge" acquired from having explored "all forms and substances/Straight homeward to their symbol-essences" (III.699-700) for "one thousand years." But, like Wordsworth's belated Solitary, his knowledge returns not as power but as the burden of self-consciousness. The return of power depends on a youthful consummation or internalization of that knowledge by a creative force in the present. Hence the youthful Endymion arrives to become both the sympathetic listener this ancient mariner needs to tell the story of his fall and thereby regain the power of speech, and the creative force necessary to "consummate" (III.710) his ripened labours. By tearing up or internalizing the ancient scroll of knowledge, he helps Glaucus release the fertile power (a kind of moly) necessary to reverse the Circean metamorphosis—the entropy of the natural and historical cycles—so that the sea of history will give up its dead. Through their power of uttering the language of "symbol-essences," Glaucus and Endymion re-unite or "interknit" the essences of the star-crossed lovers estranged by time and space (i.e., fate) in Circe's "fabric crystalline." By an act of communion, in which "the two deliverers tasted a pure wine/of happiness" (see III.801-2n.), Circe's watery abyss is transubstantiated as the "immortal drink" of Neptune's paradise within.[89] Thus, through their labors of "widening speculation to ease the Burden of the Mystery" (*Letters* I, 277), the two deliverers calm the tragic tempest of the sea to prepare a final home for the comic reunion of lovers:

> Far as the mariner on highest mast
> Can see all round upon the calmed vast
> So wide was Neptune's hall. (III.866-8)

In Neptune's "golden sphere," a world "full alchemized and free of space," Endymion has "far strayed from mortality" (III.1007). Unable to take possession of his visionary powers, to awaken the dream into his world, he swoons away. He is roused by the words of Diana, assuring him that he has freed her from the "fear of fate" (III.1023) and has won for them both an "immortal bliss." In other words, he has shown her that he has the imaginative power to break out of the prison of physical sexuality she fears, rising to a state where sexual union is, in Blake's words, "Comminglings from the Head even to the feet"—a state where the thoroughgoing intensity of sensation parts the "little curtain of flesh."

Perhaps because Endymion has dispelled the fear of his "golden age" muse which kept her a chaste and remote prisoner of an ideal past, Keats can begin the fourth book with an invocation to the "muse" of his "native land." Here he recounts the westerly progress of poesy—a motif of the third book (see II.359-63n. and III.1002n.), where the Genius of the Past, drifting the sea of history, is reborn in Neptune's western isle. But here the native muse and her poet have fallen from Renaissance "accomplishment" (IV.18) onto "latter days," and so must labor under the melancholy burden of belatedness, their "spirit's wings" confined in a "prison,/Of flesh and bone" (IV.20-2).

In this book Endymion finds himself back in physical reality, having fallen from the Renaissance glory of Neptune's golden palace, but he has also returned (by a kind of rebirth) from Circe's wintery world to the still present springtime innocence of the first book.[90] He has returned to Nature or Innocence with the truth of experience, the knowledge of the sorrow and tragic necessity to which all human love is subject. This knowledge, acquired from his descent in the second and third books, is represented by the melancholy Indian Maid, who is actually Phoebe become incarnate, fallen from her "dear native land" (IV.31) into the belated climate of physical reality. We find now that innocence and experience, Peona and the Indian Maid are "hand in hand," and that the innocent joy of the first book and the sorrow of the second and third are fused at the point of their greatest intensity in the Indian Maid's Song (IV.146-290). As in the image of children riding serpent-forms (IV.245-9), innocence now rides on the wave of a new energy springing from the sea of experience.

The scene is set, then, for the final stage of Endymion's adolescent crisis, where he is torn between the disenchantment of a naturalistic humanism (that will ripen in the odes) and the enchantment of archaic romance forms or ultimates, between the physcially present Indian Maid and the spiritually remote Phoebe. To resolve the crisis, Endymion must realize his idealistic vision of innocence (the prefigurative dreams of the first book) by assimilating experience to its form, thereby identifying the Indian Maid with Phoebe, truth with beauty. With the winged energy of "earth's splenetic fire" (IV.399), provided by the "swift magic" of Hermes's serpentine caduceus, he ascends with the Indian Maid to Jove's golden world, where he beholds "awake his very dream" (IV.436), realizing for the first time that his unknown dream-goddess is the Queen of Heaven or Phoebe. But he fails to realize that the Indian Maid is also Phoebe—a realization necessary for liberating them both from the lower world of nature's "green prison." His attempt, then, to take possession of his vision proves once again premature, and as a result he falls, like Icarus or Satan, into Chaos. Apparently the knowledge he had acquired from his descent is insufficient to overcome his fear of heights, for he "must spread/Wide pinions to keep here" (IV.355-6):

> The difference of high Sensations with and without knowledge appears to me this in the latter case we are falling continually ten thousand fathoms deep and being blown up again without wings and with all [the] horror of a bare shoulder'd Creature—in the former case, our shoulders are fledge[d], and we go thro' the same air and space without fear. (*Letters* I, 277)

As Frye remarks, "knowledge, the element of truth which is part of beauty, makes the difference between sleep and poetry, chaos and creation."[91]

The loss of "identity" attending Endymion's fall gives him the negative capability to enter the Cave of Quietude, where he experiences the dark purgatorial state in which Glaucus's "labours ripened," the state in which profound despair turns to joy. He gains from this a certain detachment, a kind of divine indifference, that enables him to renounce his dream quest, disenchanting himself from all airy "nothings" (IV.637).[92] In effect, like Prospero, he renounces the magician's willful desire to control the elemental spirits of the sublunary world, and gives himself up instead to "heaven's will" (IV.976). As Frye remarks, the "fully awakened vision of the poet, which includes truth or knowledge as well as beauty, depends, like the dream, on something beyond the conscious will."[93] Hence Endymion's "spiritualiz'd" metamorphosis comes about by an "unlook'd for change" (IV.992). On a "golden summer eve," with his roots in the ground of being (the physical and sexual underworld), he at last lifts "a golden fruit/Into the bloom of heaven," as the dusky Indian Maid is unexpectedly metamorphosed into the "full golden" Phoebe.

Keats began *Endymion* out of the "breathless desire to make 4000 Lines of one bare circumstance" in a limited period of time. This he felt would test his power of "invention"—that Elizabethan power to create nature over in gold so that it shines "Full alchemiz'd and free of space."[94] But Keats also wished to imitate the slow, quiet breathing of nature's organic rhythm, thus allowing time to reach a golden ripeness or maturity, time for the higher will of "The Genius of Poetry" to "work out its own salvation" in him. He attempts to resolve these two conflicting (primary and antithetical) desires by instilling the ideal beauty of his youthful inventions ("Nothings . . . made Great and dignified by an ardent pursuit") with the maturity and permanence of organic truths ("Things real").[95] But his attempt is willed and to that extent doomed to end in the loss of both beauty and truth. Thus near the end of the poem Endymion is separated from both Phoebe and the Indian Maid, his willful desire for poetic fruition having realized only the death-in-life despair of solitude. He has yet to learn that imposed invention only becomes discovered truth through the death or renunciation of will and the passage of slow time—a lesson Keats learned from writing *Endymion,* and one that will bear the fruit of his mature achievement. But he needs to express some sense of achievement now, if only to divine (or introject) a prefigured future of poetic maturity and apotheosis. Thus in the climax of the poem, Endymion, having renounced his antithetical quest for ideal beauty, drifts westerly toward Apollo's golden setting "with the slow move of time" (IV.922), once again, as in the Cave of Quietude, sinking under the burden of the Mystery. At this point he is judged ripe or negatively capable enough to be plucked by "heaven's will," united with his composite muse and immortal precursors in a world of "free of space."

This spaceless world appears to be by definition a post-mortal one, the "spiritual repetition" of a life of sensations here and now, or the "truth" prefigured in the beauty of Endymion's dreams.[96] Yet is also carries a sense of the "forlorn," suggesting that Endymion and Phoebe, like Porphyro and Madeline, have "vanish'd far away" (IV.1002) into a lost paradise of some previous life, like that in *Ode to a Nightingale.* But it is in actuality neither lost in a remote past nor projected into an equally remote future of post-mortal possibility. It exists in the here and now as a still potentially creative power to be realized by the sympathetic reader. However uncertainly a poet vanishes into his vision during his human spatial existence, he is fully united with that vision in his "fame," where it remains for his reader "a joy for ever."

NOTES

[1]Harold Bloom, *The Visionary Company* (Garden City: Doubleday, 1961), 387.

[2]Ernest de Selincourt, ed., *The Poems of John Keats* (New York: Dodd, Mead, 1905); Douglas Bush, ed., *Selected Poems and Letters of John Keats* (Boston: Houghton Mifflin, 1959); Miriam Allott, ed., *The Poems of John Keats* (London: Longman, 1970). Of the three, only Allott cites critical works, but her citations are far too few and arbitrary to be at all representative.

[3]Jack Stillinger, ed., *The Poems of John Keats* (Cambridge, Massachusetts: Harvard University Press, 1978).

[4]Edward Le Comte [*Endymion in England* (New York: King's Crown Press, 1944), 152] notes the "slight and elusive" (barren) quality of the myth–its inability to bear the weight of many words. Neverthless, it seems ideally suited to Keats's poetic sensibility. The action of the story, perhaps better described as pictorial passion, is slow, almost static, as Phoebe still gazes on the sculptured shepherd dreaming in a quiet bower of marmoreal sleep. This is the aesthetic state of exquisite receptivity Keats repeatedly evokes in *Endymion.* Moreover, Endymion's association with the sun and its setting (see Le Comte, pp. 11 and 32) allows for endless symbolic speculation (i.e., the sun sleeping in the Cave of Night, Apollo presiding over a western elysium, etc.). There is also an obvious personal allegory in this story of a beautiful youth beloved of the gods, who, dying young, wins an immortality with Jove.

[5]See *Endymion* I.39-57 and accompanying note.

[6]Letter to Haydon of May 10, 1817 (I,141). Murry [*Keats and Shakespeare* (London: Oxford University Press, 1925), 35], describing Keats's creative excitement at this time, believes "Shakespeare, poetry and the sea became knit together in a single thought and feeling. Each worked upon the other, till the ferment of his inward excitement became unbearable and Keats fled to the company of his brother Tom at Margate."

[7]See Letter to Taylor and Hessey of May 16, 1817 (I,146-7) and *Endymion* I.133-4. Bate [*John Keats* (Cambridge, Massachusetts: Harvard University Press, 1965), 180] believes these nervous trips "were not solely a result of his struggle to overcome inertia and create a new mementum. He was trying to express those thoughts that, as his later writing shows, were most urgent." Bate seems to suggest that since the first 400 lines of the poem anticipate many of the "thoughts" of images of Keats's later poetry, they essentially are the poem, the remaining lines being mere filler or afterthought. This is a radical instance of what happens to *Endymion* when judged by Keats's mature verse.

[8]The reviews are collected and discussed by G. M. Matthews in Keats: *The Critical Heritage* (New York: Barnes and Noble, 1971). They can also be found in a less readable (facsimile) form in Donald H. Reiman, ed., *The Romantics Reviewed: Contemporary Reviews of British Romantic Writers* (New York: Garland, 1972), pt. C, I & II.

[9]Matthews, 35.

[10]Matthews, 129; Algernon Swinburne, *Complete Works* (London: Heinemann, 1926), XIV, 296.

[11]Christopher Ricks, *Keats and Embarrassment* (London: Oxford University Press, 1974).

[12]Matthews, 327.

[13]Frances Owen, *John Keats: A Study* (London: Paul, 1880).

[14]Sidney Colvin, *John Keats* (New York: Scribners, 1925); Robert Bridges, "A Critical Introduction to Keats" in *Collected Essays* (London: Oxford University Press, 1929), IV, 85-93; Clarence Thorpe, *The Mind of John Keats* (1926; rpt. New York: Russell and Russell, 1964); J. Middleton Murry, *Keats* (New York: Noonday Press, 1962); Claude Finney, *The Evolution of Keats's Poetry* (Cambridge, Massachusetts: Harvard University Press, 1936), I. Both Keats's use of sleep and erotic idealism lent themselves to Neoplatonic interpretation. For the role of the Endymion myth in the Neoplatonic teaching (common in the Renaissance) of sleep as a portal to divine intimations, see Le Comte, 127-9.

[15]Colvin, 205; Bridges, 87.

[16]Amy Lowell, *John Keats* (Boston: Houghton Mifflin, 1925), I, 365; Newell Ford, "*Endymion*—A Neo-Platonic Allegory?", *Journal of English Literary History,* 14 (1947), 64-75; "The Meaning of 'Fellowship with Essence' in *Endymion,*" *PMLA,* 62 (December 1947), 1061-1076; *The Prefigurative Imagination of John Keats* (London: Oxford University Press, 1951).

[17]Ford, "*Endymion*—A Neo-Platonic Allegory?", 65.

[18]Ford, *The Prefigurative Imagination,* 39.

[19]E. C. Pettet, *On the Poetry of Keats* (London: Cambridge University Press, 1957).

[20]Walter Jackson Bate, *John Keats* (Cambridge, Massachusetts: Harvard University Press, 1963), 172-173.

[21]*Ibid.,* 172, no.10.

[22]Jacob Wigod, "The Meaning of *Endymion,*" *PMLA,* 68 (1953), 779-790.

[23]*Ibid.,* 784.

[24]Glen O. Allen, "The Fall of *Endymion*: A Study in Keats's Intellectual Growth," *Keats-Shelley Journal,* VI (1967), 37-57; Stuart M. Sperry, Jr., "The Allegroy of *Endymion,*" *Studies in Romanticism,* II (1962), 38-53.

[25]Sperry, 49.

[26]Morris Dickstein, *Keats and His Poetry* (Chicago: University of Chicago Press, 1971. Dickstein's study is actually more eclectic than I have suggested. It is heavily influenced by Frye's essay on the poem, and borrows important points from Bloom, Blackstone, and Paul de Man.

[27]*Ibid.*, 56.

[28]*Ibid.*, 113.

[29]Walter H. Evert, *Aesthetic and Myth in the Poetry of Keats* (Princeton: Princeton University Press, 1965).

[30]*Ibid.*, 114-115.

[31]*Ibid.*, 121.

[32]Charles I. Patterson, Jr., *The Daemonic in the Poetry of John Keats* (Urbana: University of Illinois Press, 1970).

[33]*Ibid.*, 24.

[34]Lionell Trilling, "The Poet as Hero: Keats in His Letters," in *The Opposing Self* (New York: Viking Press, 1955), 14.

[35]Northrope Frye, "*Endymion*: The Romantic Epiphanic," in *A Study of English Romanticism* (New York: Random House, 1968), 145.

[36]Bloom, *The Visionary Company,* 385-396; Frye, 125-166.

[37]Walter Jackson Bate, *The Stylistic Development of Keats* (New York: Humanities Press, 1958), 22.

[38]Colvin, 208.

[39]See Bate, *The Stylistic Development,* 21-28, for a neoclassic evaluation of Keats's use of stress-failure.

[40]George Saintsbury, *A History of English Prosody* (London: Macmillan, 1923), III, 119.

[41]*Ibid.*, 124.

[42]Colvin, 211-213.

[43]*Ibid.*, 213.

[44]Frye, 155.

[45]Saintsbury (119-20) characterizes the product of Hunt's reaction to eighteenth century poetic diction as a "rather uncomely bastard between French eighteenth-century *sensiblerie* and the 'simple' language of Wordsworth and even of Coleridge in the 'Young Ass'."

[46]Hunt, apparently, did not see any affinity between his idiom and that of *Endymion.* In fact, he even criticized Keats's diction as "high-flown." See Keats's letter to his brothers of January 23, 24, 1919: "He [Hunt] says the conversation [in the first book of *Endymion*] is unnatural & too high-flown for the Brother & Sister. Says it should be simple forgetting do ye mind, that they are both overshadowed by a Supernatural Power, & of force could not speak like Franchesca in the Rimini. He must first prove that Caliban's poetry is unnatural . . ." (I,213-4).

[47]Bate, *Stylistic Development,* 30.

[48]*Ibid.,* 94-95.

[49]*Ibid.,* 97. Of the 82 instances, 6 are relatively rare poetics (bowery, pipy, shrilly, feathery, ripply, healthy); 18 are common poeticisms (wintry, silvery, dewy, etc.); and the rest are common in and to all forms of discourse (heavy, happy, etc.).

[50]Murry in *Keats and Shakespeare* (London: Oxford University Press, 1925), 41, believes the opposition between Wordsworth and Shakespeare "is in some ways more important, as it was more continual, than the opposition between Milton and Shakespeare about which Keats' supreme poetic struggle was subsequently to be waged. His most intimate history could be written in terms of his rejection first of Wordsworth, then of Milton, in favour of a deeper and unchanging loyalty to Shakespeare."

[51]Frye, 20.

[52]*Ibid.,* 127.

[53]Geoffrey Hartman, "Romanticism and Anti-Self-Consciousness," in *Beyond Formalism* (New Haven: Yale University Press, 1970), 308.

[54]Frye, 98.

[55]Northrop Frye, *A Natural Perspective* (New York: Harcourt, Brace, and World, 1965), 131.

[56]For the most complete account of this influence see Caroline Spurgeon, *Keats's Shakespeare* (London: Oxford University Press, 1928).

[57]Frye, *A Study of English Romanticism,* 154.

[58]G. Wilson Knight, "The Priest-like Task: An Essay on Keats," in *The Starlit Dome* (1941; rpt. London: Oxford University Press, 1971), 263.

[59]Quoted by Stuart Ende in *Keats and the Sublime* (New Haven: Yale University Press, 1976), 89. See also pp. 87-98 for a discussion of Keats's annotations to Milton and their relevance for *Endymion.*

[60]Leslie Brisman, *Romantic Origins* (Ithaca: Cornell University Press, 1978), 67.

[61]Frye, *A Study of English Romanticism,* 129-130.

[62]See Angus Fletcher, *The Prophetic Moment* (Chicago: University of Chicago Press, 1971), 24-34.

[63]Frye, *A Study of English Romanticism,* 138.

[64]Of the four, Shakespeare and Marlowe are obvious influences, and Lodge a possible one. Drayton, on the other hand, is questionable. While Finney (248-55) argues in favor of Drayton's influence on internal evidence, Bush in *Mythology and the Romantic Tradition in English Poetry* (1937; rpt. New York: Norton, 1969), 99-100, believes that since few copies of *Endimion and Phoebe* were in print at Keats's time, the influence is unlikely.

[65]Frye, *Fearful Symmetry* (Princeton: Princeton University Press, 1947), 325.

[66]Frye, *Anatomy of Criticism* (Princeton: Princeton University Press, 1957), 200.

[67]*Ibid.*, 59-60.

[68]See Bloom's *Visionary Company*, 389, and his *Yeats* (New York: Oxford University Press, 1970), 87-88. For the relation of *Endymion* to *The Wandering of Oisin*, see *Yeats*, 82-103; for its affinities with *The Comedian As a Letter C*, see Jack Stillinger, "On the Interpretation of *Endymion*: The Comedian as the Letter E" in *The Hoodwinking of Madeline and Other Essays on Keats* (Urbana: University of Illinois Press, 1971), 250-263.

[69]Bloom, *Visionary Company*, 389. A. C. Bradley in "The Letters of Keats," in Oxford Lectures on Poetry (1909; rpt. London: Macmillan, 1959), 240-244, was the first to point out the relation of *Endymion* to both *Alastor* and *The Excursion*. For an extended (if not over-extended) discuscusion of Keats's use of *Alastor* as an "anti-model" for *Endymion* see Leonard Brown, "The Genesis, Growth, and Meaning of 'Endymion'," *Studies of Philology*, XXX (1933), 618-653.

[70]Bloom, *Visionary Company*, 389.

[71]Bloom, *Yeats*, 92.

[72]Bloom, "The Internalization of Quest Romance," in *The Ringers of the Tower* (Chicago: University of Chicago Press, 1971), 16.

[73]Bloom, *Visionary Company*, 389.

[74]Bloom, "The Internalization of Quest Romance," 16 & 34.

[75]Frye, *Fearful Symmetry*, 427.

[76]Fletcher in *The Prophetic Moment*, 14-21, views Spenser's Gardens of Adonis as a sacred *templum* (the root of "temper," "temperate," and "contemplate," as well as their antitype, "tempest"), which has both spatial and temporal aspects: "spatially the temple breaks into and organizes the endless extension of the labyrinth. Temporally, it arrests the ordinary unbroken duration of temporal flow."

[77]Frye in *Spiritus Mundi* (Bloomington: Indiana University Press, 1976), 134 & 140, notes that this link "between the upper mirror of the moon and the lower mirrors of seas and lakes runs all through the poetry of charm." Frye associates charm with the Circean metamorphosis, which transforms "men into animals, something once capable of speech and consciousness is obliged to fall silent."

[78]Frye, *A Study of English Romanticism*, 132.

[79]For the traditional connotations of "balm" as a generative and regenerative power (associated with Adam's birth and Christ's rebirth or resurrection) see Hartman, *Beyond Formalism*, 147-149.

[80]The youthful Endymion and the ancient Glaucus could be taken as representing the entire procreative cycle of death and rebirth, which in Spenser is represented by Mordant and Verdant of the Bower of Bliss, and by "Old Genius," the porter of the "double gates" of the Gardens of Adonis: "Th'one faire and fresh, the other old and dride" (II,vi,31). The double gates are part of the conventional architecture of the earthly paradise, extending back to the two entrances (one each for gods and mortals) in Homer's Cave of the Nymphs, and to Virgil's gates of horn and ivory (true and false dream respectively).

[81]Harry Berger, Jr., "Spenser's Gardens of Adonis: Force and Form in the Renaissance Imagination," *University of Toronto Quarterly,* XXX (1961), 144.

[82]Though recent criticism has questioned the "naive" nature of Spenserial romance, the point of view expressed here, as throughout, is Keats's. The terms "naive" and "sentimental" are Schiller's, but see Frye, *Anatomy of Criticism,* 35, for their meaning.

[83]Hartman, *Beyond Formalism,* 374.

[84]*Ibid.,* 307.

[85]Frye, *A Study of English Romanticism,* 131.

[86]See Bloom, *Yeats,* 109, for the tradition of the lower paradise as "erotic illusion, not the world as gratified desire, but the world as blocked desire, the world presided over by Sphinx and Covering Cherub."

[87]Frye, *A Study of English Romanticism,* 137.

[88]Lionel Trilling, "The Fate of Pleasure," in *Romanticism Reconsidered,* ed. Northrop Frye (New York: Columbia University Press, 1963), 83.

[89]See Keats's letter to Reynolds of May 3, 1818: "Your Third Chamber of Life shall be a lucky and a gentle one—stored with the wine of love—and the Bread of Friendship" (I,282-3).

[90]In a sense, Imagination returns to Nature, but, as Hartman (*Beyond Formalism,* 307) warns, everything depends on whether it "is a right and fruitful return. For the journey beyond self-consciousness is shadowed by cyclicity, by paralysis before the endlessness of introspection and by the lure of false ultimates."

[91]Frye, *A Study of English Romanticism,* 146.

[92]See Hartman, *Beyond Formalism,* 329, on the disenchanting process in which "vision plots the end of vision: it desires to be consummated in realities." Hartman compares Blake's disenchanting himself of the "Spectre of Prophecy" at the end of *Vala*—"The dark Religions are departed and Sweet Science reigns"—to Prospero's renunciation and Milton's "parting Genius" in the *Nativity Ode.* Of these, Prospero's is perhaps the closest analogue to Endymion's humanistic renunciation of vision, an act prefigured in Bacchus's Song, where a vital humanistic joy (rooted in sor-

row) dispels the dark enchantment of oriental gods—a Dionysian version of Christ's dispersion of the pagan gods and genii in the *Nativity Ode.*

[93]Frye, *A Study of English Romanticism,* 146.

[94]For the critical tradition of "invention," extending from Sidney down to Addison's "fairy way of writing" and the Romantics, see M. H. Abrams, *The Mirror and the Lamp* (New York: Norton, 1958), 272-285. Sidney claims that the poet "lifted up with the vigor of his owne invention, dooth growe in effect into another nature in makeing things either better than nature bringeth forth or, quite newe, formes such as never were in Nature. . . ." Keats may have had this passage in mind when, in a letter to Haydon of May 11, 1817, he claims to be one who looks "upon the Sun the Moon the Stars the Earth and its contents as materials to form greater things—that is to say ethereal things—but here I am talking like a Madman greater things tha[n] our Creator himself made!!" (I,143).

[95]See Keats's letter to Bailey of March 13, 1818: "every mental pursuit takes its reality and worth from the ardour of the pursuer—being in itself a nothing—Ethereal things[s] may at least be thus real, divided under three heads. . . Things real—such as existences of Sun Moon and Stars and passages of Shakespeare—Things semireal such as Love, the Clouds etc., which require a greeting of the Spirit to make them wholly exist—and Nothings which are made Great and dignified by an ardent pursuit. . ." (I,242-3).

[96]See Keats's famous remarks on the prefigurative truth of the imagination in his letter to Bailey of November 22, 1817: "we shall enjoy ourselves here after by having what we called happiness on Earth repeated in a finer tone and so repeated . . . Adam's dream will do here and seems to be a conviction that Imagination and its empyreal reflection is the same as human Life and its spiritual repetition" (I,185).

ENDYMION:

Text and Notes

So evenings die, in their green going,
A wave interminably flowing. . . .

Wallace Stevens

Endymion:
A Poetic Romance

"The stretched metre of an antique song"

INSCRIBED TO THE MEMORY OF THOMAS CHATTERTON

Preface

Knowing within myself the manner in which this Poem has been produced, it is not without a feeling of regret that I make it public.

What manner I mean, will be quite clear to the reader, who must soon perceive great inexperience, immaturity, and every error denoting a feverish attempt, rather than a deed accomplished. The two first books, and indeed the two last, I feel sensible are not of such completion as to warrant their passing the press; nor should they if I thought a year's castigation would do them any good;—it will not: the foundations are too sandy. It is just that this youngster should die away: a sad thought for me, if I had not some hope that while it is dwindling I may be plotting, and fitting myself for verses fit to live.

This may be speaking too presumptuously, and may deserve a punishment: but no feeling man will be forward to inflict it: he will leave me alone, with the conviction that there is not a fiercer hell than the failure in a great object. This is not written with the least atom of purpose to forestall criticisms of course, but from the desire I have to conciliate men who are competent to look, and who do look with a zealous eye, to the honour of English literature.

The imagination of a boy is healthy, and the mature imagination of a man is healthy; but there is a space of life between, in which the soul is in a ferment, the character undecided, the way of life uncertain, the ambition thick-sighted: thence proceeds mawkishness, and all the thousand bitters which those men I speak of must necessarily taste in going over the following pages.

I hope I have not in too late a day touched the beautiful mythology of Greece, and dulled its brightness: for I wish to try once more, before I bid it farewel.

Teignmouth, April 10, 1818

BOOK I

A thing of beauty is a joy for ever:
Its loveliness increases; it will never
Pass into nothingness; but still will keep
A bower quiet for us, and a sleep
Full of sweet dreams, and health, and quiet breathing.
Therefore, on every morrow, are we wreathing
A flowery band to bind us to the earth,
Spite of despondence, of the inhuman dearth
Of noble natures, of the gloomy days,
Of all the unhealthy and o'er-darkened ways
Made for our searching: yes, in spite of all,
Some shape of beauty moves away the pall
From our dark spirits. Such the sun, the moon,
Trees old, and young sprouting a shady boon
For simple sheep; and such are daffodils
With the green world they live in; and clear rills
That for themselves a cooling covert make
'Gainst the hot season; the mid forest brake,
Rich with a sprinkling of fair musk-rose blooms:
And such too is the grandeur of the dooms
We have imagined for the mighty dead;
All lovely tales that we have heard or read:
An endless fountain of immortal drink,
Pouring unto us from the heaven's brink.

Nor do we merely feel these essences
For one short hour; no, even as the trees
That whisper round a temple become soon
Dear as the temple's self, so does the moon,
The passion poesy, glories infinite,
Haunt us till they become a cheering light
Unto our souls, and bound to us so fast,
That, whether there be shine, or gloom o'ercast,
They alway must be with us, or we die.

Therefore, 'tis with full happiness that I
Will trace the story of Endymion.
The very music of the name has gone
Into my being, and each pleasant scene
Is growing fresh before me as the green
Of our own vallies: so I will begin
Now while I cannot hear the city's din;
Now while the early budders are just new,
And run in mazes of the youngest hue
About old forests; while the willow trails
Its delicate amber; and the dairy pails
Bring home increase of milk. And, as the year
Grows lush in juicy stalks, I'll smoothly steer
My little boat, for many quite hours,
With streams that deepen freshly into bowers.
Many and many a verse I hope to write,
Before the daisies, vermeil rimm'd and white,
Hide in deep herbage; and ere yet the bees
Hum about globes of clover and sweet peas,
I must be near the middle of my story.
O may no wintry season, bare and hoary,
See it half finished: but let autumn bold,
With universal tinge of sober gold,
Be all about me when I make an end.
And now at once, adventuresome, I send
My herald thought into a wilderness:
There let its trumpet blow, and quickly dress
My uncertain path with green, that I may speed
Easily onward, thorough flowers and weed.

Upon the sides of Latmos was outspread
A mighty forest; for the moist earth fed
So plenteously all weed-hidden roots
Into o'er-hanging boughs, and precious fruits.
And it had gloomy shades, sequestered deep,
Where no man went; and if from shepherd's keep
A lamb strayed far a-down those inmost glens,
Never again saw he the happy pens
Whither his brethren, bleating with content,
Over the hills at every nightfall went.
Among the shepherds, 'twas believed ever,
That not one fleecy lamb which thus did sever

From the white flock, but pass'd unworried
By angry wolf, or pard with prying head,
Until it came to some unfooted plains
Where fed the herds of Pan: ay great his gains
Who thus one lamb did lose. Paths there were many,
Winding through palmy fern, and rushes fenny,
And ivy banks; all leading pleasantly
To a wide lawn, whence one could only see
Stems thronging all around between the swell
Of turf and slanting branches: who could tell
The freshness of the space of heaven above,
Edg'd round with dark tree tops? through which a dove
Would often beat its wings, and often too
A little cloud would move across the blue.

Full in the middle of this pleasantness
There stood a marble altar, with a tress
Of flowers budded newly; and the dew
Had taken fairy phantasies to strew
Daisies upon the sacred sward last eve,
And so the dawned light in pomp receive.
For 'twas the morn: Apollo's upward fire
Made every eastern cloud a silvery pyre
Of brightness so unsullied, that therein
A melancholy spirit well might win
Oblivion, and melt out his essence fine
Into the winds: rain-scented eglantine
Gave temerate sweets to that well-wooing sun;
The lark was lost in him; cold springs had run
To warm their chilliest bubbles in the grass;
Man's voice was on the mountains; and the mass
Of nature's lives and wonders puls'd tenfold,
To feel this sun-rise and its glories old.

Now while the silent workings of the dawn
Were busiest, into that self-same lawn
All suddenly, with joyful cries, there sped
A troop of little children garlanded;
Who gathering round the altar, seemed to pry
Earnestly round as wishing to espy
Some folk of holiday: nor had they waited
For many moments, ere their ears were sated

With a faint breath of music, which ev'n then
Fill'd out its voice, and died away again.
Within a little space again it gave
Its airy swellings, with a gentle wave,
To light-hung leaves, in smoothest echoes breaking
Through copse-clad vallies,—ere their death, o'ertaking
The surgy murmurs of the lonely sea.

And now, as deep into the wood as we
Might mark a lynx's eye, there glimmered light
Fair faces and a rush of garments white,
Plainer and plainer shewing, till at last
Into the widest alley they all past,
Making directly for the woodland altar.
O kindly muse! let not my weak tongue faulter
In telling of this goodly company,
Of their old piety, and of their glee:
But let a portion of ethereal dew
Fall on my head, and presently unmew
My soul; that I may dare, in wayfaring,
To stammer where old Chaucer used to sing.

Leading the way, young damsels danced along,
Bearing the burden of a shepherd song;
Each having a white wicker over brimm'd
With April's tender younglings: next, well trimm'd,
A crowd of shepherds with as sunburnt looks
As may be read of in Arcadian books;
Such as sat listening round Apollo's pipe,
When the great deity, for earth too ripe,
Let his divinity o'er-flowing die
In music, through the vales of Thessaly:
Some idly trailed their sheep-hooks on the ground,
And some kept up a shrilly mellow sound
With ebon-tipped flutes: close after these,
Now coming from beneath the forest trees,
A venerable priest full soberly,
Begirt with ministring looks: alway his eye
Stedfast upon the matted turf he kept,
And after him his sacred vestments swept.
From his right hand there swung a vase, milk-white,
Of mingled wine, out-sparkling generous light;

And in his left he held a basket full
Of all sweet herbs that searching eye could cull:
Wild thyme, and valley-lilies whiter still
Than Leda's love, and cresses from the rill.
His aged head, crowned with beechen wreath,
Seem'd like a poll of ivy in the teeth
Of winter hoar. Then came another crowd
Of shepherds, lifting in due time aloud
Their share of the ditty. After them appear'd,
Up-followed by a multitude that rear'd
Their voices to the clouds, a fair wrought car,
Easily rolling so as scarce to mar
The freedom of three steeds of dapple brown:
Who stood therein did seem of great renown
Among the throung. His youth was fully blown,
Shewing like Ganymede to manhood grown;
And, for those simple times, his garments were
A chieftain king's: beneath his breast, half bare,
Was hung a silver bugle, and between
His nervy knees there lay a boar-spear keen.
A smile was on his countenance; he seem'd,
To common lookers on, like one who dream'd
Of idleness in groves Elysian:
But there were some who feelingly could scan
A lurking trouble in his nether lip,
And see that oftentimes the reins would slip
Through his forgotten hands: then would they sigh,
And think of yellow leaves, of owlet's cry,
Of logs piled solemnly.—Ah, well-a-day,
Why should our young Endymion pine away!

Soon the assembly, in a circle rang'd,
Stood silent round the shrine: each look was chang'd
To sudden veneration: women meek
Beckon'd their sons to silence; while each cheek
Of virgin bloom paled gently for slight fear.
Endymion too, without a forest peer,
Stood, wan, and pale, and with an awed face,
Among his brothers of the mountain chase.
In midst of all, the venerable priest
Eyed them with joy from greatest to the least,
And, after lifting up his aged hands,

Thus spake he: "Men of Latmos! shepherd bands!
Whose care it is to guard a thousand flocks:
Whether descended from beneath the rocks
That overtop your mountains; whether come
From vallies where the pipe is never dumb;
Or from your swelling downs, where sweet air stirs
Blue hare-bells lightly, and where prickly furze
Buds lavish gold; or ye, whose precious charge
Nibble their fill at ocean's very marge,
Whose mellow reeds are touch'd with sounds forlorn
By the dim echoes of old Triton's horn:
Mothers and wives! who day by day prepare
The scrip, with needments, for the mountain air;
And all ye gentle girls who foster up
Udderless lambs, and in a little cup
Will put choice honey for a favoured youth:
Yea, every one attend! for in good truth
Our vows are wanting to our great god Pan.
Are not our lowing heifers sleeker than
Night-swollen mushrooms? Are not our wide plains
Speckled with countless fleeces? Have not rains
Green'd over April's lap? No howling sad
Sickens our fearful ewes; and we have had
Great bounty from Endymion our lord.
The earth is glad: the merry lark has pour'd
His early song against yon breezy sky,
That spreads so clear o'er our solemnity."

Thus ending, on the shrine he heap'd a spire
Of teeming sweets, enkindling sacred fire;
Anon he stain'd the thick and spongy sod
With wine, in honour of the shepherd-god.
Now while the earth was drinking it, and while
Bay leaves were crackling in the fragrant pile,
And gummy frankincense was sparkling bright
'Neath smothering parsley, and a hazy light
Spread greyly eastward, thus a chorus sang:

"O thou, whose mighty palace roof doth hang
From jagged trunks, and overshadoweth
Eternal whispers, glooms, the birth, life, death
Of unseen flowers in heavy peacefulness;

Who lov'st to see the hamadryads dress
Their ruffled locks where meeting hazels darken;
And through whole solemn hours dost sit, and hearken
The dreary melody of bedded reeds—
In desolate places, where dank moisture breeds
The pipy hemlock to strange overgrowth;
Bethinking thee, how melancholy loth
Thou wast to lose fair Syrinx—do thou now,
By thy love's milky brow!
By all the trembling mazes that she ran,
Hear us, great Pan!

"O thou, for whose soul-soothing quiet, turtles
Passion their voices cooingly 'mong myrtles,
What time thou wanderest at eventide
Through sunny meadows, that outskirt the side
Of thine enmossed realms: O thou, to whom
Broad leaved fig trees even now foredoom
Their ripen'd fruitage; yellow girted bees
Their golden honeycombs; our village leas
Their fairest blossom'd beans and poppied corn;
The chuckling linnet its five young unborn,
To sing for thee; low creeping strawberries
Their summer coolness; pent up butterflies
Their freckled wings; yea, the fresh budding year
All its completions—be quickly near,
By every wind that nods the mountain pine,
O forester divine!

"Thou, to whom every faun and satyr flies
For willing service; whether to surprise
The squatted hare while in half sleeping fit;
Or upward ragged precipices flit
To save poor lambkins from the eagle's maw;
Or by mysterious enticement draw
Bewildered shepherds to their path again;
Or to tread breathless round the frothy main,
And gather up all fancifullest shells
For thee to tumble into Naiads' cells,
And, being hidden, laugh at their out-peeping;
Or to delight thee with fantastic leaping,
The while they pelt each other on the crown

With silvery oak apples, and fir cones brown—
By all the echoes that about thee ring,
Hear us, O satyr king!

"O Hearkener to the loud clapping shears,
While ever and anon to his shorn peers
A ram goes bleating: Winder of the horn,
When snouted wild-boars routing tender corn
Anger our huntsmen: Breather round our farms,
To keep off mildews, and all weather harms:
Strange ministrant of undescribed sounds,
That come a swooning over hollow grounds,
And wither drearily on barren moors:
Dread opener of the mysterious doors
Leading to universal knowledge—see,
Great son of Dryope,
The many that are come to pay their vows
With leaves about their brows!

"Be still the unimaginable lodge
For solitary thinkings; such as dodge
Conception to the very bourne of heaven,
Then leave the naked brain: be still the leaven,
That spreading in this dull and clodded earth
Gives it a touch ethereal—a new birth:
Be still a symbol of immensity;
A firmament reflected in a sea;
An element filling the space between;
An unknown—but no more: we humbly screen
With uplift hands our foreheads, lowly bending,
And giving out a shout most heaven rending,
Conjure thee to receive our humble paean.
Upon thy Mount Lycean!"

Even while they brought the burden to a close,
A shout from the whole multitude arose,
That lingered in the air like dying rolls
Of abrupt thunder, when Ionian shoals
Of dolphins bob their noses through the brine.
Meantime, on shady levels, mossy fine,
Young companies nimbly began dancing
To the swift treble pipe, and humming string.

Aye, those fair living forms swam heavenly
To tunes forgotten—out of memory:
Fair creatures! whose young children's children bred
Thermopylae its heroes—not yet dead
But in old marbles ever beautiful.
High genitors, unconscious did they cull
Time's sweet first-fruits—they danc'd to weariness
And then in quiet circles did they press
The hillock turf, and caught the latter end
Of some strange history, potent to send
A young mind from its bodily tenement.
Or they might watch the quoit-pitchers, intent
On either side; pitying the sad death
Of Hyacinthus, when the cruel breath
Of Zephyr slew him,—Zephyr penitent,
Who now, ere Phoebus mounts the firmament,
Fondles the flower amid the sobbing rain,
The archers too, upon a wider plain,
Beside the feathery whizzing of the shaft,
And the dull twanging bowstring, and the raft
Branch down sweeping from a tall ash top,
Call'd up a thousand thoughts to envelope
Those who would watch. Perhaps, the trembling knee
And frantic gape of lonely Niobe,
Poor, lonely Niobe! when her lovely young
Were dead and gone, and her caressing tongue
Lay a lost thing upon her paly lip,
And very, very deadliness did nip
Her motherly cheeks. Arous'd from this sad mood
By one, who at a distance loud hallo'd,
Uplifting his strong bow into the air,
Many night after brighter visions stare:
After the Argonauts, in blind amaze
Tossing about on Neptune's restless ways,
Until, from the horizon's vaulted side,
There shot a golden splendour far and wide,
Spangling those million poutings of the brine
With quivering ore: 'twas even an awful shine
From the exaltation of Apollo's bow;
A heavenly beacon in their dreary woe.
Who thus were ripe for high contemplating
Might turn their steps towards the sober ring

Where sat Endymion and the aged priest
'Mong shepherds gone in eld, whose looks increas'd
The silvery setting of their mortal star.
There they discours'd upon the fragile bar
That keeps us from our homes ethereal;
And what our duties there: to nightly call
Vesper, the beauty-crest of summer weather;
To summon all the downiest clouds together
For the sun's purple couch; the emulate
In ministring the potent rule of fate
With speed of fire-tailed exhalations;
To tint her pallid cheek with bloom, who cons
Sweet poesy by moonlight: besides these,
A world of other unguess'd offices.
Anon they wander'd, by divine converse,
Into Elysium; vieing to rehearse
Each one his own anticipated bliss.
One felt heart-certain that he could not miss
His quick gone love, among fair blossom'd boughs,
Where every zephyr-sigh pouts, and endows
Her lips with music for the welcoming.
Another wish'd, mid that eternal spring,
To meet his rosy child, with feathery sails,
Sweeping, eye-earnestly, through almond vales:
Who, suddenly, should stoop through the smooth wind,
And with the balmiest leaves his temples bind;
And, ever after, through those regions be
His messenger, his little Mercury.
Some were athirst in soul to see again
Their fellow huntsmen o'er the wide champaign
In times long past; to sit with them, and talk
Of all the chances in their earthly walk;
Comparing, joyfully, their plenteous stores
Of happiness, to when upon the moors,
Benighted, close they huddled from the cold,
And shar'd their famish'd scrips. Thus all out-told
Their fond imaginations,—saving him
Whose eyelids curtain'd up their jewels dim,
Endymion: yet hourly had he striven
To hide the cankering venom, that had riven
His fainting recollections. Now indeed
His senses had swoon'd off: he did not heed

The sudden silence, or the whispers low,
Or the old eyes dissolving at his woe,
Or anxious calls, or close of trembling palms,
Or maiden's sigh, that grief itself embalms:
But in the self-same fixed trance he kept,
Like one who on the earth had never stept—
Aye, even as dead-still as a marble man,
Frozen in that old tale Arabian.

Who whispers him so pantingly and close?
Peona, his sweet sister: of all those,
His friends, the dearest. Hushing signs she made,
And breath'd a sister's sorrow to persuade
A yielding up, a cradling on her care.
Her eloquence did breathe away the curse:
She led him, like some midnight spirit nurse
Of happy changes in emphatic dreams,
Along a path between two little streams,—
Guarding his forehead, with her round elbow,
From low-grown branches, and his footsteps slow
From stumbling over stumps and hillocks small;
Until they came to where these streamlets fall,
With mingled bubblings and a gentle rush,
Into a river, clear, brimful, and flush
With crystal mocking of the trees and sky.
A little shallop, floating there hard by,
Pointed its beak over the fringed bank;
And soon it lightly dipt, and rose, and sank,
And dipt again, with the young couple's weight,—
Peona guiding, through the water straight,
Towards a bowery island opposite;
Which gaining presently, she sterred light
Into a shady, fresh, and ripply cove,
Where nested was an arbour, overwove
By many a summer's silent fingering;
To whose cool bosom she was used to bring
Her playmates, with their needle broidery,
And minstrel memories of times gone by.

So she was gently glad to see him laid
Under her favourite bower's quiet shade,
On her own couch, new made of flower leaves,

Dried carefully on the cooler side of sheaves
When last the sun his autumn tresses shook,
And the tann'd harvesters rich armfuls took.
Soon was he quieted to slumbrous rest:
But, ere it crept upon him, he had prest
Peona's busy hand against his lips,
And still, a sleeping, held her finger-tips
In tender pressure. And as a willow keeps
A patient watch over the stream that creeps
Windingly by it, so the quiet maid
Held her in peace: so that a whispering blade
Of grass, a wailful gnat, a bee bustling
Down in the blue-bells, or a wren light rustling
Among sere leaves and twigs, might all be heard.

O magic sleep! O comfortable bird,
That broodest o'er the troubled sea of the mind
Till it is hush'd and smooth! O unconfin'd
Restraint! imprisoned liberty! great key
To golden palaces, strange minstrelsy,
Fountains grotesque, new trees, bespangled caves,
Echoing grottos, full of trumbling waves
And moonlight; aye, to all the mazy world
Of silvery enchantment!—who, upfurl'd
Beneath thy drowsy wing a triple hour,
But renovates and lives?—Thus, in the bower,
Endymion was calm'd to life again.
Opening his eyelids with a healthier brain,
He said: "I feel this thine endearing love
All through my bosom: thou art as a dove
Trembling its closed eyes and sleeked wings
About me; and the pearliest dew not brings
Such morning incense from the fields of May,
As do those brightest drops that twinkling stray
From those kind eyes,—the very home and haunt
Of sisterly affection. Can I want
Aught else, aught nearer heaven, than such tears?
Yet dry them up, in bidding hence all fears
That, any longer, I will pass my days
Alone and sad. No, I will once more raise
My voice upon the mountain-heights; once more
Make my horn parley from their foreheads hoar:

Again my trooping hounds their tongues shall loll
Around the breathed boar: again I'll poll
The fair-grown yew tree, for a chosen bow:
And, when the pleasant sun is getting low,
Again I'll linger in a sloping mead
To hear the speckled thrushes, and see feed
Our idle sheep. So be thou cheered, sweet,
And, if thy lute is here, softly intreat
My soul to keep in its resolved course."

Hereat Peona, in their silver source,
Shut her pure sorrow drops with glad exclaim,
And took a lute, from which there pulsing came
A lively prelude, fashioning the way
In which her voice should wander. 'Twas a lay
More subtle cadenced, more forest wild
Than Dryope's lone lulling of her child;
And nothing since has floated in the air
So mournful strange. Surely some influence rare
Went, spiritual, through the damsel's hand;
For still, with Delphic emphasis, she spann'd
The quick invisible strings, even though she saw
Endymion's spirit melt away and thaw
Before the deep intoxication.
But soon she came, with sudden burst, upon
Her self-possession—swung the lute aside,
And earnestly said: "Brother, 'tis vain to hide
That thou dost know of things mysterious,
Immortal, starry; such alone could thus
Weigh down thy nature. Hast thou sinn'd in aught
Offensive to the heavenly powers? Caught
A Paphian dove upon a message sent?
Thy deathful bow against some deer-herd bent,
Sacred to Dian? Haply, thou hast seen
Her naked limbs among the alders green;
And that, alas! is death. No, I can trace
Something more high perplexing in they face!"

Endymion look'd at her, and press'd her hand,
And said, "Art thou so pale, who wast so bland
And merry in our meadows? How is this?
Tell me thine ailment: tell me all amiss!—

Ah! thou hast been unhappy at the change
Wrought suddenly in me. What indeed more strange?
Or more complete to overwhelm surmise?
Ambition is no sluggard: 'tis no prize,
That toiling years would put within my grasp,
That I have sigh'd for: with so deadly gasp
No man e'er panted for a mortal love.
So all have set my heavier grief above
These things which happen. Rightly have they done:
I, who still saw the horizontal sun
Heave his broad shoulder o'er the edge of the world,
Out-facing Lucifer, and then had hurl'd
My spear aloft, as signal for the chace—
I, who, for very sport of heart, whould race
With my own steed from Araby; pluck down
A vulture from his towery perching; frown
A lion into growling, loth retire—
To lose, at once, all my toil breeding fire,
And sink thus low! but I will ease my breast
Of secret grief, here in this bowery nest.

"This river does not see the naked sky,
Till it begins to progress silverly
Around the western border of the wood,
Whence, from a certain spot, its winding flood
Seems at the distance like a crescent moon:
And in that nook, the very pride of June,
Had I been used to pass my weary eyes;
The rather for the sun unwilling leaves
So dear a picture of his sovereign power,
And I could witness his most kingly hour,
When he doth tighten up the golden reins,
And paces leisurely down amber plains
His snorting four. Now when his chariot last
Its beams against the zodiac-lion cast,
There blossom'd suddenly a magic bed
Of sacred ditamy, and poppies red:
At which I wondered greatly, knowing well
That but one night had wrought this flowery spell;
And, sitting down close by, began to muse
What it might mean. Perhaps, thought I, Morpheus,
In passing here, his owlet pinions shook;

Or, it may be, ere matron Night uptook
Her ebon urn, young Mercury, by stealth,
Had dipt his rod in it: such garland wealth
Came not by common growth. Thus on I thought,
Until my head was dizzy and distraught.
Moreover, through the dancing poppies stole
A breeze, most softly lulling to my soul;
And shaping visions all about my sight
Of colours, wings, and bursts of spangly light;
The which became more strange, and strange, and dim,
And then were gulph'd in a tumultuous swim:
And then I fell asleep. Ah, can I tell
The enchantment that afterwards befel?
Yet it was but a dream: yet such a dream
That never tongue, although it overteem
With mellow utterance, like a cavern spring,
Could figure out and to conception bring
All I beheld and felt. Methought I lay
Watching the zenith, where the milky way
Among the stars in virgin splendour pours;
And travelling my eye, until the doors
Of heaven appear'd to open for my flight,
I became loth and fearful to alight
From such high soaring by a downward glance:
So kept me stedfast in that airy trance,
Spreading imaginary pinions wide.
When, presently, the stars began to glide,
And faint away, before my eager view:
At which I sigh'd that I could not pursue,
And dropt my vision to the horizon's verge;
And lo! from opening clouds, I saw emerge
The loveliest moon, that ever silver'd o'er
A shell for Neptune's goblet: she did soar
So passionately bright, my dazzled soul
Commingling with her argent spheres did roll
Through clear and cloudy, even when she went
At last into a dark and vapoury tent—
Whereat, methought, the lidless-eyed train
Of planets all were in the blue again.
To commune with those orbs, once more I rais'd
My sight right upward: but it was quite dazed
By a bright something, sailing down apace,

Making me quickly veil my eyes and face:
Again I look'd, O ye deities,
Who from Olympus watch our destinies!
Whence that completed form of all completeness?
Whence came that high perfection of all sweetness?
Speak, stubborn earth, and tell me where, O where
Hast thou a symbol of her golden hair?
Not oat-sheaves drooping in the western sun;
Not—thy soft hand, fair sister! let me shun
Such follying before thee—yet she had,
Indeed, locks bright enough to make me mad;
And they were simply gordian'd up and braided,
Leaving, in naked comeliness, unshaded,
Her pearl round ears, white neck, and orbed brow;
The which were blended in, I know not how,
With such a paradise of lips and eyes,
Blush-tinted cheeks, half smiles, and faintest sighs,
That, when I think thereon, my spirit clings
And plays about its fancy, till the stings
Of human neighbourhood envenom all.
Unto what awful power shall I call?
To what high fane?—Ah! see her hovering feet,
More bluely vein'd, more soft, more whitely sweet
Than those of sea-born Venus, when she rose
From out her cradle shell. The wind out-blows
Her scarf into a fluttering pavilion;
'Tis blue, and over-spangled with a million
Of little eyes, as though thou wert to shed,
Over the darkest, lushest blue-bell bed,
Handfuls of daisies."—"Endymion, how strange!
Dream within dream!"—"She took an airy range,
And then, towards me, like a very maid,
Came blushing, waning, willing, and afraid,
And press'd me by the hand: Ah! 'twas too much;
Methought I fainted at the charmed touch,
Yet held my recollection, even as one
Who dives three fathoms where the waters run
Gurgling in beds of coral: for anon,
I felt upmounted in that region
Where falling stars dart their artillery forth,
And eagles struggle with the buffeting north
That balances the heavy meteor-stone;—

Felt too, I was not fearful, nor alone,
But lapp'd and lull'd along the dangerous sky.
Soon, as it seem'd, we left our journeying high,
And straightway into frightful eddies swoop'd;
Such as ay muster where grey time has scoop'd
Huge dens and caverns in a mountain's side:
There hollow sounds arous'd me, and I sigh'd
To faint once more by looking on my bliss—
I was distracted; madly did I kiss
The wooing arms which held me, and did give
My eyes at once to death: but 'twas to live,
To take in draughts of life from the gold fount
Of kind and passionate looks; to count, and count
The moments, by some greedy help that seem'd
A second self, that each might be redeem'd
And plunder'd of its load of blessedness.
Ah, desperate mortal! I ev'n dar'd to press
Her very cheek against my crowned lip,
And, at that moment, felt my body dip
Into a warmer air: a moment more,
Our feet were soft in flowers. There was store
Of newest joys upon that alp. Sometimes
A scent of violets, and blossoming limes,
Loiter'd around us; then of honey cells,
Made delicate from all white-flower bells;
And once, above the edges of our nest,
An arch face peep'd,—an Oread as I guess'd.

"Why did I dream that sleep o'er-power'd me
In midst of all this heaven? Why not see,
Far off, the shadows of his pinions dark,
And stare them from me? But no, like a spark
That needs must die, although its little beam
Reflects upon a diamond, my sweet dream
Fell into nothing—into stupid sleep.
And so it was, until a gentle creep,
A careful moving, caught my waking ears,
And up I started: Ah! my sighs, my tears,
My clenched hands;—for lo! the poppies hung
Dew-dabbled on their stalks, the ouzel sung
A heavy ditty, and the sullen day
Had chidden herald Hesperus away,

With leaden looks: the solitary breeze
Bluster'd, and slept, and its wild self did teaze
With wayward melancholy; and I thought,
Mark me, Peona! that sometimes it brought
Faint fare-thee-wells, and sigh-shrilled adieus!—
Away I wander'd—all the pleasant hues
Of heaven and earth had faded: deepest shades
Were deepest dungeons; heaths and sunny glades
Were full of pestilent light; our taintless rills
Seem'd sooty, and o'er-spread with upturn'd gills
Of dying fish; the vermeil rose had blown
In frightful scarlet, and its thorns out-grown
Like spiked aloe. If an innocent bird
Before my heedless footsteps stirr'd, and stirr'd
In little journeys, I beheld in it
A disguis'd demon, missioned to knit
My soul with under darkness; to entice
My stumblings down some monstrous precipice:
Therefore I eager followed, and did curse
The disappointment. Time, that aged nurse,
Rock'd me to patience. Now, thank gentle heaven!
These things, with all their comfortings, are given
To my down-sunken hours, and with thee,
Sweet sister, help to stem the ebbing sea
Of weary life."

Thus ended he, and both
Sat silent: for the maid was very loth
To answer; feeling well that breathed words
Would all be lost, unheard, and vain as swords
Against the enchased crocodile, or leaps
Of grasshoppers against the sun. She weeps,
And wonders; struggles to devise some blame;
To put on such a look as would say, *Shame*
On this poor weakness! but, for all her strife,
She could as soon have crush'd away the life
From a sick dove. At length, to break the pause,
She said with trembling chance: "Is this the cause?
This all? Yet it is strange, and sad, alas!
That one who through this middle earth should pass
Most like a sojourning demi-god, and leave
His name upon the harp-string, should achieve

No higher bard than simple maidenhood,
Singing alone, and fearfully,—how the blood
Left his young cheek; and how he used to stray
He knew not where; and how he would say, *nay,*
If any said 'twas love: and yet 'twas love;
What could it be but love? How a ring-dove
Let fall a sprig of yew tree in his path;
And how he died: and then, that love doth scathe
The gentle heart, as northern blasts do roses;
And then the ballad of his sad life closes
With sighs, and an alas!—Endymion!
Be rather in the trumpet's mouth,—anon
Among the winds at large—that all may hearken!
Although, before the crystal heavens darken,
I watch and dote upon the silver lakes
Pictur'd in western cloudiness, that takes
The semblance of gold rocks and bright gold sands,
Islands, and creeks, and amber-fretted strands
With horses prancing o'er them, palaces
And towers of amethyst,—would I so tease
My pleasant days, because I could not mount
Into those regions? The Morphean fount
Of that fine element that visions, dreams,
And fitful whims of sleep are made of, streams
Into its airy channels with so subtle,
So thin a breathing, not the spider's shuttle,
Circled a million times within the space
Of a swallow's nest-door, could delay a trace,
A tinting of its quality: how light
Must dreams themselves be; seeing they're more slight
Than the mere nothing that engenders them!
Then wherefore sully the entrusted gem
Of high and noble life with thoughts so sick?
Why pierce high-fronted honour to the quick
For nothing but a dream?" Hereat the youth
Look'd up: a conflicting of shame and ruth
Was in his plaited brow: yet, his eyelids
Widened a little, as when Zephyr bids
A little breeze to creep between the fans
Of careless butterflies: amid his pains
He seem'd to taste a drop of manna-dew,
Full palatable; and a colour grew

Upon his cheek, while thus he lifeful spake.

"Peona! ever have I long'd to slake
My thirst for the world's praises: nothing base,
No merely slumberous phantasm, could unlace
The stubborn canvas for my voyage prepar'd—
Though now 'tis tatter'd; leaving my bark bar'd
And sullenly drifting: yet my higher hope
Is of too wide, too rainbow-large a scope,
To fret at myriads of earthly wrecks.
Wherein lies happiness? In that which becks
Our ready minds to fellowship divine,
A fellowship with essence; till we shine,
Full alchemiz'd, and free of space. Behold
The clear religion of heaven! Fold
A rose leaf round thy finger's taperness,
And soothe thy lips: hist, when the airy stress
Of music's kiss impregnates the free winds,
And with a sympathetic touch unbinds
Eolian magic from their lucid wombs:
Then old songs waken from enclouded tombs;
Old ditties sigh above their father's grave;
Ghosts of melodious prophecyings rave
Round every spot where trod Apollo's foot;
Bronze clarions awake, and faintly bruit,
Where long ago a giant battle was;
And, form the turf, a lullaby doth pass
In every place where infant Orpheus slept.
Feel we these things?—that moment have we stept
Into a sort of oneness, and our state
Is like a floating spirit's. But there are
Richer entaglements, enthralments far
More self-destroying, leading, by degrees,
To the chief intensity: the crown of these
Is made of love and friendship, and sits high
Upon the forehead of humanity.
All its more ponderous and bulky worth
Is friendship, whence there ever issues forth
A steady splendour; but at the tip-top,
There hangs by unseen film, an orbed drop
Of light, and that is love: its influence,
Thrown in our eyes, genders a novel sense,

At which we start and fret; till in the end,
Melting into its radiance, we blend,
Mingle, and so become a part of it,—
Nor with aught else can our souls interknit
So wingedly: when we combine therewith,
Life's self is nourish'd by its proper pith,
And we are nurtured like a pelican brood.
Aye, so delicious is the unsating food,
That men, who might have tower'd in the van
Of all the congregated world, to fan
And winnow from the coming step of time
All chaff of custom, wipe away all slime
Left by men-slugs and human serpentry,
Have been content to let occasion die,
Whilst they did sleep in love's elysium.
And, truly, I would rather be struck dumb,
Than speak against this ardent listlessness:
For I have ever thought that it might bless
The world with benefits unknowingly;
As does the nightingale, upperched high,
And cloister'd among cool and bunched leaves—
She sings but to her love, nor e'er conceives
How tiptoe Night holds back her dark-grey hood.
Just so may love, although 'tis understood
The mere commingling of passionate breath,
Produce more than our searching witnesseth:
What I know not: but who, of men, can tell
That flowers would bloom, or that green fruit would swell
To melting pulp, that fish would have bright mail,
The earth its dower of river, wood, and vale,
The meadows runnels pebble-stones,
The seed its harvest, or the lute its tones,
Tones ravishment, or ravishment its sweet,
If human souls did never kiss and greet?

"Now, if this earthly love has power to make
Men's being mortal, immortal; to shake
Ambition from their memories, and brim
Their measure of content; what merest whim,
Seems all this poor endeavour after fame,
To one, who keeps within his stedfast aim
A love immortal, an immortal too.

Look not so wilder'd; for these things are true,
And never can be born of atomies
That buzz about our slumbers, like brain-flies,
Leaving us fancy-sick. No, no, I'm sure,
My restless spirit never could endure
To brood so long upon one luxury,
Unless it did, though fearfully, espy
A hope beyond the shadow of a dream.
My savings will the less obscured seem,
When I have told thee how my waking sight
Has made me scruple whether that same night
Was pass'd in dreaming. Hearken, sweet Peona!
Beyond the matron-temple of Latona,
Which we should see but for these darkening boughs,
Lies a deep hollow, from whose ragged brows
Bushes and trees do lean all round athwart,
And meet so nearly, that with wings outraught,
And spreaded tail, a vulture could not glide
Past them, but he must brush on every side.
Some moulder'd steps lead into this cool cell,
Far as the slabbed margin of a well,
Whose patient level peeps its crystal eye
Right upward, through the bushes, to the sky.
Oft have I brought thee flowers, on their stalks set
Like vestal primroses, but dark velvet
Edges them round, and they have golden pits:
'Twas there I got them, from the gaps and slits
In a mossy stone, that sometimes was my seat,
When all above was faint with mid-day heat.
And there in strife no burning thoughts to heed,
I'd bubble up the water through a reed;
So reaching back to boy-hood: make me ships
Of moutled feathers, touchwood, alder chips,
With leaves stuck in them; and the Neptune be
Of their petty ocean. Oftener, heavily,
When love-lorn hours had left me less a child,
I sat contemplating the figures wild
Of o'er-head clouds melting the mirror through.
Upon a day, while thus I watch'd, by flew
A cloudy Cupid, with his bow and quiver;
So plainly character'd, no breeze would shiver
The happy chance: so happy, I was fain

To follow it upon the open plain,
And, therefore, was just going; when, behold!
A wonder, fair as any I have told—
The same bright face I tasted in my sleep,
Smiling in the clear well. My heart did leap
Through the cool depth.—It moved as if to flee—
I started up, when lo! refreshfully,
There came upon my face, in plenteous showers,
Dew-drops, and dewy buds, and leaves, and flowers,
Wrapping all objects from my smothered sight,
Bathing my spirit in a new delight.
Aye, such a breathless honey-feel of bliss
Alone preserved me from the dear abyss
Of death, for the fair form had gone again.
Pleasure is oft a visitant; but pain
Clings cruelly to us, like the gnawing sloth
On the deer's tender haunches: late, and loth,
'Tis scar'd away by slow returning pleasure.
How sickening, how dark the dreadful leisure
Of weary days, made deeper exquisite,
By a fore-knowledge of unslumbrous night!
Like sorrow came upon me, heavier still,
Than when I wander'd from the poppy hill:
And a whole age of lingering moments crept
Sluggishly by, ere more contentment swept
Away at once the deadly yellow spleen.
Yes, thrice have I this fair enchantment seen;
Once more been tortured with renewed life.
When last the wintry gusts gave over strife
With the conquering sun of spring, and left the skies
Warm and serene, but yet with moistened eyes
In pity of the shatter'd infant buds,—
That time thou didst adorn, with amber studs,
My hunting cap, because I laugh'd and smil'd,
Chatted with thee, and many days exil'd
All torment from my breast;—'twas even then,
Straying about, yet, coop'd up in the den
Of helpless discontent,—hurling my lance
From place to place, and following at chance,
At last, by hap, through some young trees it struck,
And, plashing among bedded pebbles, stuck
In the middle of a brook,—whose silver ramble

Down twenty little falls, through reeds and bramble,
Tracing along, it brought me to a cave,
Whence it ran brightly forth, and white did lave
The nether sides of mossy stones and rock,–
'Mong which it gurgled blythe adieus, to mock
Its own sweet grief at parting. Overhead,
Hung a lush screen of drooping weeds, and spread
Thick, as to curtain up some wood-nymph's home.
'Ah! impious mortal, whither do I roam?'
Said I, low voic'd: 'Ah, whither! 'Tis the grot
Of Proserpine, when Hell, obscure and hot,
Doth her resign; and where her tender hands
She dabbles, on the cool and sluicy sands:
Or 'tis the cell of Echo, where she sits,
And babbles thorough silence, till her wits
Are gone in tender madness, and anon,
Faints into sleep, with many a dying tone
Of sadness. O that she would take my vows,
And breathe them sighingly among the boughs,
To sue her gentle ears for whose fair head,
Daily, I pluck sweet flowerets from their bed,
And weave them dyingly–send honey-whispers
Round every leaf, that all those gentle lispers
May sigh my love unto her pitying!
O charitable Echo! hear, and sing
This ditty to her'–so I stay'd
My foolish tongue, and listening, half afraid,
Stood stupefied with my own empty folly,
And blushing for the freaks of melancholy.
Salt tears were coming, when I heard my name
Most fondly lipp'd, and then these accents came:
'Endymion! the cave is secreter
Than the isle of Delos. Echo hence shall stir
No sighs but sigh-warm kisses, or light noise
Of thy combing hand, the while it travelling cloys
And trembles through my labyrinthine hair.'
At that opress'd I hurried in.–Ah! where
Are those swift moments? Whither are they fled?
I'll smile no more, Peona; nor will wed
Sorrow the way to death; but patiently
Bear up against it: so farewel, sad sigh;
And come instead demurest meditation,

To occupy me wholly, and to fashion
My pilgrimage for the world's dusky brink.
No more will I count over, link by link,
My chain of grief: no longer strive to find
A half-forgetfulness in mountain wind
Blustering about my ears: aye, thou shalt see,
Dearest of sisters, what my life shall be;
What a calm round of hours shall make my days.
There is a paly flame of hope that plays
Where'er I look: but yet, I'll say 'tis naught—
And here I bid it die. Have not I caught,
Already, a more healthy countenance?
By this the sun is setting; we may chance
Meet some of our near-dwellers with my car."

This said, he rose, faint-smiling like a star
Through autumn mists, and took Peona's hand:
They stept into the boat, and launch'd from land.

BOOK II

O sovereign power of love! O grief! O balm!
All records, saving thine, come cool, and calm,
And shadowy, through the mist of passed years:
For others, good or bad, hatred and tears
Have become indolent; but touching thine,
One sigh doth echo, one poor sob doth pine,
One kiss brings honey-dew from buried days.
The woes of Troy, towers smothering o'er their blaze,
Stiff-holden shields, far-piercing spears, keen blades,
Struggling, and blood, and shrieks—all dimly fades
Into some backward corner of the brain;
Yet, in our very souls, we feel amain
The close of Troilus and Cressid sweet.
Hence, pageant history! hence, gilded cheat!
Swart planet in the universe of deeds!
Wide sea, that one continuous murmur breeds
Along the pebbled shore of memory!
Many old rotten-timber'd boats there be
Upon thy vaporous bosom, magnified
To goodly vessels; many a sail of pride,

And golden keel'd, is left unlaunch'd and dry.
But wherefore this? What care, though owl did fly
About the great Athenian admiral's mast?
What care, though striding Alexander past
The Indus with his Macedonian numbers?
Though old Ulysses tortured from his slumbers
The glutted Cyclops, what care?—Juliet leaning
Amid her window-flowers,—sighing,—weaning
Tenderly her fancy from its maiden snow,
Doth more avail than these: the silver flow
Of Hero's tears, the swoon of Imogen,
Fair Pastorella in the bandit's den,
Are things to brood on with more ardency
Than the death-day of empires. Fearfully
Must such conviction come upon his head,
Who, thus far, discontent, has dared to tread,
Without one muse's smile, or kind behest,
The path of love and poesy. But rest,
In chafing restlessness, is yet more drear
Than to be crush'd, in striving to uprear
Love's standard on the battlements of song.
So once more days and nights aid me along,
Like legion'd soldiers.

Brain-sick shepherd prince,
What promise hast thou faithful guarded since
The day of sacrifice? Or, have new sorrows
Come with the constant dawn upon thy morrows?
Alas! 'tis his old grief. For many days,
Has he been wandering in uncertain ways:
Through wilderness, and woods of mossed oaks;
Counting his woe-worn minutes, by the strokes
Of the lone woodcutter; and listening still,
Hour after hour, to each lush-leav'd rill.
Now he is sitting by a shady spring,
And elbow-deep with feverous fingering
Stems the upbursting cold: a wild rose tree
Pavilions him in bloom, and he doth see
A bud which snares his fancy: lo! but now
He plucks it, dips its stalk in the water: how!
It swells, it buds, it flowers beneath his sight;
And, in the middle, there is softly pight

A golden butterfly; upon whose wings
There must be surely character'd strange things,
For with wide eye he wonders, and smiles oft.

Lightly this little herald flew aloft,
Follow'd by glad Endymion's clasped hands:
Onward it flies. From languor's sullen bands
His limbs are loos'd, and eager, on he hies
Dazzled to trace it in the sunny skies.
It seem'd he flew, the way so easy was;
And like a new-born spirit did he pass
Through the green evening quiet in the sun,
O'er many a heath, through many a woodland dun,
Through buried paths, where sleepy twilight dreams
The summer time away. One track unseams
A wooded cleft, and, far away, the blue
Of ocean fades upon him; then, anew,
He sinks adown a solitary glen,
Where there was never sound of mortal men,
Saving, perhaps, some snow-light cadences
Melting to silence, when upon the breeze
Some holy bark let forth an anthem sweet,
To cheer itself to Delphi. Still his feet
Went swift beneath the merry-winged guide,
Until it reached a splashing fountain's side
That, near a cavern's mouth, for ever pour'd
Unto the temperate air: then high it soar'd,
And, downward, suddenly began to dip,
As if, athirst with so much toil, 'twould sip
The crystal spout-head: so it did, with touch
Most delicate, as though afraid to smutch
Even with mealy gold the waters clear.
But, at that very touch, to disappear
So fairy-quick, was strange! Bewildered,
Endymion sought around, and shook each bed
Of covert flowers in vain; and then he flung
Himself along the grass. What gentle tongue,
What whisperer disturb'd his gloomy rest?
It was a nymph uprisen to the breast
In the fountain's pebbly margin, and she stood
'Mong lilies, like the youngest of the brood.
To him her dripping hand she softly kist,

And anxiously began to plait and twist
Her ringlets round her fingers, saying: "Youth!
Too long, alas, hast thou starv'd on the ruth,
The bitterness of love: too long indeed,
Seeing thou art so gentle. Could I weed
Thy soul of care, by heavens, I would offer
All the bright riches of my crystal coffer
To Amphitrite; all my clear-eyed fish,
Golden, or rainbow-sided, or purplish,
Vermilion-tail'd, or finn'd with silvery gauze;
Yea, or my veined pebble-floor, that draws
A virgin light to the deep; my grotto-sands
Tawny and gold, ooz'd slowly from far lands
By my diligent springs; my levels lilies, shells,
My charming rod, my potent river spells;
Yes, every thing, even to the pearly cup
Meander gave me,—for I bubbled up
To fainting creatures in a desert wild.
But woe is me, I am but as a child
To gladden thee; and all I dare to say,
Is, that I pity thee; that on this day
I've been thy guide; that thou must wander far
In other regions, past the scanty bar
To mortal steps, before thou canst be ta'en
From every wasting sigh, from every pain,
Into the gentle bosom of thy love.
Why it is thus, one knows in heaven above:
But, a poor Naiad, I guess not. Farewel!
I have a ditty for my hollow cell."

Hereat, she vanished from Endymion's gaze,
Who brooded o'er the water in amaze:
The dashing fount pour'd on, and where its pool
Lay, half asleep, in grass and rushes cool,
Quick waterflies and gnats were sporting still,
And fish were dimpling, as if good nor ill
Had fallen out that hour. The wanderer,
Holding his forehead, to keep off the burr
Of smothering fancies, patiently sat down;
And, while beneath the evening's sleepy frown
Glow-worms began to trim their starry lamps,
Thus breath'd he to himself: "Whoso encamps

To take a fancied city of delight,
O what a wretch is he! and when 'tis his,
After long toil and travelling, to miss
The kernel of his hopes, how more than vile:
Yet, for him there's refreshment even in toil;
Another city doth he set about,
Free from the smallest pebble-bead of doubt
That he will seize on trickling honey-combs:
Alas, he finds them dry; and then he foams,
And onward to another city speeds.
But this is human life: the war, the deeds,
The disappointment, the anxiety,
Imagination's struggles, far and nigh,
All human; bearing in themselves this good,
That they are still the air, the subtle food,
To make us feel existence, and to shew
How quiet death is. Where soil is men grow,
Whether to weeds or flowers; but for me,
There is no depth to strike in: I can see
Nought earthly worth my compassing; so stand
Upon a misty, jutting head of land—
Alone? No, no; and by the Orphean lute,
When mad Eurydice is listening to't;
I'd rather stand upon this misty peak,
With not a thing to sigh for, or to seek,
But the soft shadow of my thrice-seen love,
Than be—I care not what. O meekest dove
Of heaven! O Cynthia, ten-times bright and fair!
From thy blue throne, now filling all the air,
Glance but one little beam of temper'd light
Into my bosom, that the dreadful might
And tryanny of love be somewhat scar'd!
Yet do not so, sweet queen; one torment spar'd
Would give a pang to jealous misery,
Worse than the torment's self: but rather tie
Large wings upon my shoulders, and point out
My love's far dwelling. Though the playful rout
Of Cupids shun thee, too divine art thou,
Too keen in beauty, for thy silver prow
Not to have dipp'd in love's most gentle stream.
O be propitious, nor severely deem
My madness impious; for, by all the stars

That tend thy bidding, I do think the bars
That kept my spirit in are burst—that I
Am sailing with thee through the dizzy sky!
How beautiful thou art! The world how deep!
How tremulous-dazzlingly the wheels sweep
Around their axle! Then these gleaming reins,
How lithe! When this thy chariot attains
Its airy goal, haply some bower veils
Those twilight eyes? Those eyes!—my spirit fails—
Dear goddess, help! or the wide-gaping air
Will gulph me—help!"—At this with madden'd stare,
And lifted hands, and trembling lips he stood;
Like old Deucalion mountain'd o'er the flood,
Or blind Orion hungry for the morn.
And, but from the deep cavern there was borne
A voice, he had been froze to senseless stone;
Nor sigh of his, nor plaint, nor passion'd moan
Had more been heard. Thus swell'd it forth: "Descend,
Young mountaineer! descend where alleys bend
Into the sparry hollows of the world!
Oft hast thou seen bolts of the thunder hurl'd
As from thy threshold; day by day hast been
A little lower than the chilly sheen
Of icy pinnalces, and dipp'dst thine arms
Into the deadening ether that still charms
Their marble being: now, as deep profound
As those are high, descend! He ne'er is crown'd
With immortality, who fears to follow
Where airy voices lead: so through the hollow,
The silent mysteries of earth, descend!"

He heard but the last words, nor could contend
One moment in reflection: for he fled
Into the fearful deep, to hide his head
From the clear moon, the trees, and coming madness.

'Twas far too strange, and wonderful for sadness;
Sharpening, by degrees, his appetite
To dive into the deepest. Dark, nor light,
The region; nor bright, nor sombre wholly,
But mingled up; a gleaming melancholy;
A dusky empire and its diadems;

One faint eternal eventide of gems.
Aye, millions sparkled on a vein of gold,
Along whose track the prince quick footsteps told,
With all its lines abrupt and angular:
Out-shooting sometimes, like a meteor-star,
Through a vast antre; then the metal woof,
Like Vulcan's rainbow, with some monstrous roof
Curves hugely: now, far in the deep abyss,
It seems an angry lightning, and doth hiss
Fancy into belief: anon it leads
Through winding passages, where sameness breeds
Vexing conceptions of some sudden change;
Whether to silver grots, or giant range
Of sapphire columns, or fantastic bridge
Athwart a flood of crystal. On a ridge
Now fareth he, that o'er the vast beneath
Towers like an ocean-cliff, and whence he seeth
A hundred waterfalls, whose voices come
But as the murmuring surge. Chilly and numb
His bosom grew, when first he, far away,
Descried and orbed diamond, set to fray
Old darkness from his throne: 'twas like the sun
Uprisen o'er chaos: and with such a stun
Came the amazement, that, absorb'd in it,
He saw not fiercer wonders—past the wit
Of any spirit to tell, but one of those
Who, when this planet's sphering time doth close,
Will be its high remembrancers: who they?
The mighty ones who have made eternal day
For Greece and England. While astonishment
With deep-drawn sighs was quieting, he went
Into a marble gallery, passing through
A mimic temple, so complete and true
In sacred custom, that he well nigh fear'd
To search it inwards; whence far off appear'd,
Through a long pillar'd vista, a fair shrine,
And, just beyond, on light tiptoe divine,
A quiver'd Dian. Stepping awfully,
The youth approach'd; oft turning his veil'd eye
Down sidelong aisles, and into niches old.
And when, more near against the marble cold
He had touch'd his forehead, he began to thread

All courts and passages, where silence dead
Rous'd by his whispering footsteps murmured faint:
And long he travers'd to and fro, to acquaint
Himself with every mystery, and awe;
Till, weary, he sat down before the maw
Of a wide outlet, fathomless and dim,
To wild uncertainty and shadows grim.
There, when new wonders ceas'd to float before,
And thoughts of self came on, how crude and sore
The journey homeward to habitual self!
A mad-pursuing of the fog-horn elf,
Whose flitting lantern, through rude nettle-briar,
Cheats us into a swamp, into a fire,
Into the bosom of a hated thing.

What misery most drowningly doth sing
In lone Endymion's ear, now he has raught
The goal of consciousness? Ah, 'tis the thought,
The deadly feel of solitude: for lo!
He cannot see the heavens, nor the flow
Of rivers, nor hill-flowers running wild
In pink and purple chequer, nor, up-pil'd,
The cloudy rack slow journeying in the west,
Like herded elephants; nor felt, nor prest
Cool grass, nor tasted the fresh slumberous air;
But far from such companionship to wear
An unknown time, surcharg'd with grief, away,
Was now his lot. And must he patient stay,
Tracing fantastic figures with his spear?
"No!" exclaimed hi, "why should I tarry here?"
No! loudly echoed times innumerable.
At which he straightway started, and 'gan tell
His paces back into the temple's chief;
Warming and glowing strong in the belief
Of help from Dian: so that when again
He caught her airy form, thus did he plain,
Moving more near the while, "O Haunter chaste
Of river sides, and woods, and heathy waste,
Where with thy silver bow and arrows keen
Art thou now forested? O woodland Queen,
What smoothest air thy smoother forehead woos?
Where dost thou listen to the wide halloos

Of thy disparted nymphs? Through what dark tree
Glimmers thy crescent? Wheresoe'er it be,
'Tis in the breath of heaven: thou dost taste
Freedom as none can taste it, nor dost waste
Thy loveliness in dismal elements;
But, finding in our green earth sweet contents,
There livest blissfully. Ah, if to thee
It feels Elysian, how rich to me,
An exil'd mortal, sounds its pleasant name!
Within my breast there lives a choking flame—
O let me cool it the zephyr-boughs among!
A homeward fever parches up my tongue—
O let me slake it at the running springs!
Upon my ear a noisy nothing rings—
O let me once more hear the linnet's note!
Before mine eyes thick films and shadows float—
O let me 'noint them with the heaven's light!
Dost thou now lave thy feet and ankles white?
O think how sweet to me the freshening sluice!
Dost thou now please thy thirst with berry-juice?
O think how this dry palate would rejoice!
If in soft slumber thou dost hear my voice,
O think how I should love a bed of flowers!—
Young goddess! let me see my native bowers!
Deliver me from this rapacious deep!"

Thus ending loudly, as he would o'erleap
His destiny, alert he stood: but when
Obstinate silence came heavily again,
Feeling about for its old couch of space
And airy cradle, lowly bow'd his face
Desponding, o'er the marble floor's cold thrill.
But 'twas not long; for, sweeter than the rill
To its old channel, or a swollen tide
To margin sallows, were the leaves he spied,
And flowers, and wreaths, and ready myrtle crowns
Up heaping through the slab: refreshment drowns
Itself, and strives its own delights to hide—
Nor in one spot alone; the floral pride
In a long whispering birth enchanted grew
Before his footsteps; as when heav'd anew
Old ocean rolls a lengthened wave to the shore,

Down whose green back the short-liv'd foam, all hoar,
Bursts gradual, with a wayward indolence.

Increasing still in heart, and pleasant sense,
Upon his fairy journey on he hastes;
So anxious for the end, he scarcely wastes
One moment with his hand among the sweets:
Onward he goes—he stops—his bosom beats
As plainly in his ear, as the faint charm
Of which the throbs were born. This still alarm,
This sleepy music, forc'd him walk tiptoe:
For it came more softly than the east could blow
Arion's magic to the Atlantic isles;
Or than the west, made jealous by the smiles
Of thron'd Apollo, could breathe back the lyre
To seas Ionian and Tyrian.

O did he ever live, that lonely man,
Who lov'd—and music slew not? 'Tis the pest
Of love, that fairest joys give most unrest;
That things of delicate and tenderest worth
Are swallow'd all, and made a seared dearth,
By one consuming flame: it doth immerse
And suffocate true blessings in a curse.
Half-happy, by comparsion of bliss,
Is miserable. 'Twas even so with this
Dew-dropping melody, in the Carian's ear;
First heaven, then hell, and then forgotten clear,
Vanish'd in elemental passion.

And down some swart abysm he had gone,
Had not a heavenly guide benignant led
To where thick myrtle branches, 'gainst his head
Brushing, awakened: then the sounds again
Went noiseless as a passing noontide rain
Over a bower, where little space he stood;
For, as the sunset peeps into a wood,
So saw he panting light, and towards it went
Through winding alleys; and lo, wonderment!
Upon soft verdure saw, one here, one there,
Cupids a slumbering on their pinions fair.

After a thousand mazes overgone,
At last, with sudden step, he came upon
A chamber, myrtle wall'd, embowered high,
Full of light, incense, tender minstrelsy,
And more of beautiful and strange beside:
For on a silken couch of rosy pride,
In midst of all, there lay a sleeping youth
Of fondest beauty; fonder, in fair sooth,
Than sighs could fathom, or contentment reach:
And coverlids gold-tinted like the peach,
Or ripe October's faded marigolds,
Fell sleek about him in a thousand folds—
Not hiding up an Apollonian curve
Of neck and shoulder, nor the tenting swerve
Of knee, nor ankles pointing light;
But rather, giving them to the filled sight
Officiously. Sideway his face repos'd
On one white arm, and tenderly unclos'd,
By tenderest pressure, a faint damask mouth
To slumbery pout; just as the morning south
Disparts a dew-lipp'd rose. Above his head,
Four lily stalks did their white honours wed
To make a coronal; and round him grew
All tendrils green, of every bloom and hue,
Together intertwin'd and trammel'd fresh:
The vine of glossy sprout; the ivy mesh,
Shading its Ethiop berries; and woodbine,
Of velvet leaves and bugle-blooms divine;
Convolvulus in streaked vases flush;
The creeper, mellowing for an autumn blush;
And virgin's bower, trailing airily;
With others of the sisterhood. Hard by,
Stood serene Cupids watching silently.
One, kneeling to a lyre, touch'd the strings,
Muffling to death the pathos with his wings;
And, ever and anon, uprose to look
At the youth's slumber; while another took
A willow-bouth, distilling odorous dew,
And shook it on his hair; another flew
In through the woven roof, and fluttering-wise
Rain'd violets upon his sleeping eyes.

At these enchantments, and yet many more,
The breathless Latmian wonder'd o'er and o'er;
Until, impatient in embarrassment,
He forthright pass'd, and lightly treading went
To that same feather'd lyrist, who straightway,
Smiling, thus whisper'd: "Though from upper day
Thou art a wanderer, and thy presence here
Might seem unholy, be of happy cheer!
For 'tis the nicest touch of human honour,
When some ethereal and high-favouring donor
Presents immortal bowers to mortal sense;
As now 'tis done to thee, Endymion. Hence
Was I in no wise startled. So recline
Upon these living flowers. Here is wine,
Alive with sparkles—never, I aver,
Since Ariadne was a vintager,
So cool a purple: taste these juicy pears,
Sent me by sad Vertumnus, when his fears
Were high about Pomona: here is cream,
Deepening to richness from a snowy gleam;
Sweeter than that nurse Amalthea skimm'd
For the boy Jupiter: and here, undimm'd
By any touch, a bunch of blooming plums
Ready to melt between an infant's gums:
And here is manna pick'd from Syrian trees,
In starlight, by the three Hesperides.
Feast on, and meanwhile I will let thee know
Of all these things around us." He did so,
Still brooding o'er the cadence of his lyre;
And thus: "I need not any hearing tire
By telling how the sea-born goddess pin'd
For a mortal youth, and how she strove to bind
Him all in all unto her doting self.
Who would not be so prison'd? but, fond elf,
He was content to let her amorous plea
Faint through his careless arms; content to see
An unseiz'd heaven dying at his feet;
Content, O fool! to make a cold retreat,
When on the pleasant grass such love, lovelorn,
Lay sorrowing; when every tear was born
Of diverse passion; when her lips and eyes
Were clos'd in sullen moisture, and quick sighs

Came vex'd and pettish through her nostrils small.
Hush! no exclaim—yet, justly mightst thou call
Curses upon his head.—I was half glad,
But my poor mistress went distract and mad,
When the boar tusk'd him: so away she flew
To Jove's high throne, and by her plainings drew
Immortal tear-drops down the thunderer's beard;
Whereon, it was decreed he should be rear'd
Each summer time to life. Lo! this is he,
That same Adonis, safe in the privacy
Of this still region all his winter-sleep.
Aye, sleep; for when our love-sick queen did weep
Over his waned corse, the tremulous shower
Heal'd up the wound, and, with a balmy power,
Medicined death to a lengthened drowsiness:
The which she fills with visions, and doth dress
In all this quiet luxury; and hath set
Us young immortals, without any let,
To watch his slumber through. 'Tis well nigh pass'd,
Even to a moment's filling up, and fast
She scuds with summer breezes, to pant through
The first long kiss, warm firstling, to renew
Embower'd sports in Cytherea's isle.
Look! how those winged listeners all this while
Stand anxious: see! behold!"—This clamant word
Broke through the careful silence; for they heard
A rustling noise of leaves, and out there flutter'd
Pigeons and doves: Adonis something mutter'd,
The while one hand, that erst upon his thigh
Lay dormant, mov'd convuls'd and gradually
Up to his forehead. Then there was a hum
Of sudden voices, echoing, "Come! come!
Arise! awake! Clear summer has forth walk'd
Unto the clover-sward, and she has talk'd
Full soothingly to every nested finch:
Rise, Cupids! or we'll give the blue-bell pinch
To your dimpled arms. Once more sweet life begin!"
At this, from every side they hurried in,
Rubbing their sleepy eyes with lazy wrists,
And doubling over head their little fists
In backward yawns. But all were soon alive:
For as delicious wine doth, sparkling, dive

In nectar'd clouds and curls through water fair,
So from the arbour roof down swell'd an air
Odorous and enlivening; making all
To laugh, and play, and sing, and loudly call
For their sweet queen: when lo! the wreathed green
Disparted, and far upward could be seen
Blue heaven, and a silver car, air-borne,
Whose silent wheels, fresh wet from clouds of morn,
Spun off a drizzling dew,—which falling chill
On soft Adonis' shoulders, made him still
Nestle and turn uneasily about.
Soon were the white doves plain, with necks stretch'd out,
And silken traces tighten'd in descent;
And soon, returning form love's banishment,
Queen Venus leaning downward open arm'd:
Her shadow fell upon his breast, and charm'd
A tumult to his heart, and a new life
Into his eyes. Ah, miserable strife,
But for her comforting! unhappy sight,
But meeting her blue orbs! Who, who can write
Of these first minutes? The unchariest muse
To embracements warm as theirs makes coy excuse.

O it has ruffled every spirit there,
Saving Love's self, who stands superb to share
The general gladness: awfully he stands;
A sovereign quell is in his waving hands;
No sight can bear the lightning of his bow;
His quiver is mysterious, none can know
What themselves think of it; from forth his eyes
There darts strange light of varied hues and dyes:
A scowl is sometimes on his brow, but who
Look full upon it feel anon the blue
Of his fair eyes run liquid through their souls.
Endymion feels it, and no more controls
The burning prayer within him; so, bent low,
He had begun a plaining of his woe.
But Venus, bending forward, said: "My child,
Favour this gentle youth; his days are wild
With love—he—but alas! too well I see
Thou know'st the deepness of his misery.
Ah, smile not so, my son: I tell thee true,

That when through heavy hours I used to rue
The endless sleep of his new-born Adon',
This stranger ay I pitied. For upon
A dreary morning once I fled away
Into the breezy clouds, to weep and pray
For this my love: for vexing Mars had teaz'd
Me even to tears: thence, when a little eas'd,
Down-looking, vacant, through a hazy wood,
I saw this youth as he despairing stood:
Those same dark curls blown vagrant in the wind;
Those same full fringed lids a constant blind
Over his sullen eyes: I saw him throw
Himself on wither'd leaves, even as though
Death had come sudden; for no jot he mov'd,
Yet mutter'd wildly. I could hear he lov'd
Some fair immortal, and that his embrace
Had zoned her through the night. There is no trace
Of this in heaven: I have mark'd each cheek,
And find it is the vainest thing to seek;
And that of all things 'tis kept secretest.
Endymion! one day thou wilt be blest:
So still obey the guiding hand that fends
Thee safely through these wonders for sweet ends.
'Tis a concealment needful in extreme;
And if I guess'd not so, the sunny beam
Thou shouldst mount up to with me. Now adieu!
Here must we leave thee."—At these words up flew
The impatient doves, up rose the floating car,
Up went the hum celestial. High afar
The Latmian saw them minish into nought;
And, when all were clear vanish'd, still he caught
A vivid lightning from that dreadful bow.
When all was darkened, with Etnean throe
The earth clos'd—gave a solitary moan—
And left him once again in twilight lone.

He did not rave, he did not stare aghast,
For all those visions were o'ergone, and past,
And he in loneliness: he felt assur'd
Of happy times, when all he had endur'd
Would seem a feather to the mighty prize.
So, with unusual gladness, on he hies

Through caves, and palaces of mottled ore,
Gold dome, and crystal wall, and turquois floor,
Black polish'd porticos of awful shade,
And, at the last, a diamond balustrade,
Leading afar past wild magnificence,
Spiral through ruggedest loopholes, and thence
Stretching across a void, then guiding o'er
Enormous chasms, where, all foam and roar,
Streams subterranean tease their granite beds,
Then heighten'd just above the silvery heads
Of a thousand fountains, so that he could dash
The waters with his spear; but at the splash,
Done heedlessly, those spouting columns rose
Sudden a poplar's height, and 'gan to enclose
His diamond path with fretwork, streaming round
Alive, and dazzling cool, and with a sound,
Haply, like dolphin tumults, when sweet shells
Welcome the float of Thetis. Long he dwells
On this delight; for, every minute's space,
The streams with changed magic interlace:
Sometimes like delicatest lattices,
Cover'd with crystal vines; then weeping trees,
Moving about as in a gentle wind,
Which, in a wink, to watery gauze refin'd,
Pour'd into shapes of curtain'd canopies,
Spangled, and rich with liquid broideries
Of flowers, peacocks, swans, and naiads fair.
Swifter than lightning went these wonders rare;
And then the water, into stubborn streams
Collecting, mimick'd the wrought oaken beams,
Pillars, and frieze, and high fantastic roof,
Of those dusk places in times far aloof
Cathedrals call'd. He bade a loth farewel
To these founts Protean, passing gulph, and dell,
And torrent, and ten thousand jutting shapes,
Half seen through deepest gloom, and griesly gapes,
Blackening on every side, and overhead
A vaulted dome like heaven's, far bespread
With starlight gems: aye, all so huge and strange,
The solitary felt a hurried change
Working within him into something dreary,—
Vex'd like a morning eagle, lost, and weary,

And purblind amid foggy, midnight wolds.
But he revives at once: for who beholds
New sudden things, nor casts his mental slough?
Forth from a rugged arch, in the dusk below,
Came mother Cybele! alone—alone—
In sombre chariot; dark foldings thrown
About her majesty, and front death-pale,
With turrets crown'd. Four maned lions hale
The sluggish wheels; solemn their toothed maws,
Their surly eyes brow-hidden, heavy paws
Uplifted drowsily, and nervy tails
Cowering their tawny brushes. Silent sails
This shadowy queen athwart, and faints away
In another gloomy arch.

Wherefore delay,
Young traveller, in such a mournful place?
Art thou wayworn, or canst not further trace
The diamond path? And does it indeed end
Abrupt in middle air? Yet earthward bend
Thy forehead, and to Jupiter cloud-borne
Call ardently! He was indeed wayworn;
Abrupt, in middle air, his way was lost;
To cloud-borne Jove he bowed, and there crost
Towards him a large eagle, 'twixt whose wings,
Without one impious word, himself he flings,
Committed to the darkness and the gloom:
Down, down, uncertain to what pleasant doom,
Swift as a fathoming plummet down he fell
Through unknown things; till exhaled asphodel,
And rose, with spicy fannings interbreath'd,
Came swelling forth where little caves were wreath'd
So thick with leaves and mosses, that they seem'd
Large honey-combs of green, and freshly teem'd
With airs delicious. In the greenest nook
The eagle landed him, and farewel took.

It was a jasmine bower, all bestrown
With golden moss. His every sense had grown
Ethereal for pleasure; 'bove his head
Flew a delight half-graspable; his tread
Was Hesperean; to his capable ears

Silence was music from the holy spheres;
A dewy luxury was in his eyes;
The little flowers felt his pleasant sighs
And stirr'd them faintly. Verdant cave and cell
He wander'd through, oft wondering at such swell
Of sudden exaltation: but, "Alas!"
Said he, "will all this gush of feeling pass
Away in solitude? And must they wane,
Like melodies upon a sandy plain,
Without an echo? Then shall I be left
So sad, so melancholy, so bereft!
Yet still I feel immortal! O my love,
My breath of life, where art thou? High above,
Dancing before the morning gates of heaven?
Or keeping watch among those starry seven,
Old Atlas' children? Art a maid of the waters,
One of shell-winding Triton's bright-hair'd daughters?
Or art, impossible! a nymph of Dian's,
Weaving a coronal of tender scions
For very idleness? Where'er thou art,
Methinks it now is at my will to start
Into thine arms; to scare Aurora's train,
And snatch thee from the morning; o'er the main
To scud like a wild bird, and take thee off
From thy sea-foamy cradle; or to doff
Thy shepherd vest, and woo thee mid fresh leaves.
No, no, too eagerly my soul deceives
Its powerless self: I know this cannot be.
O let me then by some sweet dreaming flee
To her entrancements: hither, sleep, awhile!
Hither, most gentle sleep! and soothing foil
For some few hours the coming solitude."

Thus spake he, and that moment felt endued
With power to dream deliciously; so wound
Through a dim passage, searching till he found
The smoothest mossy bed and deepest, where
He threw himself, and just into the air
Stretching his indolent arms, he took, O bliss!
A naked waist: "Fair Cupid, whence is this?"
A well-known voice sigh'd, "Sweetest, here am I!"
At which soft ravishment, with doating cry

They trembled to each other.—Helicon!
O fountain'd hill! Old Homer's Helicon!
That thou wouldst spout a little streamlet o'er
These sorry pages; then the verse would soar
And sing above this gentle pair, like lark
Over his nested young: but all is dark
Around thine aged top, and thy clear fount
Exhales in mists to heaven. Aye, the count
Of mighty Poets is made up; the scroll
Is folded by the Muses; the bright roll
Is in Apollo's hand: our dazed eyes
Have seen a new tinge in the western skies:
The world has done its duty. Yet, oh yet,
Although the sun of poesy is set,
These lovers did embrace, and we must weep
That there is no old power left to steep
A quill immortal in their joyous tears.
Long time in silence did their anxious fears
Question that thus it was; long time they lay
Fondling and kissing every doubt away;
Long time ere soft caressing sobs began
To mellow into words, and then there ran
Two bubbling springs of talk from their sweet lips.
"O known Unknown! from whom my being sips
Such darling essence, wherefore may I not
Be ever in these arms? in this sweet spot
Pillow my chin for ever? ever press
These toying hands and kiss their smooth excess?
Why not for ever and for ever feel
That breath about my eyes? Ah, thou wilt steal
Away from me again, indeed, indeed—
Thou wilt be gone away, and wilt not heed
My lonely madness. Speak, delicious fair!
Is—is it to be so? No! Who will dare
To pluck thee from me? And, of thine own will,
Full well I feel thou wouldst not leave me. Still
Let me entwine thee surer, surer—now
How can we part? Elysium! who art thou?
Who, that thou canst not be for ever here,
Or lift me with thee to some starry sphere?
Enchantress! tell me by this soft embrace,
By the most soft completion of thy face,

Those lips, O slippery blisses, twinkling eyes,
And by these tenderest, milky sovereignties—
These tenderest, and by the nectar-wine,
The passion"—"O dov'd Ida the divine!
Endymion! dearest! Ah, unhappy me!
His soul will 'scape us—O felicity!
How he does love me! His poor temples beat
To the very tune of love—how sweet, sweet, sweet.
Revive, dear youth, or I shall faint and die;
Revive, or these soft hours will hurry by
In tranced dulness; speak, and let that spell
Affright this lethargy! I cannot quell
Its heavy pressure, and will press at least
My lips to thine, that they may richly feast
Until we taste the life of love again.
What! dost thou move? dost kiss? O bliss! O pain!
I love thee, youth, more than I can conceive;
And so long absence from thee doth bereave
My soul of any rest: yet must I hence:
Yet, can I not to starry eminence
Uplift thee; nor for very shame can own
Myself to thee. Ah, dearest, do not groan
Or thou wilt force me from this secrecy,
And I must blush in heaven. O that I
Had done't already; that the dreadful smiles
At my lost brightness, my impassion'd wiles,
Had waned from Olympus' solemn height,
And from all serious Gods; that our delight
Was quite forgotten, save of us alone!
And wherefore so ashamed? 'Tis but to atone
For endless pleasure, by some coward blushes:
Yet must I be a coward!—Horror rushes
Too palpable before me—the sad look
Of Jove—Minerva's start—no bosom shook
With awe of purity—no Cupid pinion
In reverence vailed—my crystalline dominion
Half lost, and all old hymns made nullity!
But what is this to love? O I could fly
With thee into the ken of heavenly powers,
So thou wouldst thus, for many sequent hours,
Press me so sweetly. Now I swear at once
That I am wise, that Pallas is a dunce—

Perhaps her love like mine is but unknown—
O I do think that I have been alone
In chastity: yes, Pallas has been sighing,
While every eve saw me my hair uptying
With fingers cool as aspen leaves. Sweet love,
I was as vague as solitary dove,
Nor knew that nests were built. Now a soft kiss—
Aye, by that kiss, I vow an endless bliss,
An immortality of passion's thine:
Ere long I will exalt thee to the shine
Of heaven ambrosial; and we will shade
Ourselves whole summers by a river glade;
And I will tell thee stories of the sky,
And breath thee whispers of its minstrelsy.
My happy love will overwing all bounds!
O let me melt into thee; let the sounds
Of our close voices marry at their birth;
Let us entwine hoveringly—O dearth
O human words! roughness of mortal speech!
Lispings empyrean will I sometime teach
Thine honied tongue—lute-breathings, which I gasp
To have thee understand, now while I clasp
Thee thus, and weep for fondness—I am pain'd,
Endymion: woe! woe! is grief contain'd
In the very deeps of pleasure, my sole life?"—
Hereat, with many sobs, her gentle strife
Melted into a languor. He return'd
Entranced vows and tears.

Ye who have yearn'd
With too much passion, will here stay and pity,
For the mere sake of truth; as 'tis a ditty
Not of these days, but long ago 'twas told
By a cavern wind unto a forest old;
And then the forest told it in a dream
To a sleeping lake, whose cool and level gleam
A poet caught as he was journeying
To Phoebus' shrine; and in it he did fling
His weary limbs, bathing an hour's space,
And after, straight in that inspired place
He sang the story up into the air,
Giving it universal freedom. There

Has it been ever sounding for those ears
Whose tips are glowing hot. The legend cheers
Yon centinel stars; and he who listens to it
Must surely be self-doomed or he will rue it:
For quenchless burnings come upon the heart,
Made fiercer by a fear lest any part
Should be engulphed in the eddying wind.
As much as here is penn'd doth always find
A resting place, thus much comes clear and plain;
Anon the strange voice is upon the wane—
And 'tis but echo'd from departing sound,
That the fair visitant at last unwound
Her gentle limbs, and left the youth asleep.—
Thus the tradition of the gusty deep.

Now turn we to our former chroniclers.—
Endymion awoke, that grief of hers
Sweet paining on his ear: he sickly guess'd
How lone he was once more, and sadly press'd
His empty arms together, hung his head,
And most forlorn upon that widow'd bed
Sat silently. Love's madness he had known:
Often with more than tortured lion's groan
Moanings had burst from him; but now that rage
Had pass'd away: no longer did he wage
A rough-voic'd war against the dooming stars.
No, he had felt too much for such harsh jars:
The lyre of his soul Eolian tun'd
Forgot all violence, and but commun'd
With melancholy thought: O he had swoon'd
Drunken from pleasure's nipple; and his love
Henceforth was dove-like.—Loth was he to move
From the imprinted couch, and when he did,
'Twas with slow, languid paces, and face hid
In muffling hands. So temper'd, out he stray'd
Half seeing visions that might have dismay'd
Alecto's serpents; ravishments more keen
Than Hermes' pipe, when anxious he did lean
Over eclipsing eyes: and at the last
It was a sounding grotto, vaulted, vast,
O'er studded with a thousand, thousand pearls,
And crimson mouthed shells with stubborn curls,

Of every shape and size, even to the bulk
In which whales harbour close, to brood and sulk
Against an endless storm. Moreover too,
Fish-semblances, of green and azure hue,
Ready to snort their streams. In this cool wonder
Endymion sat down, and 'gan to ponder
On all his life: his youth, up to the day
When 'mid acclaim, and feasts, and garlands gay,
He stept upon his shepherd throne: the look
Of his white palace in wild forest nook,
And all the revels he had lorded there:
Each tender maiden whom he once thought fair,
With every friend and fellow-woodlander—
Pass'd like a dream before him. Then the spur
Of the old bards to mighty deeds: his plans
To nurse the golden age 'mong shepherd clans:
That wonderous night: the great Pan-festival:
His sister's sorrow; and his wanderings all,
Until into the earth's deep maw he rush'd:
Then all its buried magic, till it flush'd
High with excessive love. "And now," thought he,
"How long must I remain in jeopardy
Of blank amazements that amaze no more?
Now I have tasted her sweet soul to the core
All other depths are shallow: essences,
Once spiritual, are like muddy lees,
Meant but to fertilize my earthly root,
And make my branches lift a golden fruit
Into the bloom of heaven: other light,
Though it be quick and sharp enough to blight
The Olympian eagle's vision, is dark,
Dark as the parentage of chaos. Hark!
My silent thoughts are echoing from these shells;
Or they are but the ghosts, the dying swells
Of noises far away?—list!"—Hereupon
He kept an anxious ear. The humming tone
Came louder, and behold, there as he lay,
On either side outgush'd, with misty spray,
A copious spring; and both together dash'd
Swift, mad, fantastic round the rocks, and lash'd
Among the conchs and shells of the lofty grot,
Leaving a trickling dew. At last they shot

Down from the ceiling's height, pouring a noise
As of some breathless racers whose hopes poize
Upon the last few steps, and with spent force
Along the ground they took a winding course.
Endymion follow'd—for it seem'd that one
Every pursued, the other strove to shun—
Follow'd their languid mazes, till well nigh
He had left thinking of the mystery,—
And was now rapt in tender hoverings
Over the vanish'd bliss. Ah! what is it sings
His dream away? What melodies are these?
They sound as through the whispering of trees,
Not native in such barren vaults. Give ear!

"O Arethusa, peerless nymph! why fear
such tenderness as mine? Great Dian, why,
Why didst thou hear her prayer? O that I
Were rippling round her dainty fairness now,
Circling about her waist, and striving how
To entice her to a dive! then stealing in
Between her luscious lips and eyelids thin.
O that her shining hair was in the sun,
And I distilling from it thence to run
In amorous rillets down her shrinking form!
To linger on her lily shoulders, warm
Between her kissing breasts, and every charm
Touch raptur'd!—See how painfully I flow:
Fair maid, be pitiful to my great woe.
Stay, stay thy weary course, and let me lead,
A happy wooer, to the flowery mead
Where all that beauty snar'd me."—"Cruel god,
Desist! or my offended mistress' nod
Will stagnate all thy fountains:—tease me not
With syren words—Ah, have I really got
Such power to madden thee? And is it true—
Away, away, or I shall dearly rue
My very thoughts: in mercy then away,
Kindest Alpheus, for should I obey
My own dear will, 'twould be a deadly bane.
O, Oread-Queen! would that thou hadst a pain
Like this of mine, then would I fearless turn
And be a criminal. Alas, I burn,

I shudder—gentle river, get thee hence.
Alpheus! thou enchanter! every sense
O mine was once made perfect in these woods.
Fresh breezes, bowery lawns, and innocent floods,
Ripe fruits, and lonely couch, contentment gave;
But every since I heedlessly did lave
In thy deceitful stream, a panting glow
Grew strong within me: wherefore serve me so,
And call it love? Alas, 'twas cruelty.
Not once more did I close my happy eye
Amid the thrush's song. Away! Avaunt!
O 'twas a cruel thing."—"Now thou dost taunt
So softly, Arethusa, that I think
If thou wast playing on my shady brink,
Thou wouldst bathe once again. Innocent maid!
Stifle thine heart no more;—nor be afraid
Of angry powers: there are deities
Will shade us with their wings. Those fitful sighs
'Tis almost death to hear: O let me pour
A dewy balm upon them!—fear no more,
Sweet Arethusa! Dian's self must feel
Sometimes these very pangs. Dear maiden, steal
Blushing into my soul, and let us fly
These dreary caverns for the open sky.
I will delight thee all my winding course,
From the green sea up to my hidden source
About Arcadian forests; and will shew
The channels where my coolest waters flow
Through mossy rocks; where, 'mid exuberant green,
I roam in pleasant darkness, more unseen
Than Saturn in his exile; where I brim
Round flowery islands, and take thence a skim
Of mealy sweets, which myriads of bees
Buzz from their honied wings: and thou shouldst please
Thyself to choose the richest, where we might
Be incense-pillow'd every summer night.
Doff all sad fears, thou white deliciousness,
And let us be thus comforted; unless
Thou couldst rejoice to see my hopeless stream
Hurry distracted from Sol's temperate beam,
And pour to death along some hungry sands."—
"What can I do, Alpheus? Dian stands

Severe before me: persecuting fate!
Unhappy Arethusa! thou wast late
A huntress free in"—At this, sudden fell
Those two sad streams adown a fearful dell.
The Latmian listen'd, but he heard no more,
Save echo, faint repeating o'er and o'er
The name of Arethusa. On the verge
Of that dark gulph he wept, and said: "I urge
Thee, gentle Goddess of my pilgrimage,
By our eternal hopes, to soothe, to assuage,
If thou art powerful, these lovers' pains;
And make them happy in some happy plains."

He turn'd—there was a whelming sound—he stept,
There was a cooler light; and so he kept
Towards it by a sandy path, and lo!
More suddenly than doth a moment go,
The visions of the earth were gone and fled—
He saw the giant sea above his head.

BOOK III

There are who lord it o'er their fellow-men
With most prevailing tinsel: who unpen
Their baaing vanities, to browse away
The comfortable green and juicy hay
From human pastures; or, O torturing fact!
Who, through an idiot blink, will see unpack'd
Fire-branded foxes to sear up and singe
Our gold and ripe-ear'd hopes. With not one tinge
Of sanctuary splendour, not a sight
Able to face an owl's, they still are dight
By the blear-eyed nations in empurpled vests,
And crowns, and turbans. With unladen breasts,
Save of blown self-applause, they proudly mount
To their spirit's perch, their being's high account,
Their tiptop nothings, their dull skies, their thrones—
Amid the fierce intoxicating tones
Of trumpets, shootings, and belabor'd drums,
And sudden cannon. Ah! how all this hums,
In wakeful ears, like uproar past and gone—

Like thunder clouds that spake to Babylon,
And set those old Chaldeans to their tasks.—
Are then regalities all gilded masks?
No, there are throned seats unscalable
But by a patient wing, a constant spell,
Or by ethereal things that, unconfin'd,
Can make a ladder of the eternal wind,
And poise about in cloudy thunder-tents
To watch the abysm-birth of elements.
Aye, 'bove the withering of old-lipp'd Fate
A thousand Powers kepp religious state,
In water, fiery realm, and airy bourne;
And, silent as a consecrated urn,
Hold sphery sessions for a season due.
Yet few of these far majesties, ah, few!
Have bared their operations to this globe—
Few, who with gorgeous pageantry enrobe
Our piece of heaven—whose benevolence
Shakes hand with our own Ceres; every sense
Filling with spiritual sweets to plenitude,
As bees gorge full their cells. And, by the feud
'Twixt Nothing and Creation, I here swear,
Eterne Apollo! that thy Sister fair
Is of all these the gentlier-mightiest.
When thy gold breath is misting in the west,
She unobserved steals unto her throne,
And there she sits most meek and most alone;
As if she had not pomp subservient;
As if thine eye, high Poet! was not bent
Towards her with the Muses in thine heart;
As if the ministring stars kept not apart,
Waiting for silver-footed messages.
O Moon! the oldest shades 'mong oldest trees
Feel palpitations when thou lookest in:
O Moon! old boughs lisp forth a holier din
The while they feel thine airy fellowship.
Thou dost bless every where, with silver lip
Kissing dead things to life. The sleeping kine,
Couched in thy brightness, dream of fields divine:
Innumerable mountains rise, and rise,
Ambitious for the hallowing of thine eyes;
And yet thy benediction passeth not

One obscure hiding-place, one little spot
Where pleasure may be sent: the nested wren
Has thy fair face within its tranquil ken,
And from beneath a sheltering ivy leaf
Takes glimpses of thee; thou art a relief
To the poor patient oyster, where it sleeps
Within its pearly house.—The mighty deeps,
The monstrous sea is thine—thy myriad sea!
O Moon! far-spooming Ocean bows to thee,
And Tellus feels his forehead's cumbrous load.

Cynthia! where art thou now? What far abode
Of green or silvery bower doth enshrine
Such utmost beauty? Alas, thou dost pine
For one as sorrowful: thy cheek is pale
For one whose cheek is pale: thou dost bewail
His tears, who weeps for thee. Where dost thou sigh?
Ah! surely that light peeps from Vesper's eye,
Or what a thing is love! 'Tis She, but lo!
How chang'd, how full of ache, how gone in woe!
She dies at the thinnest cloud; her loveliness
Is wan on Neptune's blue: yet there's a stress
Of love-spangles, just off yon cape of trees,
Dancing upon the waves, as if to please
The curly foam with amorous influence.
O, not so idle: for down-glancing thence
She fathoms eddies, and runs wild about
O'erwhelming water-courses; scaring out
The thorny sharks from hiding-holes, and fright'ning
Their savage eyes with unaccustomed lightning.
Where will the splendor be content to reach?
O love! how potent hast thou been to teach
Strange journeyings! Wherever beauty dwells,
In gulf or aerie, mountains or deep dells,
In light, in gloom, in star or blazing sun,
Thou pointest out the way, and straight 'tis won.
Amid his toil thou gav'st Leander breath;
Thou leddest Orpheus through the gleams of death;
Thou madest Pluto bear thin element;
And now, O winged Chieftain! thou hast sent
A moon-beam to the deep, deep water-world,
To find Endymion.

On gold sand impearl'd
With lily shells, and pebbles milky white,
Poor Cynthia greeted him, and sooth'd her light
Against his pallid face: he felt the charm
To breathlessness, and suddenly a warm
Of his heart's blood: 'twas very sweet; he stay'd
His wandering steps, and half-entranced laid
His head upon a tuft of straggling weeds,
To taste the gentle moon, and freshening beads,
Lashed from the crystal roof by fishes' tails.
And so he kept, until the rosy veils
Mantling the east, by Aurora's peering hand
Were lifted from the water's breast, and fann'd
Into sweet air; and sober'd morning came
Meekly through billows:—when like taper-flame
Left sudden by a dallying breath of air,
He rose in silence, and once more 'gan fare
Along his fated way.

Far had he roam'd,
With nothing save the hollow vast, that foam'd
Above, around, and at his feet; save things
More dead than Morpheus' imaginings:
Old rusted anchors, helmets, breast-plates large
Of gone sea-warriors; brazen beaks and targe;
Rudders that for a hundred years had lost
The sway of human hand; gold vase emboss'd
With long-forgotten story, and wherein
No reveller had ever dipp'd a chin
But those of Saturn's vintage; mouldering scrolls,
Writ in the tongue of heaven, by those souls
Who first were on the earth; and sculptures rude
In ponderous stone, developing the mood
Of ancient Nox;—then skeletons of man,
Of beast, behemoth, and leviathan,
And elephant, and eagle, and huge jaw
Of nameless monster. A cold leaden awe
These secrets struck into him; and unless
Dian had chaced away that heaviness,
He might have died: but now, with cheered feel,
He onward kept; wooing these thoughts to steal
About the labyrinth in his soul of love.

"What is there in thee, Moon! that thou shouldst move
My heart so potently? When yet a child
I oft have dried my tears when thou hast smil'd.
Thou seem'dst my sister: hand in hand we went
From eve to morn across the firmament.
No apples would I gather from the tree,
Till thou hadst cool'd their cheeks deliciously:
No tumbling water ever spake romance,
But when my eyes with thine thereon could dance:
No woods were green enough, no bower divine,
Until thou liftedst up thine eyelids fine:
In sowing time ne'er would I dibble take,
Or drop a seed, till thou wast wide awake;
And, in the summer tide of blossoming,
No one but thee hath heard me blithely sing
And mesh my dewy flowers all the night.
No melody was like a passing spright
If it went not to solemnize thy reign.
Yes, in my boyhood, every joy and pain
By thee were fashion'd to the self-same end;
And as I grew in years, still didst thou blend
With all my ardours: thou wast the deep glen;
Thou wast the mountain-top—the sage's pen—
The poet's harp—the voice of friends—the sun;
Thou wast the river—thou wast glory won;
Thou wast my clarion's blast—thou wast my steed—
My goblet full of wine—my topmost deed:—
Thou wast the charm of women, lovely Moon!
O what a wild and harmonized tune
My spirit struck from all the beautiful!
On some bright essence could I lean, and lull
Myself to immortality: I prest
Nature's soft pillow in a wakeful rest.
But, gentle Orb! there came a nearer bliss—
My strange love came—Felicity's abyss!
She came, and thou didst fade, and fade away—
Yet not entirely; no, thy starry sway
Has been an under-passion to this hour.
Now I begin to feel thine orby power
Is coming fresh upon me: O be kind,
Keep back thine influence, and do not blind
My sovereign vision.—Dearest love, forgive

That I can think away from thee and live!—
Pardon me, airy planet, that I prize
One thought beyond thine argent luxuries!
How far beyond!" At this a surpris'd start
Frosted the springing verdure of his heart;
For as he lifted up his eyes to swear
How his own goddess was past all things fair,
He saw far in the concave green of the sea
An old man sitting calm and peacefully.
Upon a weeded rock this old man sat,
And his white hair was awful, and a mat
Of weeds were cold beneath his cold thin feet;
And, ample as the largest winding-sheet,
A cloak of blue wrapp'd up his aged bones,
O'erwrought with symbols by the deepest groans
Of ambitious magic: every ocean-form
Was woven in with black distinctness; storm,
And calm, and whispering, and hideous roar,
Quicksand and whirlpool, and deserted shore
Were emblem'd in the woof; with every shape
That skims, or dives, or sleeps, 'twixt cape and cape.
The gulphing whale was like a dot in the spell,
Yet look upon it, and 'twould size and swell
To its huge self; and the minutest fish
Would pass the very hardest gazer's wish,
And shew his little eye's anatomy.
Then there was pictur'd the regality
Of Neptune; and the sea nymphs round his state,
In beauteous vassalage, look up and wait.
Beside this old man lay a pearly wand,
And in his lap a book, the which he conn'd
So stedfastly, that the new denizen
Had time to keep him in amazed ken,
To mark these shadowings, and stand in awe.

The old man rais'd his hoary head and saw
The wilder'd stranger—seeming not to see,
His features were so lifeless. Suddenly
He woke as from a trance; his snow-white brows
Went arching up, and like two magic ploughs
Furrow'd deep wrinkles in his forehead-large,
Which kept as fixedly as rocky marge,

Till round his wither'd lips had gone a smile.
Then up he rose, like one whose tedious toil
Had watch'd for years in forlorn hermitage,
Who had not from mid-life to utmost age
Eas'd in one accent his o'er-burden'd soul,
Even to the trees. He rose: he grasp'd his stole,
With convuls'd clenches waving it abroad,
And in a voice of solemn joy, that aw'd
Echo into oblivion, he said:—

"Thou art the man! Now shall I lay my head
In peace upon my watery pillow: now
Sleep will come smoothly to my weary brow.
O Jove! I shall be young again, be young!
O shell-borne Neptune, I am pierc'd and stung
With new-born life! What shall I do? Where go,
When I have cast this serpent-skin of woe?—
I'll swim to the syrens, and one moment listen
Their melodies, and see their long hair glisten;
Anon upon that giant's arm I'll be,
That writhes about the roots of Sicily:
To northern seas I'll in a twinkling sail,
And mount upon the snortings of a whale
To some black cloud; thence down I'll madly sweep
On forked lightning, to the deepest deep,
Where through some sucking pool I will be hurl'd
With rapture to the other side of the world!
O, I am full of gladness! Sisters three,
I bow full hearted to your old decree!
Yes, every god be thank'd, and power benign,
For I no more shall wither, droop, and pine.
Thou art the man!" Endymion started back
Dismay'd; and, like a wretch from whom the rack
Tortures hot breath, and speech of agony,
Mutter'd: "What lonely death am I to die
In this cold region? Will he let me freeze,
And float my brittle limbs o'er polar seas?
Or will he touch me with his searing hand,
And leave a black memorial on the sand?
Or tear me piece-meal with a bony saw,
And keep me as a chosen food to draw
His magian fish through hated fire and flame?

O misery of hell! resistless, tame,
Am I to be burnt up? No, I will shout,
Until the gods through heaven's blue look out!—
O Tartarus! but some few days agone
Her soft arms were entwining me, and on
Her voice I hung like fruit among green leaves:
Her lips were all my own, and—ah, ripe sheaves
Of happiness! ye on the stubble droop,
But never may be garner'd. I must stoop
My head, and kiss death's foot. Love! farewel!
Is there no hope from thee? This horrid spell
Would melt at thy sweet breath.—By Dian's hind
Feeding from her white fingers, on the wind
I see thy streaming hair! and now, by Pan,
I care not for this old mysterious man!"

He spake, and walking to that aged form,
Look'd high defiance. Lo! his heart 'gan warm
With pity, for the grey-hair'd creature wept.
Had he then wrong'd a heart where sorrow kept?
Had he, though blindly contumelious, brought
Rheum to kind eyes, a sting to humane thought,
Convulsion to a mouth of many years?
He had in truth; and he was ripe for tears.
The penitent shower fell, as down he knelt
Before that care-worn sage, who trembling felt
About his large dark locks, and faultering spake:

"Arise, good youth, for sacred Phoebus' sake!
I know thine inmost bosom, and I feel
A very brother's yearning for thee steal
Into mine own: for why? thou openest
The prison gates that have so long opprest
My weary watching. Though thou know'st it not,
Thou art commission'd to this fated spot
For great enfranchisement. O weep no more;
I am a friend to love, to loves of yore:
Aye, hadst thou never lov'd an unknown power,
I had been grieving at this joyous hour.
But even now most miserable old,
I saw thee, and my blood no longer cold
Gave mighty pulses: in this tottering case

Grew a new heart, which at this moment plays
As dancingly as thine. Be not afraid,
For thou shalt hear this secret all display'd,
Now as we speed towards our joyous task."

So saying, this young soul in age's mask
Went forward with the Carian side by side:
Resuming quickly thus; while ocean's tide
Hung swollen at their backs, and jewel'd sands
Took silently their foot-prints.

"My soul stands
Now past the midway from mortality,
And so I can prepare without a sigh
To tell thee briefly all my joy and pain.
I was a fisher once, upon this main,
And my boat danc'd in every creek and bay;
Rough billows were my home by night and day,—
The sea-gulls not more constant; for I had
No housing from the storm and tempests mad,
But hollow rocks,—and they were palaces
Of silent happiness, of slumberous ease:
Long years of misery have told me so.
Aye, thus it was one thousand years ago.
One thousand years!—Is it then possible
To look so plainly through them? to dispel
A thousand years with backward glance sublime?
To breathe away as 'twere all scummy slime
From off a crystal pool, to see its deep,
And one's own image from the bottom peep?
Yes: now I am no longer wretched thrall,
My long captivity and moanings all
Are but a slime, a thin pervading scum,
The which I breathe away, and thronging come
Like thinks of yesterday my youthful pleasures.

"I touch'd no lute, I sang not, trod no measures:
I was a lonely youth on desert shores.
My sports were lonely, 'mid continuous roars,
And craggy isles, and sea-mew's plaintive cry
Plaining discrepant between sea and sky.
Dolphins were still my playmates; shapes unseen

Would let me feel their scales of gold and green,
Nor be my desolation; and, full oft,
When a dread waterspout had rear'd aloft
Its hungry hugeness, seeming ready ripe
To burst with hoarsest thunderings, and wipe
My life away like a vast sponge of fate,
Some friendly monster, pitying my sad state,
Has dived to its foundations, gulph'd it down,
And left me tossing safely. But the crown
Of all my life was utmost quietude:
More did I love to lie in cavern rude,
Keeping in wait whole days for Neptune's voice,
And if it came at last, hark, and rejoice!
There blush'd no summer eve but I would steer
My skiff along green shelving coasts, to hear
The shepherd's pipe come clear from airy steep,
Mingled with ceaseless bleatings of his sheep:
And never was a day of summer shine,
But I beheld its birth upon the brine:
For I would watch all night to see unfold
Heaven's gates, and Aethon snort his morning gold
Wide o'er the swelling streams: and constantly
At brim of day-tide, on some grassy lea,
My nets would be spread out, and I at rest.
The poor folk of the sea-country I blest
With daily boon of fish most delicate:
They knew not whence this bounty, and elate
Would strew sweet flowers on a sterile beach.

"Why was I not contented? Wherefore reach
At things which, but for thee, O Latmian!
Had been my dreary death? Fool! I began
To feel distemper'd longings: to desire
The utmost privilege that ocean's sire
Could grant in benediction: to be free
Of all his kingdom. Long in misery
I wasted, ere in one extremest fit
I plung'd for life or death. To interknit
One's senses with so dense a breathing stuff
Might seem a work of pain; so not enough
Can I admire how crystal-smooth it felt,
And buoyant round my limbs. At first I dwelt

Whole days and days of sheer astonishment;
Forgetful utterly of self-intent;
Moving but with the mighty ebb and flow.
Then, like a new fledg'd bird that first doth shew
His spreaded feathers to the morrow chill,
I tried in fear the pinions of my will.
'Twas freedom! and at once I visited
The ceaseless wonders of this ocean-bed.
No need to tell thee of them, for I see
That thou hast been a witness—it must be—
For these I know thou canst not feel a drouth,
By the melancholy corners of that mouth.
So I will in my story straightway pass
To more immediate matter. Woe, alas!
That love should be my bane! Ah, Scylla fair!
Why did poor Glaucus ever—ever dare
To sue thee to his heart? Kind stranger-youth!
I lov'd her to the very white of truth,
And she would not conceive it. Timid thing!
She fled me swift as sea-bird on the wing,
Round every isle, and point, and promontory,
From where large Hercules wound up his story
Far as Egyptian Nile. My passion grew
The more, the more I saw her dainty hue
Gleam delicately through the azure clear:
Until 'twas too fierce agony to bear;
And in that agony, across my grief
It flash'd, that Circe might find some relief—
Cruel enchantress! So above the water
I rear'd my head, and look'd for Phoebus' daughter.
Aeaea's isle was wondering at the moon:—
It seem'd to whirl around me, and a swoon
Left me dead-drifting to that fatal power.

"When I awoke, 'twas in a twilight bower;
Just when the light of morn, with hum of bees,
Stole through its verdurous matting of fresh trees.
How sweet, and sweeter! for I heard a lyre,
And over it a sighing voice expire.
It ceased—I caught light footsteps; and anon
The fairest face that morn e'er look'd upon
Push'd through a screen of roses. Starry Jove!

With tears, and smiles, and honey-words she wove
A net whose thraldom was more bliss than all
The range of flower'd Elysium. Thus did fall
The dew of her rich speech: 'Ah! Art awake?
O let me hear thee speak, for Cupid's sake!
I am so oppress'd with joy! Why, I have shed
An urn of tears, as though thou wert cold dead;
And now I find thee living, I will pour
From these devoted eyes their silver store,
Until exhausted of the latest drop,
So it will pleasure thee, and force thee stop
Here, that I too may live: but if beyond
Such cool and sorrowful offerings, thou art fond
Of soothing warmth, of dalliance supreme;
If thou art ripe to taste a long love dream;
If smiles, if dimples, tongues for ardour mute,
Hang in thy vision like a tempting fruit,
O let me pluck it for thee.' Thus she link'd
Her charming syllables, till indistinct
Their music came to my o'er-sweeten'd soul;
And then she hover'd over me, and stole
So near, that if no nearer it had been
This furrow'd visage thou hadst never seen.

"Young man of Latmos! thus particular
Am I, that thou may'st plainly see how far
This fierce temptation went: and thou may'st not
Exclaim, How then, was Scylla quite forgot?

"Who could resist? Who in this universe?
She did so breath ambrosia; so immerse
My fine existence in a golden clime.
She took me like a child of suckling time,
And cradled me in roses. Thus condemn'd,
The current of my former life was stemm'd,
And to this arbitrary queen of sense
I bow'd a tranced vassal: nor would thence
Have mov'd, even though Amphion's harp had woo'd
Me back to Scylla o'er the billows rude.
For as Apollo each eve doth devise
A new appareling for western skies;
So every eve, nay every spendthrift hour

Shed balmy consciousness within that bower.
And I was free of haunts umbrageous;
Could wander in the mazy forest-house
Of squirrels, foxes shy, and antler'd deer,
And birds from coverts innermost and drear
Warbling for very joy mellifluous sorrow—
To me new born delights!

"Now let me borrow,
For moments few, a temperament as stern
As Pluto's sceptre, that my words not burn
These uttering lips, while I in calm speech tell
How specious heaven was changed to real hell.

"One morn she left me sleeping: half awake
I sought for her smooth arms and lips, and slake
My greedy thirst with nectarous camel-draughts;
But she was gone. Whereat the barbed shafts
Of disappointment stuck in me so sore,
That out I ran and search'd the forest o'er.
Wandering about in pine and cedar gloom
Damp awe assail'd me; for there 'gan to boom
A sound of moan, an agony of sound,
Sepulchral from the distance all around.
Then came a conquering earth-thunder, and rumbled
That fierce complain to silence: while I stumbled
Down a precipitous path, as if impell'd.
I came to a dark valley.—Groanings swell'd
Poisonous about my ears, and louder grew,
The nearer I approach'd a flame's gaunt blue,
That glar'd before me through a thorny brake.
This fire, like the eye of gordian snake,
Bewitch'd me towards; and I soon was near
A sight too fearful for the feel of fear:
In thicket hid I curs'd the haggard scene—
The banquet of my arms, my arbour queen,
Seated upon an uptorn forest root;
And all around her shapes, wizard and brute,
Laughing, and wailing, groveling, serpenting,
Shewing tooth, tusk, and venom-bag, and sting!
O such deformities! Old Charon's self,
Should he give up awhile his penny pelf,

And take a dream 'mong rushes Stygian,
It could not be so phantasied. Fierce, wan,
And tyrannizing was the lady's look,
As over them a gnarled staff she shook.
Oft-times upon the sudden she laugh'd out,
And from a basket emptied to the rout
Clusters of grapes, the which they raven'd quick
And roar'd for more; with many a hungry lick
About their shaggy jaws. Avenging, slow,
Anon she took a branch of mistletoe,
And emptied on't a black dull-gurgling phial:
Groan'd one and all, as if some piercing trial
Was sharpening for their pitiable bones.
She lifted up the charm: appealing groans
From their poor breasts went sueing to her ear
In vain; remorseless as an infant's bier
She whisk'd against their eyes the sooty oil.
Whereat was heard a noise of painful toil,
Increasing gradual to a tempest rage,
Shrieks, yells, and groans of torture-pilgrimage;
Until their grieved bodies 'gan to bloat
And puff from the tail's end to stifled throat:
Then was appalling silence: then a sight
More wildering than all that hoarse affright;
For the whole herd, as by a whirlwind writhen,
Went through the dismal air like one huge Python
Antagonizing Boreas,—and so vanish'd.
Yet there was not a breath of wind: she banish'd
These phantoms with a nod. Lo! from the dark
Came waggish fauns, and nymphs, and satyrs stark,
With dancing and loud revelry,—and went
Swifter than centaurs after rapine bent.—
Sighing, an elephant appear'd and bow'd
Before the fierce witch, speaking thus aloud
In human accent: 'Potent goddess! chief
Of pains resistless! make my being brief,
Or let me from this heavy prison fly:
Or give me to the air, or let me die!
I sue not for my happy crown again;
I sue not for my phalanx on the plain;
I sue not for my lone, my widow'd wife;
I sue not for my ruddy drops of life,

My children fair, my lovely girls and boys!
I will forget them; I will pass these joys;
Ask nought so heavenward, so too—too high:
Only I pray, as fairest boon, to die,
Or be deliver'd from this cumbrous flesh,
From this gross, detestable, filthy mesh,
And merely given to the cold bleak air.
Have mercy, Goddess! Circe, feel my prayer!'

"That curst magician's name fell icy numb
Upon my wild conjecturing: truth had come
Naked and sabre-like against my heart.
I saw a fury whetting a death-dart;
And my slain spirit, overwrought with fright,
Fainted away in that dark lair of night.
Think, my deliverer, how desolate
My waking must have been! disgust, and hate,
And terrors manifold divided me
A spoil amongst them. I prepar'd to flee
Into the dungeon core of that wild wood:
I fled three days—when lo! before me stood
Glaring the angry witch. O Dis, even now,
A clammy dew is beading on my brow,
At mere remembering her pale laugh, and curse.
'Ha! ha! Sir Dainty! there must be a nurse
Made of rose leaves and thistledown, express,
To cradle thee, my sweet, and lull thee: yes,
I am too flinty-hard for thy nice touch:
My tenderest squeeze is but a giant's clutch.
So, fairy-thing, it shall have lullabies
Unheard of yet; and it shall still its cries
Upon some breast more lily-feminine.
Oh, no—it shall not pine, and pine, and pine
More than one pretty, trifling thousand years;
And then 'twere pity, but fate's gentle shears
Cut short its immortality. Sea-flirt!
Young dove of the waters! truly I'll not hurt
One hair of thine: see how I weep and sigh,
That our heart-broken parting is so nigh.
And must we part? Ah, yes, it must be so.
Yet ere thou leavest me in utter woe,
Let me sob over thee my last adieus,

And speak a blessing: Mark me! Thou hast thews
Immortal, for thou art of heavenly race:
But such a love is mine, that here I chase
Eternally away from thee all bloom
Of youth, and destine thee towards a tomb.
Hence shalt thou quickly to the watery vast;
And there, ere many days be overpast,
Disabled age shall seize thee; and even then
Thou shalt not go the way of aged men;
But live and wither, cripple and still breathe
Ten hundred years: which gone, I then bequeath
Thy fragile bones to unknown burial.
Adieu, sweet love, adieu!"—As shot stars fall,
She fled ere I could groan for mercy. Stung
And poisoned was my spirit: despair sung
A war-song of defiance 'gainst all hell.
A hand was at my shoulder to compel
My sullen steps; another 'fore my eyes
Moved on with pointed finger. In this guise
Enforced, at the last by ocean's foam
I found me; by my fresh, my native home.
Its tempering coolness, to my life akin,
Came salutary as I waded in;
And, with a blind voluptuous rage, I gave
Battle to the swollen billow-ridge, and drave
Large froth before me, while there yet remain'd
Hale strength, nor from my bones all marrow drain'd.

"Young lover, I must weep—such hellish spite
With dry cheek who can tell? While thus my might
Proving upon this element, dismay'd,
Upon a dead thing's face my hand I laid;
I look'd—'twas Scylla! Cursed, cursed Circe!
O vulture-witch, hast never heard of mercy?
Could not thy harshest vengeance be content,
But thou must nip this tender innocent
Because I lov'd her?—Cold, O cold indeed
Were her fair limbs, and like a common weed
The sea-swell took her hair. Dead as she was
I clung about her waist, nor ceas'd to pass
Fleet as an arrow through unfathom'd brine,
Until there shone a fabric crystalline,

Ribb'd and inlaid with coral, pebble, and pearl.
Headlong I darted; at one eager swirl
Gain'd its bright portal, enter'd, and behold!
'Twas vast, and desolate, and icy-cold;
And all around—But wherefore this to thee
Who in few minutes more thyself shalt see?—
I left poor Scylla in a niche and fled.
My fever'd parchings up, my scathing dread
Met palsy half way: soon these limbs became
Gaunt, wither'd, sapless, feeble, cramp'd, and lame.

"Now let me pass a cruel, cruel space,
Without one hope, without one faintest trace
Of mitigation, or redeeming bubble
Of colour'd phantasy; for I fear 'twould trouble
Thy brain to loss of reason: and next tell
How a restoring chance came down to quell
One half of the witch in me.

"On a day,
Sitting upon a rock above the spray,
I saw grow up from the horizon's brink
A gallant vessel: soon she seem'd to sink
Away from me again, as though her course
Had been resum'd in spite of hindering force—
So vanish'd: and not long, before arose
Dark clouds, and muttering of winds morose.
Old Eolus would stifle his mad spleen,
But could not: therefore all the billows green
Toss'd up the silver spume against the clouds.
The tempest came: I saw that vessel's shrouds
In perilous bustle; while upon the deck
Stood trembling creatures. I beheld the wreck;
The final gulphing; the poor struggling souls:
I heard their cries amid loud thunder-rolls.
O they had all been sav'd but crazed eld
Annull'd my vigorous cravings: and thus quell'd
And curb'd, think on't, O Latmian! did I sit
Writhing with pity, and a cursing fit
Against that hell-born Circe. The crew had gone,
By one and one, to pale oblivion;
And I was gazing on the surges prone,

With many a scalding tear and many a groan,
When at my feet emerg'd an old man's hand,
Grasping this scroll, and this same slender wand.
I knelt with pain—reached out my hand—had grasp'd
These treasures—touch'd the knuckles—they unclasp'd—
I caught a finger: but the downward weight
O'erpowered me—it sank. Then 'gan abate
The storm, and through chill aguish gloom outburst
The comfortable sun. I was athirst
To search the book, and in the warming air
Parted its dripping leaves with eager care.
Strange matters did it treat of, and drew on
My soul page after page, till well-nigh won
Into forgetfulness; when, stupefied,
I read these words, and read again, and tried
My eyes against the heavens, and read again.
O what a load of misery and pain
Each Atlas-line bore off!—a shine of hope
Came gold around me, cheering me to cope
Strenuous with hellish tyranny. Attend!
For thou hast brought their promise to an end.

"In the wide sea there lives a forlorn wretch,
Doom'd with enfeebled carcase to outstretch
His loath'd existencethrough ten centuries,
And then to die alone. Who can devise
A total opposition? No one. So
One million times ocean must ebb and flow,
And he oppressed. Yet he shall not die,
These things accomplish'd:—If he utterly
Scans all the depths of magic, and expounds
The meanings of all motions, shapes, and sounds;
If he explores all forms and substances
Straight homeward to their symbol-essences;
He shall not die. Moreover, and in chief,
He must pursue this task of joy and grief
Most piously;—all lovers tempest-tost,
And in the savage overwhelming lost,
He shall deposit side by side, until
Time's creeping shall the dreary space fulfil:
Which done, and all these labours ripened,
A youth, by heavenly power lov'd and led,

Shall stand before him; whom he shall direct
How to consummate all. The youth elect
Must do the thing, or both will be destroy'd."—

"Then," cried the young Endymion, overjoy'd,
"We are twin brothers in this destiny!
Say, I intreat thee, what achievement high
Is, in this restless world, for me reserv'd.
What! if from thee my wandering feet had swerv'd,
Had we both perish'd?"—"Look!" the sage replied,
"Dost thou not mark a gleaming through the tide,
Of divers brilliances? 'tis the edifice
I told thee of, where lovely Scylla lies;
And where I have enshrined piously
All lovers, whom fell storms have doom'd to die
Throughout my bondage." Thus discoursing, on
They went till unobscur'd the porches shone;
Which hurryingly they gain'd, and enter'd straight.
Sure never since king Neptune held his state
Was seen such wonder underneath the stars.
Turn to some level plain where haughty Mars
Has legion'd all his battle; and behold
How every soldier, with firm foot, doth hold
His even breast: see, many steeled squares,
And rigid ranks of iron—whence who dares
One step? Imagine further, line by line,
These warrior thousands on the field supine:—
So in that crystal place, in silent rows,
Poor lovers lay at rest from joys and woes.—
The stranger from the mountains, breathless, trac'd
Such thousands of shut eyes in order plac'd;
Such ranges of white feet, and patient lips
All ruddy,—for here death no blossom nips.
He mark'd their brows and foreheads; saw their hair
Put sleekly on one side with nicest care;
And each one's gentle wrists, with reverence,
Put cross-wise to its heart.

"Let us commence,"
Whisper'd the guide, stuttering with joy, "even now."
He spake, and, trembling like an aspen-bough,
Began to tear his scroll in pieces small,

Uttering the while some mumblings funeral.
He tore it into pieces small as snow
That drifts unfeather'd when bleak northerns blow;
And having done it, took his dark blue cloak
And bound it round Endymion: then struck
His wand against the empty air times nine.—
"What more there is to do, young man, is thine:
But first a little patience; first undo
This tangled thread, and wind it to a clue.
Ah, gentle! 'tis as weak as spider's skein;
And shouldst thou break it—What, is it done so clean?
A power overshadows thee! Oh, brave!
The spite of hell is tumbling to its grave.
Here is a shell; 'tis pearly blank to me,
Nor mark'd with any sign or charactery—
Canst thou read aught? O read for pity's sake!
Olympus! we are safe! Now, Carian, break
This wand against yon lyre on the pedestal."

'Twas done: and straight with sudden swell and fall
Sweet music breath'd her soul away, and sigh'd
A lullaby to silence.—"Youth! now strew
These minced leaves on me, and passing through
Those files of dead, scatter the same around,
And thou wilt see the issue."—'Mid the sound
Of flutes and viols, ravishing his heart,
Endymion from Glaucus stood apart,
And scatter'd in his face some fragments light.
How lightning-swift the change! a youthful wight
Smiling beneath a coral diadem,
Out-sparkling sudden like an upturn'd gem,
Appear'd, and, stepping to a beauteous corse,
Kneel'd down beside it, and with tenderest force
Press'd its cold hand, and wept,—and Scylla sigh'd!
Endymion, with quick hand, the charm applied—
The nymph arose: he left them to their joy,
And onward went upon his high employ,
Showering those powerful fragments on the dead.
And, as he pass'd, each lifted up its head,
As doth a flower at Apollo's touch.
Death felt it to his inwards: 'twas too much:
Death fell a weeping in his charnel-house.

The Latmian persever'd along, and thus
All were re-animated. There arose
A noise of harmony, pulses and throes
Of gladness in the air—while many, who
Had died in mutual arms devout and true,
Sprang to each other madly; and the rest
Felt a high certainty of being blest.
They gaz'd upon Endymion. Enchantment
Grew drunken, and would have its head and bent.
Delicious symphonies, like airy flowers,
Budded, and swell'd, and, full-blown, shed full showers
Of light, soft, unseen leaves of sounds divine.
The two deliverers tasted a pure wine
Of happiness, from fairy-press ooz'd out.
Speechless they eyed each other, and about
The fair assembly wander'd to and fro,
Distracted with the richest overflow
Of joy that ever pour'd from heaven.

——"Away!"
Shouted the new born god; "Follow, and pay
Our piety to Neptunus supreme!"—
Then Scylla, blushing sweetly from her dream,
They led on first, bent to her meek surprise,
Through portal columns of a giant size,
Into the vaulted, boundless emerald.
Joyous all follow'd, as the leader call'd,
Down marble steps; pouring as easily
As hour-glass sand,—and fast, as you might see
Swallows obeying the south summer's call,
Or swans upon a gentle waterfall.

Thus went that beautiful multitude, nor far,
Ere from among some rocks of glittering spar,
Just within ken, they saw descending thick
Another multitude. Whereat more quick
Moved either host. On a wide sand they met,
And of those numbers every eye was wet;
For each their old love found. A murmuring rose,
Like what was never heard in all the throes
Of wind and waters: 'tis past human wit
To tell; 'tis dizziness to think of it.

Tis mighty consummation made, the host
Mov'd on for many a league; and gain'd, and lost
Huge sea-marks; vanward swelling in array,
And from the rear diminishing away,—
Till a faint dawn surpris'd them. Glaucus cried,
"Behold! behold, the palace of his pride!
God Neptune's palaces!" With noise increas'd,
They shoulder'd on towards that brightening east.
At every onward step proud domes arose
In prospect,—diamond gleams, and golden glows
Of amber 'gainst their faces levelling.
Joyous, and many as the leaves in spring,
Still onward; still the splendour gradual swell'd.
Rich opal domes were seen, on high upheld
By jasper pillars, letting through their shafts
A blush of coral. Copious wonder-draughts
Each gazer drank; and deeper drank more near:
For what poor mortals fragment up, as mere
As marble was there lavish, to the vast
Of one fair palace, that far far surpass'd,
Even for common bulk, those olden three,
Memphis, and Babylon, and Nineveh.

As large, as bright, as colour'd as the bow
Of Iris, when unfading it doth shew
Beyond a silvery shower, was the arch
Through which his Paphian army took its march,
Into the outer courts of Neptune's state:
Whence could be seen, direct, a golden gate,
To which the leaders sped; but not half raught
Ere it burst open swift as fairy thought,
And made those dazzled thousands veil their eyes
Like callow eagles at the first sunrise.
Soon with an eagle nativeness their gaze
Ripe from hue-golden swoons took all the blaze,
And then, behold! large Neptune on his throne
Of emerald deep: yet not exalt alone;
At his right hand stood winged Love, and on
His left sat smiling Beauty's paragon.

Far as the mariner on highest mast
Can see all round upon the calmed vast,

So wide was Neptune's hall: and as the blue
Doth vault the waters, so the waters drew
Their doming curtains, high, magnificent,
Aw'd from the throne aloof;—and when storm-rent
Disclos'd the thunder-gloomings in love's air;
But sooth'd as now, flash'd sudden everywhere,
Noiseless, sub-marine cloudlets, glittering
Death to a human eye: for there did spring
From natural west, and east, and south, and north,
A light as of four sunsets, blazing forth
A gold-green zenith 'bove the Sea-God's head.
Of lucid depth the floor, and far outspread
As breezeless lake, on which the slim canoe
Of feather'd Indian darts about, as through
The delicatest air: air verily,
But for the portraiture of clouds and sky:
This palace floor breath-air,—but for the amaze
Of deep-seen wonders motionless,—and blaze
Of the dome pomp, reflected in extremes,
Globing a golden sphere.

They stood in dreams
Till Triton blew his horn. The palace rang;
The Nereids danc'd; the Syrens faintly sang;
And the great Sea-King bow'd his dripping head.
Then Love took wing, and from his pinions shed
On all the multitude a nectarous dew.
The ooze-born Goddess beckoned and drew
Fair Scylla and her guides to conference;
And when they reach'd the throned eminence
She kist the sea-numph's cheek,—who sat her down
A toying with the doves. Then,—"Mighty crown
And sceptre of this kingdom!" Venus said,
"Thy vows were on a time to Nais paid:
Behold!"—Two copious tear-drops instant fell
From the God's large eyes; he smil'd delectable,
And over Galucus held his blessing hands.—
"Endymion! Ah! still wandering in the bands
Of love? Now this is cruel. Since the hour
I met thee in earth's bosom, all my power
Have I put forth to serve thee. What, not yet
Escap'd from dull mortality's harsh net?

A little patience, youth! 'twill not be long,
Or I am skilless quite: an idle tongue,
A humid eye, and steps luxurious,
Where these are new and strange, are ominous.
Aye, I have seen these signs in one of heaven,
When others were all blind; and were I given
To utter secrets, haply I might say
Some pleasant words:—but Love will have his day.
So wait awhile expectant. Pr'ythee soon,
Even in the passing of thine honey-moon,
Visit my Cytherea: thou wilt find
Cupid well-natured, my Adonis kind;
And pray persuade with thee—Ah, I have done,
All blisses be upon thee, my sweet son!"—
Thus the fair goddess: while Endymion
Knelt to receive those accents halcyon.

Meantime a glorious revelry began
Before the Water-Monarch. Nectar ran
In courteous fountains to all cups outreach'd;
And plunder'd vines, teeming exhaustless, pleach'd
New growth about each shell and pendent lyre;
The which, in disentangling for their fire,
Pull'd down fresh foliage and coverture
For dainty toying. Cupid, empire-sure,
Flutter'd and laugh'd, and oft-times through the throng
Made a delighted way. Then dance, and song,
And garlanding grew wild; and pleasure reign'd.
In harmless tendril they each other chain'd,
And strove who should be smother'd deepest in
Fresh crush of leaves.

O 'tis a very sin
For one so weak to venture his poor verse
In such a place as this. O do not curse,
High Muses! let him hurry to the ending.

All suddenly were silent. A soft blending
Of dulcet instruments came charmingly;
And then a hymn.

"King of the stormy sea!

Brother of Jove, and co-inheritor
Of elements! Eternally before
Thee the waves awful bow. Fast, stubborn rock,
At thy fear'd trident shrinking, doth unlock
Its deep foundations, hissing into foam.
All mountain-rivers lost in the wide home
Of thy capacious bosom ever flow.
Thou frownest, and old Eolus thy foe
Skulks to his cavern, 'mid the gruff complaint
Of all his rebel tempests. Dark clouds faint
When, from they diadem, a silver gleam
Slants over blue dominion. Thy bright team
Gulphs in the morning light, and scuds along
To bring thee nearer to that golden song
Apollo singeth, while his chariot
Waits at the doors of heaven. Thou art not
For scenes like this: an empire stern hast thou;
And it hath furrow'd that large front: yet now,
As newly come of heaven, dost thou sit
To blend and interknit
Subdued majesty with this glad time.
O shell-borne King sublime!
We lay our hearts before thee evermore—
We sing, and we adore!

"Breathe softly, flutes;
Be tender of your strings, ye soothing lutes;
Nor be the trumpet heard! O vain, O vain;
Not flowers budding in an April rain,
Nor breath of sleeping dove, nor river's flow,—
No, nor the Eolian twang of Love's own bow,
Can mingle music fit for the soft ear
Of goddess Cytherea!
Yet deign, white Queen of Beauty, thy fair eyes
On our souls' sacrifice.

"Bright-winged Child!
Who has another care when thou hast smil'd?
Unfortunates on earth, we see at last
All death-shadows, and glooms that overcast
Our spirits, fann'd away by thy light pinions.
O sweetest essence! sweetest of all minions!

God of warm pulses, and dishevell'd hair,
And panting bosoms bare!
Dear unseen light in darkness! eclipser
Of light in light! delicious poisoner!
Thy venom'd goblet will we quaff until
We fill—we fill!
And by thy Mother's lips——"

Was heard no more
For clamour, when the golden palace door
Opened again, and from without, in shone
A new magnificence. On oozy throne
Smooth-moving came Oceanus the old,
To take a latest glimpse at his sheep-fold,
Before he went into his quiet cave
To muse for ever—Then a lucid wave,
Scoop'd from its trembling sisters of mid-sea,
Afloat, and pillowing up the majesty
Of Doris, and the Egean seer, her spouse—
Next, on a dolphin, clad in laurel boughs,
Theban Amphion leaning on his lute:
His fingers went across it—All were mute
To gaze on Amphitrite, queen of pearls,
And Thetis pearly too—

The palace whirls
Around giddy Endymion; seeing he
Was there far strayed from mortality.
He could not bear it—shut his eyes in vain;
Imagination gave a dizzier pain.
"O I shall die! sweet Venus, be my stay!
Where is my lovely mistress? Well-away!
I die—I hear her voice—I feel my wing—"
At Neptune's feet he sank. A sudden ring
Of Nereids were about him, in kind strife
To usher back his spirit into life:
But still he slept. At last they interwove
Their cradling arms, and purpos'd to convey
Towards a crystal bower far away.

Lo! while slow carried through the pitying crowd,
To his inward senses these words spake aloud;

Written in star-light on the dark above:
Dearest Endymion! my entire love!
How have I dwelt in fear of fate: 'tis done—
Immortal bliss for me too hast thou won.
Arise then! for the hen-dove shall not hatch
Her ready eggs, before I'll kissing snatch
Thee into endless heaven. Awake! awake!

The youth at once arose: a placid lake
Came quiet to his eyes; and forest green,
Cooler than all the wonders he had seen,
Lull'd with its simple song his fluttering breast.
How happy once again in grassy nest!

BOOK IV

Muse of my native land! loftiest Muse!
O first-born on the mountains! by the hues
Of heaven on the spiritual air begot:
Long didst thou sit alone in northern grot,
While yet our England was a wolfish den;
Before our forests heard the talk of men;
Before the first of Druids was a child;—
Long didst thou sit amid our regions wild
Rapt in a deep prophetic solitude.
There came an eastern voice of solemn mood:—
Yet wast thou patient. Then sang forth the Nine,
Apollo's garland:—yet didst thou divine
Such home-bred glory, that they cry'd in vain,
"Come hither, Sister of the Island!" Plain
Spake fair Ausonia; and once more she spake
A higher summons:—still didst thou betake
Thee to thy native hopes. O thou hast won
A full accomplishment! The thing is done,
Which undone, these our latter days had risen
On barren souls. Great Muse, thou know'st what prison,
Of flesh and bone, curbs, and confines, and frets
Our spirit's wings: despondency besets
Our pillows; and the fresh to-morrow morn
Seems to give forth its light in very scorn
Of our dull, uninspired, snail-paced lives.

Long have I said, how happy he who shrives
To thee! But then I thought on poets gone,
And could not pray:—nor can I now—so on
I move to the end in lowliness of heart.——

"Ah, woe is me! that I should fondly part
From my dear native land! Ah, foolish maid!
Glad was the hour, when, with thee, myriads bade
Adieu to Ganges and their pleasant fields!
To one so friendless the clear freshet yields
A bitter coolness; the ripe grape is sour:
Yet I would have, great gods! but one short hour
Of native air—let me but die at home."

Endymion to heaven's airy dome
Was offering up a hecatomb of vows,
When these words reach'd him. Whereupon he bows
His head through thorny-green entanglement
Of underwood, and to the sound is bent,
Anxious as hind towards her hidden fawn.

"Is no one near to help me? No fair dawn
Of life from charitable voice? No sweet saying
To set my dull and sadden'd spirit playing?
No hand to toy with mine? No lips so sweet
That I may worship them? No eyelids meet
To twinkle on my bosom? No one dies
Before me, till from these enslaving eyes
Redemption sparkles!—I am sad and lost."

Thou, Carian lord, hadst better have been tost
Into a whirlpool. Vanish into air,
Warm mountaineer! for canst thou only bear
A woman's sigh alone and in distress?
See not her charms! Is Phoebe passionless?
Phoebe is fairer far—O gaze no more:—
Yet if thou wilt behold all beauty's store,
Behold her panting in the forest grass!
Do not those curls of glossy jet surpass
For tenderness the arms so idly lain
Amongst them? Feelest not a kindred pain,
To see such lovely eyes in swimming search

After some warm delight, that seems to perch
Dovelike in the dim cell lying beyond
Their upper lids?—Hist!

"O for Hermes' wand,
To touch this flower into human shape!
That woodland Hyacinthus could escape
From his green prison, and here kneeling down
Call me his queen, his second life's fair crown!
Ah me, how I could love!—My soul doth melt
For the unhappy youth—Love! I have felt
So faint a kindness, such a meek surrender
To what my own full thoughts had made too tender,
That but for tears my life had fled away!—
Ye deaf and senseless minutes of the day,
And thou, old forest, hold ye this for true,
There is no lightning, no authentic dew
But in the eye of love: there's not a sound,
Melodious howsoever, can confound
The heavens and earth in one to such a death
As doth the voice of love: there's not a breath
Will mingle kindly with the meadow air,
Till it has panted round, and stolen a share
Of passion from the heart!"—

Upon a bough
He leant, wretched. He surely cannot now
Thirst for another love: O impious,
That he can even dream upon it thus!
Thought he, "Why am I not as are the dead,
Since to a woe like this I have been led
Through the dark earth, and through the wondrous sea?
Goddess! I love thee not the less: from thee
By Juno's smile I turn not—no, no, no—
While the great waters are at ebb and flow.—
I have a triple soul! O fond pretence—
For both, for both my love is so immense,
I feel my heart is cut for them in twain."

And so he groan'd, as one by beauty slain.
The lady's heart beat quick, and he could see
Her gentle bosom heave tumultuously.

He sprang from his green covert: there she lay,
Sweet as a muskrose upon new-made hay;
With all her limbs on tremble, and her eyes
Shut softly up alive. To speak he tries.
"Fair damsel, pity me! forgive that I
Thus violate thy bower's sanctity!
O pardon me, for I am full of grief—
Grief born of thee, young angel! fairest thief!
Who stolen hast away the wings wherewith
I was to top the heavens. Dear maid, sith
Thou art my executioner, and I feel
Loving and hatred, misery and weal,
Will in a few short hours be nothing to me,
And all my story that much passion slew me;
Do smile upon the evening of my days:
And, for my tortur'd brain begins to craze,
Be thou my nurse; and let my understand
How dying I shall kiss that lily hand.—
Dost weep for me? Then should I be content.
Scowl on, ye fates! until the firmament
Outblackens Erebus, and the full-cavern'd earth
Crumbles into itself. By the cloud girth
Of Jove, those tears have given me a thirst
To meet oblivion."—As her heart would burst
The maiden sobb'd awhile, and then replied:
"Why must such desolation betide
As that thou speakest of? Are not these green nooks
Empty of all misfortune? Do the brooks
Utter a gorgon voice? Does yonder thrush,
Schooling its half-fledg'd little ones to brush
About the dewy forest, whisper tales?—
Speak not of grief, young stranger, or cold snails
Will slime the rose to night. Though if thou wilt,
Methinks 'twould be a guilt—a very guilt—
Not to companion thee, and sigh away
The light—the dusk—the dark—till break of day!"
"Dear lady," said Endymion, " 'tis past:
I love thee! and my days can never last.
That I may pass in patience still speak:
Let me have music dying, and I seek
No more delight—I bid adieu to all.
Didst thou not after other climates call,

And murmur about Indian streams?"—Then she,
Sitting beneath the midmost forest tree,
For pity sang this roundelay—
    "O Sorrow,
    Why dost borrow
The natural hue of health, from vermeil lips?—
    To give maiden blushes
    To the white rose bushes?
Or is't thy dewy hand the daisy tips?

    "O Sorrow,
    Why dost borrow
The lustrous passion from a falcon-eye?—
    To give the glow-worm light?
    Or, on a moonless night,
To tinge, on syren shores, the salt sea-spry?

    "O Sorrow,
    Why dost borrow
The mellow ditties from a mourning tongue?—
    To give at evening pale
    Unto the nightingale,
That thou mayst listen the cold dews among?

    "O Sorrow,
    Why dost borrow
Heart's lightness from the merriment of May?—
    A lover would not tread
    A cowslip on the head,
Though he should dance from eve till peep of day—
    Nor any drooping flower
    Held sacred for thy bower,
Wherever he may sport himself and play.

    "To Sorrow,
    I bade good-morrow,
And thought it leave her far away behind;
    But cheerly, cheerly,
    She loves me dearly;
She is so constant to me, and so kind:
    I would deceive her
    And so leave her,

But ah! she is so constant and so kind.

"Beneath my palm trees, by the river side,
I sat a weeping: in the whole world wide
There was no one to ask me why I wept,—
    And so I kept
Brimming the water-lily cups with tears
    Cold as my fears.

"Beneath my palm trees, by the river side,
I sat a weeping: what enamour'd bride,
Cheated by shadowy wooer from the clouds,
    But hides and shrouds
Beneath dark palm trees by a river side?

"And as I sat, over the light blue hills
There came a noise of revellers: the rills
Into the wide stream came of purple hue—
    'Twas Bacchus and his crew!
The earnest trumpet spake, and silver thrills
From kissing cymbals made a merry din—
    'Twas Bacchus and his kin!
Like to a moving vintage down they came,
Crown'd with green leaves, and faces all on flame;
All madly dancing through the pleasant valley,
    To scare thee, Melancholy!
O then, O then, thou wast a simple name!
And I forgot thee, as the berried holly
By shepherds is forgotten, when, in June,
Tall chesnuts keep away the sun and moon:—
    I rush'd into the folly!

"Within his car, aloft, young Bacchus stood,
Trifling his ivy-dart, in dancing mood,
    Wtih sidelong laughing;
And little rills of crimson wine imbrued
His plump white arms, and shoulders, enough white
    For Venus' pearly bite;
And near him rode Silenus on his ass,
Pelted with flowers as he on did pass
    Tipsily quaffing.

"Whence came ye, merry Damsels! whence came ye!
So many, and so many, and such glee?
Why have ye left your bowers desolate,
    Your lutes, and gentler fate?—
'We follow Bacchus! Bacchus on the wing,
    A conquering!
Bacchus, young Bacchus! good or ill betide,
We dance before him thorough kingdoms wide:—
Come hither, lady fair, and joined be
    To our wild minstrelsy!'

"Whence came ye, jolly Satyrs! whence came ye!
So many, and so many, and such glee?
Why have ye left your forest haunts, why left
    Your nuts in oak-tree cleft?—
'For wine, for wine we left our kernel tree;
For wine we left our heath, and yellow brooms,
    And cold mushrooms;
For wine we follow Bacchus through the earth;
Great God of breathless cups and chirping mirth!—
Come hither, lady fair, and joined be
    To our mad minstrelsy!'

"Over wide streams and mountains great we went,
And, save when Bacchus kept his ivy tent,
Onward the tiger and the leopard pants,
    With Asian elephants:
Onward these myriads—with song and dance,
With zebras striped, and sleek Arabians' prance,
Web-footed alligators, crocodiles,
Bearing upon their scaly backs, in files,
Plump infant laughers mimicking the coil
Of seamen, and stout galley-rowers' toil:
With toying oars and silken sails they glide,
    Nor care for wind and tide.

"Mounted on panthers' furs and lions' manes,
From rear to van they scour about the plains;
A three days' journey in a moment done:
And always, at the rising of the sun,
About the wilds they hunt with spear and horn,
    On spleenful unicorn.

"I saw Osirian Egypt kneel adown
Before the vine-wreath crown!
I saw parch'd Abyssinia rouse and sing
To the silver cymblas' ring!
I saw the whelming vintage hotly pierce
Old Tartary the fierce!
The kings of Inde their jewel-sceptres vail,
And from their treasures scatter pearled hail;
Great Brahma from his mystic heaven groans,
And all his priesthood moans;
Before young Bacchus' eye-wink turning pale.—
Into these regions came I following him,
Sick hearted, weary—so I took a whim
To stray away into these forests drear
Alone, without a peer:
And I have told thee all thou mayest hear.

"Young stranger!
I've been a ranger
In search of pleasure throughout every clime:
Alas, 'tis not for me!
Bewitch'd I sure must be,
To lose in grieving all my maiden prime.

"Come then, Sorrow!
Sweetest Sorrow!
Like an own babe I nurse thee on my breast:
I thought to leave thee
And deceive thee,
But now of all the world I love thee best.

"There is not one,
No, no, not one
But thee to comfort a poor lonely maid;
Thou art her mother,
And her brother,
Her playmate, and her wooer in the shade."

O what a sigh she gave in finishing,
And look, quite dead to every worldly thing!
Endymion could not speak, but gazed on her;
And listened to the wind that now did stir

About the crisped oaks full drearily,
Yet with as sweet a softness as might be
Remember'd from its velvet summer song.
At last he said: "Poor lady, how thus long
Have I been able to endure that voice?
Fair Melody! kind Syren! I've no choice;
I must be thy sad servant evermore:
I cannot choose but kneel here and adore.
Alas, I must not think—by Phoebe, no!
Let me not think, soft Angel! shall it be so?
Say, beautifullest, shall I never think?
O thou could'st foster me beyond the brink
Of recollection! make my watchful care
Close up its bloodshot eyes, nor see despair!
Do gently murder half my soul, and I
Shall feel the other half so utterly!—
I'm giddy at that cheek so fair and smooth;
O let it blush so ever! let it soothe
My madness! let it mantle rosy-warm
With the tinge of love, panting in safe alarm.—
This cannot be thy hand, and yet it is;
And this is sure thine other softling—this
Thine own fair bosom, and I am so near!
Wilt fall asleep? O let me sip that tear!
And whisper one sweet word that I may know
This is this world—sweet dewy blossom!"—*Woe!*
Woe! Woe to that Endymion! Where is he?—
Even these words went echoing dismally
Through the wide forest—a most fearful tone,
Like one repenting in his latest moan;
And while it died away a shade pass'd by,
As of a thunder cloud. When arrows fly
Through the thick branches, poor ring-doves sleek forth
Their timid necks and tremble; so these both
Leant to each other trembling, and sat so
Waiting for some destruction—when lo,
Foot-feather'd Mercury appear'd sublime
Beyond the tall tree tops; and in less time
Than shoots the slanted hail-storm, down he dropt
Towards the ground; but rested not, nor stopt
One moment from his home: only the sward
He with his wand light touch'd, and heavenward

Swifter than sight was gone—even before
The teeming earth a sudden witness bore
Of his swift magic. Diving swans appear
Above the crystal circlings white and clear;
And catch the cheated eye in wide surprise,
How they can dive in sight and unseen rise—
So from the turf outsprang two steeds jet-black,
Each with large dark blue wings upon his back.
The youth of Caria plac'd the lovely dame
On one, and felt himself in spleen to tame
The other's fierceness. Through the air they flew,
High as the eagles. Like two drops of dew
Exhal'd to Phoebus' lips, away they are gone,
Far from the earth away—unseen, alone,
Among cool clouds and winds, but that the free,
The buoyant life of song can floating be
Above their heads, and follow them untir'd.—
Muse of my native land, am I inspir'd?
This is the giddy air, and I must spread
Wide pinions to keep here; nor do I dread
Or height, or depth, or width, or any chance
Precipitous: I have beneath my glance
Those towering horses and their mournful freight.
Could I thus sail, and see, and thus await
Fearless for power of thought, without thine aid?—

There is a sleepy dusk, an odorous shade
From some approaching wonder, and behold
Those winged steeds, with snorting nostrils bold
Snuff at its faint extreme, and seem to tire,
Dying to embers from their native fire!

There curl'd a purple mist around them; soon,
It seem'd as when around the pale new moon
Sad Zephyr droops the clouds like weeping willow:
'Twas Sleep slow journeying with head on pillow.
For the first time, since he came nigh dead born
From the old womb of night, his cave forlorn
Had he left more forlorn; for the first time,
He felt aloof the day and morning's prime—
Because into his depth Cimmerian
There came a dream, shewing how a young man,

Ere a lean bat could plump its wintery skin,
Would at high Jove's empyreal footstool win
An immortality, and how espouse
Jove's daughter, and be reckon'd of his house.
Now was he slumbering towards heaven's gate,
That he might at the threshold one hour wait
To hear the marriage melodies, and then
Sink downward to his dusky cave again.
His litter of smooth semilucent mist,
Diversely ting'd with rose and amethyst,
Puzzled those eyes that for the centre sought;
And scarcely for one moment could be caught
His sluggish form reposing motionless.
Those two on winged steeds, with all the stress
Of vision search'd for him, as one would look
Athwart the sallows of a river nook
To catch a glance at silver throated eels,—
Or from old Skiddaw's top, when fog conceals
His rugged forehead in a mantle pale,
With an eye-guess towards some pleasant vale
Descry a favourite hamlet faint and far.

These raven horses, though they foster'd are
Of earth's splenetic fire, dully drop
Their full-veined ears, nostrils blood wide, and stop:
Upon the spiritless mist have they outspread
Their ample feathers, are in slumber dead,—
And on those pinions, level in mid air,
Endymion sleepeth and the lady fair.
Slowly the sail, slowly as icy isle
Upon a calm sea drifting: and meanwhile
The mournful wanderer dreams. Behold! he walks
On heaven's pavement; brotherly he talks
To divine powers: from his hand full fain
Juno's proud birds are pecking pearly grain:
He tries the nerve of Phoebus' golden bow,
And asketh where the golden apples grow:
Upon his arm he braces Pallas' shield,
And strives in vain to unsettle and wield
A Jovian thunderbolt: arch Hebe brings
A full-brimm'd goblet, dances lightly, sings
And tantalizes long; at last he drinks,

And lost in pleasure at her feet he sinks,
Touching with dazzled lips her starlight hand.
He blows a bugle,—an ethereal band
Are visible above: the Seasons four,—
Green-kyrtled Spring, flush Summer, golden store
In Autumn's sickle, Winter frosty hoar,
Join dance with shadowy Hours; while still the blast,
In swells unmitigated, still doth last
To sway their floating morris. "Whose is this?
Whose bugle?" he inquires: they smile—"O Dis!
Why is this mortal here? Dost thou not know
Its mistress' lips? Not thou?—'Tis Dian's: lo!
She rises crescented!" He looks, 'tis she,
His very goddess: good-bye earth, and sea,
And air, and pains, and care, and suffering;
Good-bye to all but love! Then doth he spring
Towards her, and awakes—and, strange, o'erhead,
Of those same fragrant exhalations bred,
Beheld awake his very dream: the gods
Stood smiling; merry Hebe laughs and nods;
And Phoebe bends towards him crescented.
O state perplexing! On the pinion bed,
Too well awake, he feels the panting side
Of his delicious lady. He who died
For soaring too audacious in the sun,
When that same treacherous wax began to run,
Felt not more tongue-tied than Endymion.
His heart leapt up as to its rightful throne,
To that fair shadow'd passion puls'd its way—
Ah, what perplexity! Ah, well a day!
So fond, so beauteous was his bed-fellow,
He could not help but kiss her: then he grew
Awhile forgetful of all beauty save
Young Phoebe's, golden hair'd; and so 'gan crave
Forgiveness: yet he turn'd once more to look
At the sweet sleeper,—all his soul was shook,—
She press'd his hand in slumber; so once more
He could not help but kiss her and adore.
At this the shadow wept, melting away.
The Latmian started up: "Bright goddess, stay!
Search my most hidden breast! By truth's own tongue,
I have no daedale heart: why is it wrung

To desperation? Is there nought for me,
Upon the bourne of bliss, but misery?"

These words awoke the stranger of dark tresses:
Her dawning love-look rapt Endymion blesses
With 'haviour soft. Sleep yawned from underneath.
"Thou swan of Ganges, let us no more breathe
This murky phantasm! thou contented seem'st
Pillow'd in lovely idleness, nor dream'st
What horrors may discomfort thee and me.
Ah, shouldst thou die from my heart-treachery!—
Yet did she merely weep—her gentle soul
Hath no revenge in it: as it is whole
In tenderness, would I were whole in love!
Can I prize thee, fair maid, all price above,
Even when I feel as true as innocence?
I do, I do.—What is this soul then? Whence
Came it? It does not seem my own, and I
Have no self-passion or identity.
Some fearful end must be: where, where is it?
By Nemesis, I see my spirit flit
Alone about the dark—Forgive me, sweet:
Shall we away?" He rous'd the steeds: they beat
Their wings chivalrous into the clear air,
Leaving old Sleep within his vapoury lair.

The good-night blush of eve was waning slow,
And Vesper, risen star, began to throe
In the dusk heavens silverly, when they
Thus sprang direct towards the Galaxy.
Nor did speed hinder converse soft and strange—
Eternal oaths and vows they interchange,
In such wise, in such temper, so aloof
Up in the winds, beneath a starry roof,
So witless of their doom, that verily
'Tis well nigh past man's search their hearts to see;
Whether they wept, or laugh'd, or griev'd, or toy'd—
Most like with joy gone mad, with sorrow cloy'd.

Full facing their swift flight, from ebon streak,
The moon put forth a little diamond peak,
No bigger than an unobserved star,

Or tiny point of fairy scymetar;
Bright signal that she only stoop'd to tie
Her silver sandals, ere deliciously
She bow'd into the heavens her timid head.
Slowly she rose, as though she would have fled,
While to his lady meek the Carian turn'd,
To mark if her dark eyes had yet discern'd
This beauty in its birth—Despair! despair!
He saw her body fading gaunt and spare
In the cold moonshine. Straight he seiz'd her wrist;
It melted from his grasp: her hand he kiss'd,
And, horror! kiss'd his own—he was alone.
Her steed a little higher soar'd, and then
Dropt hawkwise to the earth.

There lies a den,
Beyond the seeming confines of the space
Made for the soul to wander in and trace
Its own existence, of remotest glooms.
Dark regions are around it, where the tombs
Of buried griefs the spirit sees, but scarce
One hour doth linger weeping, for the pierce
Of new-born woe it feels more inly smart:
And in these regions many a venom'd dart
At random flies; they are the proper home
Of every ill: the man is yet to come
Who hath not journeyed in this native hell.
But few have ever felt how calm and well
Sleep may be had in that deep den of all.
There anguish does not sting; nor pleasure pall:
Woe-hurricanes beat ever at the gate,
Yet all is still within and desolate.
Beset with plainful gusts, within ye hear
No sound so loud as when on curtain'd bier
The death-watch tick is stifled. Enter none
Who strive therefore: on the sudden it is won.
Just when the sufferer begins to burn,
Then it is free to him; and from an urn,
Still fed by melting ice, he takes a draught—
Young Semele such richness never quaft
In her maternal longing! Happy gloom!
Dark paradise! where pale becomes the bloom

Of health by due; where silence dreariest
Is most articulate; where hopes infest;
Where those eyes are the brightest far that keep
Their lids shut longest in a dreamless sleep.
O happy spirit-home! O wondrous soul!
Pregnant with such a den to save the whole
In thine own depth. Hail, gentle Carian!
For, never since they griefs and woes began,
Hast thou felt so content: a grievous feud
Hath led thee to this Cave of Quietude.
Aye, his lull'd soul was there, although upborne
With dangerous speed: and so he did not mourn
Because he knew not whither he was going.
So happy was he, not the aerial blowing
Of trumpets at clear parley from the east
Could rouse from that fine relish, that high feast.
They stung the feather'd horse: with fierce alarm
He flapp'd towards the sound. Alas, no charm
Could lift Endymion's head, or he had view'd
A skyey masque, a pinion'd multitude,—
And silvery was its passing: voices sweet
Warbling the while as if to lull and greet
The wanderer in his path. Thus warbled they,
While past the vision went in bright array.

"Who, who from Dian's feast would be away?
For all the golden bowers of the day
Are empty left? Who, who away would be
From Cynthia's wedding and festivity?
Not Hesperus: lo! upon his silver wings
He leans away for highest heaven and sings,
Snapping his lucid fingers merrily!—
Ah, Zephyrus! art here, and Flora too!
Ye tender bibbers of the rain and dew,
Young playmates of the rose and daffodil,
Be careful, ere ye enter in, to fill
        Your baskets high
With fennel green, and balm, and golden pines,
Savory, latter-mint, and columbines,
Cool parsley, basil sweet, and sunny thyme;
Yea, every flower and leaf of every clime,
All gather'd in the dewy morning: hie

Away! fly, fly!—
Crystalline brother of the belt of heaven,
Aquarius! to whom king Jove has given
Two liquid pulse streams 'stead of feather'd wings,
Two fan-like fountains,—thine illuminings
For Dian play:
Dissolve the frozen purity of air;
Let thy white shoulders silvery and bare
Shew cold through watery pinions; make more bright
The Star-Queen's crescent on her marriage night:
Haste, haste away!—
Castor has tamed the planet Lion, see!
And of the Bear has Pollux mastery:
A third is in the race! who is the third,
Speeding away swift as the eagle bird?
The ramping Centaur!
The Lion's mane's on end: the Bear how fierce!
The Centaur's arrow ready seems to pierce
Some enemy: far forth his bow is bent
Into the blue of heaven. He'll be shent,
Pale unrelentor,
When he shall hear the wedding lutes a playing.—
Andromeda! sweet woman! why delaying
So timidly among the stars: come hither!
Join this bright throng, and nimbly follow whither
They all are going.
Danae's Son, before Jove newly bow'd,
Has wept for thee, calling to Jove aloud.
Thee, gentle lady, did he disenthral:
Ye shall for ever live and love, for all
Thy tears are flowing.—
By Daphne's fright, behold Apollo!—"

More
Endymion heard not: down his steed him bore,
Prone to the green head of a misty hill.

His first touch of the earth went nigh to kill.
"Alas!" said he, "were I but always borne
Through dangerous winds, had but my footsteps worn
A path in hell, for ever would I bless
Horrors which nourish an uneasiness

For my own sullen conquering: to him
Who lives beyond earth's boundary, grief is dim,
Sorrow is but a shadow: now I see
The grass; I feel the solid ground—Ah, me!
It is thy voice—divinest! Where?—who? who
Left thee so quiet on this bed of dew?
Behold upon this happy earth we are;
Let us ay love each other; let us fare
On forest-fruits, and never, never go
Among the abodes of mortals here below,
Or be by phantoms duped. O destiny!
Into a labyrinth now my soul would fly,
But with thy beauty will I deaden it.
Where didst thou melt to? By thee will I sit
For ever: let our fate stop here—a kid
I on this spot will offer: Pan will bid
Us live in peace, in love and peace among
His forest wildernesses. I have clung
To nothing, lov'd a nothing, nothing seen
Or felt but a great dream! O I have been
Presumptuous against love, against the sky,
Against all elements, against the tie
Of mortals each to each, against the blooms
Of flowers, rush of rivers, and the tombs
Of heroes gone! Against his proper glory
Has my own soul conspired: so my story
Will I to children utter, and repent.
There never liv'd a mortal man, who bent
His appetite beyond his natural sphere,
But starv'd and died. My sweetest Indian, here,
Here will I kneel, for thou redeemed hast
My life from too thin breathing: gone and past
Are cloudy phantasms. Caverns lone, farewel!
And air of visions, and the monstrous swell
Of visionary seas! No, never more
Shall airy voices cheat me to the shore
Of tangled wonder, breathless and aghast.
Adieu, my daintiest Dream! although so vast
My love is still for thee. The hour may come
When we shall meet in pure elysium.
On earth I may not love thee; and therefore
Doves will I offer up, and sweetest store

All through the teeming year: so thou wilt shine
On me, and on this damsel fair of mine,
And bless our simple lives. My Indian bliss!
My river-lily bud! one human kiss!
One sigh of real breath—one gentle squeeze,
Warm as a dove's nest among summer trees,
And warm with dew at ooze from living blood!
Whither didst melt? Ah, what of that!—all good
We'll talk about—no more of dreaming.—Now,
Where shall our dwelling be? Under the brow
Of some steep mossy hill, where ivy dun
Would hide us up, although spring leaves were none;
And where dark yew trees, as we rustle through,
Will drop their scarlet berry cups of dew?
O thou wouldst joy to live in such a place;
Dusk for our loves, yet light enough to grace
Those gentle limbs on mossy bed reclin'd:
For by one step the blue sky shouldst thou find,
And by another, in deep dell below,
See, through the trees, a little river go
All in its mid-day gold and glimmering.
Honey from out the gnarled hive I'll bring,
And apples, wan with sweetness, gather thee,—
Cresses that grow where no man may them see,
And sorrel untorn by the dew-claw'd stag:
Pipes will I fashion of the syrinx flag,
That thou mayst always know whither I roam,
When it shall please thee in our quiet home
To listen and think of love. Still let me speak;
Still let me dive into the joy I seek,—
For yet the past doth prison me. The rill,
Thou haply mayst delight in, will I fill
With fairy fishes from the mountain tarn,
And thou shalt feed them from the squirrel's barn.
Its bottom will I strew with amber shells,
And pebbles blue from deep enchanted wells.
Its sides I'll plant with dew-sweet eglantine,
And honeysuckles full of clear bee-wine.
I will entice this crystal rill to trace
Love's silver name upon the meadow's face.
I'll kneel to Vesta, for a flame of fire;
And to god Phoebus, for a golden lyre;

To Empress Dian, for a hunting spear;
To Vesper, for a taper silver-clear,
That I may see thy beauty through the night;
To Flora, and a nightingale shall light
Tame on thy finger; to the River-gods,
And they shall bring thee taper fishing-rods
Of gold, and lines of Naiads' long bright tress.
Heaven shield thee for thine utter loveliness!
Thy mossy footstool shall the altar be
'Fore which I'll bend, bending, dear love, to thee:
Those lips shall be my Delphos, and shall speak
Laws to my footsteps, colour to my cheek,
Trembling or stedfastness to this same voice,
And of three sweetest pleasurings the choice:
And that affectionate light, those diamond things,
Those eyes, those passions, those supreme pearl springs,
Shall be my grief, or twinkle me to pleasure.
Say, is not bliss within our perfect seisure?
O that I could not doubt!"

The mountaineer
Thus strove by fancies vain and crude to clear
His briar'd path to some tranquillity.
It gave bright gladness to his lady's eye,
And yet the tears she wept were tears of sorrow;
Answering thus, just as the golden morrow
Beam'd upward from the vallies of the east:
"O that the flutter of this heart had ceas'd,
Or the sweet name of love had pass'd away.
Young feather'd tyrant! by a swift decay
Wilt thou devote this body to the earth:
And I do think that at my very birth
I lisp'd thy blooming titles inwardly;
For at the first, first dawn and thought of thee,
With uplift hands I blest the stars of heaven.
Art thou not cruel? Ever have I striven
To think thee kind, but ah, it will not do!
When yet a child, I heard that kisses drew
Favour from thee, and so I kisses gave
To the void air, bidding them find out love:
But when I came to feel how far above
All fancy, pride, and fickle maidenhood,

All earthly pleasure, all imagin'd good,
Was the warm tremble of a devout kiss,—
Even then, that moment, at the thought of this,
Fainting I fell into a bed of flowers,
And languish'd there three days. Ye milder powers,
Am I not cruelly wrong'd? Believe, believe
Me, dear Endymion, were I to weave
With my own fancies garlands of sweet life,
Thou shouldst be one of all. Ah, bitter strife!
I may not be thy love: I am forbidden—
Indeed I am—thwarted, affrighted, chidden,
By things I trembled at, and gorgon wrath.
Twice hast thou ask'd whither I went: henceforth
Ask me no more! I may not utter it,
Nor may I be thy love. We might commit
Ourselves at once to vengeance; we might die;
We might embrace and die: voluptuous thought!
Enlarge not to my hunger, or I'm caught
In trammels of perverse deliciousness.
No, no, that shall not be: thee will I bless,
And bid a long adieu."

The Carian
No word return'd: both lovelorn, silent, wan,
Into the vallies green together went.
Far wandering, they were perforce content
To sit beneath a fair lone beechen tree;
Nor at each other gaz'd, but heavily
Por'd on its hazle cirque of shedded leaves.

Endymion! unhappy! it nigh grieves
Me to behold thee thus in last extreme:
Ensky'd ere this, but truly that I deem
Truth the best music in a first-born song.
Thy lute-voic'd brother will I sing ere long,
And thou shalt aid—hast thou not aided me?
Yes, moonlight Emperor! felicity
Has been thy meed for many thousand years;
Yet often have I, on the brink of tears,
Mourn'd as if yet thou wert a forester;—
Forgetting the old tale.

He did not stir
His eyes from the dead leaves, or one small pulse
Of joy he might have felt. The spirit culls
Unfaded amaranth, when wild it strays
Through the old garden-ground of boyish days.
A little onward ran the very stream
By which he took his first soft poppy dream;
And on the very bark 'gainst which he leant
A crescent he had carv'd, and round it spent
His skill in little stars. The teeming tree
Had swollen and green'd the pious charactery,
But not ta'en out. Why, there was not a slope
Up which he had not fear'd the antelope;
And not a tree, beneath whose rooty shade
He had not with his tamed leopards play'd:
Nor could an arrow light, or javelin,
Fly in the air where his had never been—
And yet he knew it not.

O treachery!
Why does his lady smile, pleasing her eye
With all his sorrowing? He sees her not.
But who so stares on him; His sister sure!
Peona of the woods!—Can she endure—
Impossible—how dearly they embrace!
His lady smiles; delight is in her face;
It is no treachery.

"Dear brother mine!
Endymion, weep not so! Why shouldst thou pine
When all great Latmos so exalt will be?
Thank the great gods, and look not bitterly;
And speak not one pale word, and sigh no more.
Sure I will not believe thou hast such store
Of grief, to last thee to my kiss again.
Thou surely canst not bear a mind in pain,
Come hand in hand with one so beautiful.
Be happy both of you! for I will pull
The flowers of autumn for your coronals.
Pan's holy priest for young Endymion calls;
And when he is restor'd, thou, fairest dame,
Shalt be our queen. Now, is it not a shame

To see ye thus,—not very, very sad?
Perhaps ye are too happy to be glad:
O feel as if it were a common day;
Free-voic'd as one who never was away.
No tongue shall ask, whence come ye? but ye shall
Be gods of your own rest imperial.
Not even I, for one whole month, will pry
Into the hours that have pass'd us by,
Since in my arbour I did sing to thee.
O Hermes! on this very night will be
A hymning up to Cynthia, queen of light;
For the soothsayers old saw yesternight
Good visions in the air,—whence will befal,
As say these sages, health perpetual
To shepherds and their flocks; and furthermore,
In Dian's face they read the gentle lore:
Therefore for her these vesper-carols are.
Our friends will all be there from nigh and far.
Many upon the death have ditties made;
And many, even now, their foreheads shade
With cypress, on a day of sacrifice.
New singing for our maids shalt thou devise,
And pluck the sorrow from our huntsmen's brows.
Tell me, my lady-queen, how to espouse
This wayward brother to his rightful joys!
His eyes are on thee bent, as thou didst poise
His fate most goddess-like. Help me, I pray,
To lure—Endymion, dear brother, say
What ails thee?" He could bear no more, and so
Bent his soul fiercely like a spiritual bow,
And twang'd it inwardly, and calmly said:
"I would have thee my only friend, sweet maid!
My only visitor! not ignorant though,
That those deceptions which for pleasure go
'Mong men, are pleasures real as real may be:
But there are higher ones I may not see,
If impiously an earthly realm I take.
Since I saw thee, I have been wide awake
Night after night, and day by day, until
Of the empyrean I have drunk my fill.
Let it content thee, sister, seeing me
More happy than betides mortality.

A hermit young, I'll live in mossy cave,
Where thou alone shalt come to me, and lave
Thy spirit in the wonders I shall tell.
Through me the shepherd realm shall prosper well;
For to thy tongue will I all health confide.
And, for my sake, let this young maid abide
With thee as a dear sister. Thou alone,
Peona, mayst return to me. I own
This may sound strangely: but when, dearest girl,
Thou seest it for my happiness, no pearl
Will trespass down those cheeks. Companion fair!
Wilt be content to dwell with her, to share
This sister's love with me?" Like one resign'd
And bent by circumstance, and thereby blind
In self-commitment, thus that meek unknown:
"Aye, but a buzzing by my ears has flown,
Of jubilee to Dian:—truth I heard?
Well then, I see there is no little bird,
Tender soever, but is Jove's own care.
Long have I sought for rest, and, unaware,
Behold I find it! so exalted too!
So after my own heart! I knew, I knew
There was a place untenanted in it:
In that same void white Chastity shall sit,
And monitor me nightly to lone slumber.
With sanest lips I vow me to the number
Of Dian's sisterhood; and, kind lady,
With thy good help, this very night shall see
My future days to her fane consecrate."

As feels a dreamer what doth most create
His own particular fright, so these three felt:
Or like one who, in after ages, knelt
To Lucifer or Baal, when he'd pine
After a little sleep: or when in mine
Far under-ground, a sleeper meets his friends
Who know him not. Each diligently bends
Towards common thoughts and things for very fear;
Striving their ghastly malady to cheer,
By thinking it a thing of yes and no,
That housewives talk of. But the spirit-blow
Was struck, and all were dreamers. At the last

Endymion said: "Are not our fates all cast?
Why stand we here? Adieu, ye tender pair!
Adieu!" Whereat those maidens, with wild stare,
Walk'd dizzily away. Pained and hot
His eyes went after them, until they got
Near to a cypress grove, whose deadly maw,
In one swift moment, would what then he saw
Engulph for ever. "Stay!" he cried, "ah, stay!
Turn, damsels! hist! one word I have to say.
Sweet Indian, I would see thee once again.
It is a thing I dote on: so I'd fain,
Peona, ye should hand in hand repair
Into those holy groves, that silent are
Behind great Dian's temple. I'll be yon,
At Vesper's earliest twinkle—they are gone—
But once, once, once again—" At this he press'd
His hands against his face, and then did rest
His head upon a mossy hillock green,
And so remain'd as he a corpse had been
All the long day; save when he scantly lifted
His eyes abroad, to see how shadows shifted
With the slow move of time,—sluggish and weary
Until the poplar tops, in journey dreary,
Had reach'd the river's brim. Then up he rose,
And, slowly as that very river flows,
Walk'd towards the temple grove with this lament:
"Why such a golden eve? The breeze is sent
Careful and soft, that not a leaf may fall
Before the serene father of them all
Bows down his summer head below the west.
Now am I of breath, speech, and speed possest,
But at the setting I must bid adieu
To her for the last time. Night will strew
On the damp grass myriads of lingering leaves,
And with them shall I die; nor much it grieves
To die, when summer dies on the cold sward.
Why, I have been a butterfly, a lord
Of flowers, garlands, love-knots, silly posies,
Groves, meadows, melodies, and arbour roses;
My kingdom's at its death, and just it is
That I should die with it: so in all this
We miscal grief, bale, sorrow, heartbreak, woe,

What is there to plain of? By Titan's foe
I am but rightly serv'd." So saying, he
Tripp'd lightly on, in sort of deathful glee;
Laughing at the clear stream and setting sun,
As though they jests had been: nor had he done
His laugh at nature's holy countenance,
Until that grove appear'd, as if perchance,
And then his tongue with sober seemlihed
Gave utterance as he entered: "Ha! I said,
King of the butterflies; but by this gloom,
And by old Rhadamanthus' tongue of doom,
This dusk religion, pomp of solitude,
And the Promethean clay by thief endued,
By old Saturnus' forelock, by his head
Shook with eternal palsy, I did wed
Myself to things of light from infancy;
And thus to be cast out, thus lorn to die,
Is sure enough to make a mortal man
Grow impious." So he inwardly began
On things for which no wording can be found;
Deeper and deeper sinking, until drown'd
Beyond the reach of music: for the choir
Of Cynthia he heard not, though rough briar
Nor muffling thicket interpos'd to dull
The vesper hymn, far swollen, soft and full,
Through the dark pillars of those sylvan aisles.
He saw not the two maidens, nor their smiles,
Wan as primroses gather'd at midnight
By chilly finger'd spring. "Unhappy wight!
Endymion!" said Peona, "we are here!
What wouldst thou ere we all are laid on bier?"
Then he embrac'd her, and his lady's hand
Press'd, saying: "Sister, I would have command,
If it were heaven's will, on our sad fate."
At which that dark-eyed stranger stood elate
And said, in a new voice, but sweet as love,
To Endymion's amaze: "By Cupid's dove,
And so thou shalt! and by the lily truth
Of my own breast thou shalt, beloved youth!"
And as she spake, into her face there came
Light, as reflected from a silver flame:
Her long black hair swell'd ampler, in display

Full golden; in her eyes a brighter day
Dawn'd blue and full of love. Aye, he beheld
Phoebe, his passion! joyous she upheld
Her lucid bow, continuing thus: "Drear, drear
Has our delaying been; but foolish fear
Withheld me first; and then decrees of fate;
And then 'twas fit that from this mortal state
Thou shouldst, my love, by some unlook'd for change
Be spiritualiz'd. Peona, we shall range
These forests, and to thee they safe shall be
As was thy cradle; hither shalt thou flee
To meet us many a time." Next Cynthia bright
Peona kiss'd, and bless'd with fair good night:
Her brother kiss'd her too, and knelt adown
Before his goddess, in a blissful swoon.
She gave her fair hands to him, and behold,
Before three swiftest kisses he had told,
They vanish'd far away!—Peona went
Home through the gloomy wood in wonderment.

Notes to Book I

Motto: From Shakespeare's Sonnet xvii, "Who will believe my verse in time to come?" Dickstein (55-6) notes that K.'s use of the line, which is spoken "not by the poet but by a mocking and skeptical posterity," reflects an "ironic double perspective," since he both asserts the claims of the imagination and is skeptical about them. See K.'s letter to Reynolds of Nov. 22, 1817, where he says Shakespeare "overwhelms a genuine Lover of Poesy with all manner of abuse, talking about—'a poet's rage and stretched metre of an antique song'—Which by the by will be a capital Motto for my Poem—wont it?" (I, 189).

Dedication: K. viewed Chatterton, like himself, not only as another Endymion, but as a poet of "the native music" (see K.'s letter to the George Keatses of Sept. 21, 1819 and IV.1-29n.). Although Bailey heard the "charm" of Chatterton's style in *Endymion* (see Bate 216), Gittings[2] (49) feels it "does not appear anywhere in *Endymion,* which is largely dominated by the greater charm of Shakespeare."

1-33. Dickstein (54) argues that "the proem is not the poem's actual beginning, but a sort of Argument, not fully comprehensi--ble until we have gone through the whole poem." It is also, he adds, "an apologetic assertion about the nature of poetry and about *this* poem's relation to reality." According to Evert (165), it states "the lesson Endymion will have to learn . . . that the natural beauty of the external world and of humanity at its best reflects the condition of, and places us in touch with the divine." (4-6)

1-13. Finney (297) believes K. derived "This principle of the comforting power in beautiful objects" from "Wordsworth's philosophy of nature," and compares *Tintern Abbey* (23-31). For Frye[6] (127), the awareness of beauty here is "not a mere solace in sorrow, though it is also that, but a more intensely experienced kind of reality . . . where truth is created as well as recognized. . ." For a further discussion of the passage, see Intro.

1-3. Ende (60) claims the passage "affirms the permanence of beauty at the same time that it implys doubt," and compares the post-visionary doubt in *Sleep and Poetry* (157-9): "A sense of real things comes doubly strong, / And, like a muddy stream, would bear along / My soul to nothingness" (cf. IV.637n.).

1. Originally, according to Henry Stephens, a fellow medical student with K., "A thing of beauty is a constant joy." If the story is true (Bate 178 finds it "hackneyed and questionable"), constancy has been revised to permanence. Ende (60-1) notes K.'s insistence here upon beauty as a concrete "thing" as opposed to Wordsworth's sense of beauty as a "Presence" or numinous quality.

3-4. *still . . . quiet:* Anticipates what Brisman (93) calls "the arrest of time" in "Thou still unravish'd bride of quietness" of *Ode on a Grecian Urn.*

6-13. See Murry's (180-1) comment on the poem's dialectic: "Essentially, the poem is the effort to create a thing of beauty before the spirit is darkened; to make the creation of the poem itself a defence against the onset of the doubts and miseries and feverous speculations, of which he had a clear presentiment. It is the poem of maiden experience and maiden though, indeed, but they are conscious of their doom."

6-7. Ende (62) compares *Tintern Abbey* (134-5): "Therefore let the moon / Shine on thee in thy solitary walk," and Coleridge's *Frost at Midnight* 65: "Therefore all seasons shall be sweet to thee," and claims "All three 'Therefores' conclude arguments that make possible the self's willing submission to natural relationship."

8-10. See K.'s letter to Haydon of May 11, 1817: "I have a horrid Morbidity of Temperament which has shown itself at intervals —it is I have no doubt the greatest Enemy and stumbling block I have to fear" (I, 142).

12-24. Allot calls a "Keatsian catalogue of 'luxuries,' " citing as other examples *Sleep and Poetry* 1-10 and *I stood tip-toe* 1-115. But it is more than a catalogue, for, among other things, it establishes the temperature or creative clime of Book I as "the cool of the day." We retreat from hot light ("sun") to cool light ("moon") to shade ("shady boon"), "cooling covert" and "fountain," receding into a temperate realm where "Some shape of beauty" (which includes morning "sun" and shady "trees") tempers the extremes of cold darkness ("dark spirits") and hot light ("the hot season"). Cf. *Lycidas* 133-53.

12. Bate[2] (57) cites as one of the few instances in K.'s early verse of consecutive or patterned assonance.

14-5. *Trees . . . sheep:* Cf. Shakespeare's Sonnet xii 5-6: "When lofty trees I see barren of leaves / Which erst from heat did canopy the herd." K. praises the lines in his letter to Reynolds of Nov. 22, 1817 (I, 188).

14. *Trees:* Blackstone (117) finds that "*Endymion* is all trees. It begins and ends, and develops its main action within 'a mighty forest' . . . trees are always magical for Keats: they whisper secrets, they shelter, instruct and console." See I.64n., Iv. 994, and Intro.

16. *the green world:* See Intro. for its Shakespearean analogue.

19. *musk-rose:* One of K.'s favorite flowers. See "To a Friend who sent me some Roses" 5-6, and *Ode to a Nightingale* 49. Though not a common pastoral flower, it is included in the flower anthologies of *A Midsummer Night's Dream* II,i,252 and *Lycidas* 146.

20-1. *the dooms . . . mighty dead:* De Selincourt compares Thomson's *The Seasons*, Winter 432: "And hold high converse with the mighty dead." Ford[3] (42) regards it as one of many instances of K.'s belief in a real Elysium for poets. See I.177n.

23-4. See Abrams[2] (58) on the Romantic revival of the Neoplatonic image of "an overflowing fountain of light," instanced in Wordsworth's "the fountain light of all our day" (*Intimations* Ode 155). K. often identifies this "light" with wine, as in *Hence Burgundy, Claret and Port* 6-8. See also his letter to Bailey of Nov. 22, 1817, where he speaks of the "old Wine of Heaven" as the "redigestion of our most ethereal Musings on earth" (I, 186). For other forms of the image see I.143-4 and 154.

25-33. Evokes for Bloom[3] (385) the world of the poem: "An enclosed world, frequently likened to a bower and covert, it is a natural temple, dominated by the moon, which is scarcely differentiated from the poetry made by its celebrants. . ." For Ende (66-7) the passage reflects K.'s "belief in the 'essences' of natural relationship . . rather than in the sublime."

25. *essences:* A controversial term in Keats criticism. See I.779n. While Bate (182) feels the plural form refers to "concrete objects and experiences," Dickstein (60) regards it as abstract and transcendental.

32. *shine:* On K.'s use of verbs as nouns see Intro.

34. *happiness:* See I.777n.

38. *growing:* Perkins (198) observes K.'s "pronounced reliance on the present participle . . . serving to vivity and dramatize the sense of process taking place, re-enacting it, so to speak, in the texture of his poetry."

39-57. *So I will begin . . . end.* K.'s timetable for the composition of the poem. See K.'s letter to Haydon of May 11, 1817: "I revoke my Promise of finishing my Poem by Autumn which I should have done had I gone on as I have done" (I, 142). See also the letter to Taylor of Feb. 27, 1818: "That if Poetry does not come as naturally as the Leaves to a tree it had better not come at all" (I, 238-9). By comparing the progress of the poem to the progress of the seasons, K. is suggesting that his poetic powers, though now young and green, will have matured and ripened by the end of the poem, at which time the vernal promise of his poetic calling will be fulfilled and the first fruits of his labor harvested. Evert (30-1) believes this analogy to be the substance of K.'s poetic metaphysics: "the human spiritual cycle is comparable to the annual cycle of nature, and both are subject to the harmonizing and ripening influences of Apollo." What Evert (166) calls the "slow, natural, organic growth" here, however, does not tally well with the actual process of composition. For further discussion see Intro.

40. A common pastoral and Wordsworthian motif. Cf. K.'s sonnet "To one who has been long in city pent."

41. *budders:* A coinage.

47. *boat:* A conventional metaphor for poetic composition. See K.'s letter to Bailey of Oct. 8, 1817: "a long Poem is a test of Invention which I take to be the Polar Star of Poetry, as Fancy is the Sails, and Imagination the rudder" (I, 170).

51. *bees:* Traditionally, seekers of pleasure, and are sometimes associated with the moon. They also serve as a metaphor for the poet, since they distill from nature's floral beauty nectar and

honey, the food of the gods.

56. *gold:* For an excellent discussion of K.'s autumnal and Apollonian "golden world," see Evert (45-52). See I.608-10n.

63-4. *Upon . . . forest:* The mountain, as a traditional point of epiphany, carries the connotation of "outspread" wings. See I.85-6n.

63. *Latmos:* A mountain in Caria, Asia Minor, where Phoebe, the goddess of the moon, visited the shepherd Endymion. K.'s Endymion returns to Latmos at the climax of the poem.

64. *A mighty forest:* See K.'s letter to Reynolds of Feb. 9, 1818, where he speaks of an ideal society as "a grand democracy of Forest Trees" where "every human might become great" (I,232).

73-9. *Among . . . lose.* See the parable of the lost sheep, Matt. 18.10-14. The contrapuntal use of classical and Biblical pastoral imagery is common in Renaissance poetry, though rare in K. Notcutt (13) interprets the lines allegorically: the angry wolves are K.'s critics and the lost sheep his unpublished poems, which he "felt had not perished, but had joined the herds of Pan . . . for they lived on in his mind as beautiful ideals, unmarred by foolish or unfriendly criticism."

78. *Pan:* The classical god of universal nature and "the shepherds God" of pastoral poetry. Bush[3] (101-2) feels "Keats's conception of Pan, however un-Greek, is in accordance with the allegorical tradition, but . . . greatly enriches 'the All' of the mythographers . . ." and agrees with Garrod (81) that "Pan is, in fact, the symbol of the romantic imagination, concrete in a thousand objective shapes, the very life itself of 'sensation rather than thought.' " Similarly, Knight (268) regards Pan as "a deification of Keats's own loved poetic earthiness." In implicitly associating Pan with Christ, K. is drawing on the "allegorical tradition" in such works as Sandys (267), Spenser's *The Shepheards Calendar, Julye* 49-68, and Milton's "Nativity Ode" 89. He seems also to be following Wordsworth's description of Pan as "The simple shepherd's awe-inspiring God!" in *The Excursion* IV,887. ay: ever.

85-6. De Selincourt cites "Ode to Psyche" 54-5: "Far, far around shall those dark-cluster'd trees / Fledge the wild-ridged mountains steep by steep."

89f. De Selincourt believes the idea of beginning the poem with the feast of Pan may have been suggested by Drayton's *Man in the Moone.*

95-106. Dickstein (71) notes that "behind the tone of celebration" in the "wonderful evocation of harmonious reciprocity within nature and between nature and man" "a more ambiguous note" of "benign destructiveness" is sounded.

95-100. Frye[6] (131-2) compares the innocent and fragile world of Blake's *The Book of Thel,* "with its shadowy, dissolving imagery, where things melt into other things without taking on definite existence . . ." Cf. I.501.

95. *Apollo's upward fire:* the rising sun; but the wording suggests a sacrificial "altar" (90) fire as well. See *Sleep and Poetry* 58-61, where the young poet prays to "Poesy" "that I may die a death / Of luxury and my young spirit follow / The morning sunbeams to the great Apollo / Like a fresh sacrifice. . ." For the symbolic significance of Apollo see Evert and I.139-43 n.

98-100. Allott compares *Hamlet* I.ii, 129-30: "O! that this too too solid flesh would melt, / Thaw and resolve itself into a dew."

107-13. Jack (149) compares Titian's "The Worship of Venus" and Rubens's "Sacrifice to Venus": "In each of these paintings a crowd of putti come rushing in to surround an altar surmounted by a statue of Venus . . . the image of an altar approached by a number of classical figures came early in Keats, and remained in his imagination, developing and increasing in significance, throughout his poetic career." Cf. K.'s Dedication Sonnet to Leigh Hunt.

114. *sated:* satisifed. K.'s only use of the word.

120-1. *ere their death . . . sea.* Murry[2] (37) believes that at the Isle of Wight, poetry, the murmur of the sea, and Shakespeare became inextricably one for K. See II.243n.

123. *light:* Placed at the end of the line it carries the weight of both adjective and substantive, a syntactic device frequent in Milton.

124. *a rush of garments white:* Cinematically renders the immediate visual impressions of a distant object in the order they would be perceived, i.e. movement followed by color. Cf. "glimmered light." Close up the order is reversed, as in "that white rush" of Yeats's *Leda and the Swan.*

129. *goodly company:* Cf. Coleridge's *The Ancient Mariner* 601-4: "O sweeter than the marriage-feast, / 'Tis sweeter far to me, / To walk together to the kirk / With a goodly company!"

132. *unmew:* set free.

134. See K.'s letter to Taylor and Hessey of May 16, 1817: "This Evening I go to Canterbury . . I hope the Remembrance of Chaucer will set me forward like a Billard-Ball" (I, 146-7).

139-44. A reference to Apollo's period of exile as a shepherd in Thessaly, recorded in Ovid's *Met.* II, 677-82. Evert (70-1), speaking of Apollo's identity with images of light, wine, music, and poetry, claims (in referring to I.154) that the overflowing of Apollo's divinity as music (or pastoral poetry) here is "a typical Keatsian compression of imagery, in which the god is conceived as his essence of light, in himself and in the effects of that essence on the world of organic nature, and that the processes between the ripening of grapes under this influence and the overflowing of the wine goblet are allusively implicit in lines 142-3."

139. *sunburnt looks:* Another effect of Apollo's descent. Cf. "sunburnt mirth" in *Ode to a Nightingale* 14. Spurgeon (62) cites *The Tempest* IV,i, 134-5: "You sunburned sicklemen, of August weary, / Come hither from the furrow and be merry." Cf. I.441.

140. *Arcadian books:* pastoral poetry.

150. *Begirt . . . looks:* Allott interprets as "Surrounded by ready attendants." But K. seems to be referring to the priest's appearance (cf. "sunburnt looks"): his down-cast "eye" and "sacred vestments" express a "ministring" attitude.

154. Evert (69-70) interprets as a symbol of poetry, since in K.'s

thinking poetry is "sufficiently identified with light by having its source and sanction in the god of light . . .As for wine, it is the concentrated essence of a fruit that has grown to ripeness through the absorption of the sun's rays. It is . . . the same thing in the physical sphere that poetry is in the intellectual, for poetry is the concentrated essence of human experience, nurtured, in another capacity, by the same god who ripens the fruit. And finally, wine and poetry . . . may be equated in their effects [i.e. intoxication]." We may grant Evert's point even though wine here appears to be identified with starlight rather than sunlight. Cf. *To My Brother George* 39-42.

157-8. *whiter . . . love:* See Spenser's *Prothalamium* 39-45.

160. *poll:* the part of the head on which the hair grows. Cf. *Hamlet* IV,v,192-3: "His beard was a white as snow, / All flaxen was his poll."

164. *Up-followed:* See Croker's review of *Endymion:* K. "has formed new verbs by the process of cutting off their natural tails, the adverbs, and affixing them to their foreheads. . ." See I.561 and 708 for other instances.

165. *car:* Cf. *Sleep and Poetry* 151-7, where Apollo looks out of his "car" with "glorious fear" or what Bloom (116) calls "the repression of the daemonic force of belated creativity." Cf. Endymion's "lurking trouble" (179).

169-74. *His youth . . . keen.* An instance for Fogle (160) of "Keats's ability to endow static figures with organic life. . ." The image is "built around *nervy,* which projects the detail which precedes it into life. By virtue of its organic and kinesthetic force Endymion is a sturdy young man, capable of physical action; without it he would have been a mere lay-figure."

170. *Ganymede:* Like Endymion, a beautiful prince or shepherd beloved of the gods. Jove, in the form of an eagle (cf. II.658) abducted the youth to Olympus to be his cup-bearer. See Ovid, *Met.* X,155-61, and also *As You Like It,* where Rosalind, a bisexual Eros figure, disguises as Ganymede (whose bisexuality is implied in the myth), is wooed by "Phebe," and eventually

marries "Hercules." In Endymion's prefigurative dream, Ganymede's female counterpart, the goddess Phebe (Jove's daughter and Hercules's wife), pours his wine (see IV.415f. and 415n.). Ganymede and Endymion are occasionally linked metonymically as wine (or intoxication) and sleep (see Apuleius 39).

172. *A chieftain king's:* In some versions of the myth, Endymion was said to be the son of the King of Elis (Elysium?). See Le Comte (4-5).

173. *silver bugle:* Diana's hunting horn. See IV.427 where Diana's bugle is the key to the recognition scene.

174. *boar-spear:* Bloom[3] (386) sees here an intimation of "Adonis-like" self-destruction, "reinforced by a comparison to Ganymede and by a 'lurking trouble' in his countenance." Adonis was mortally wounded when his spear failed to stop the onset of a wild boar. See Ovid, *Met.* X,708-16, and also *As You Like It*, where Rosalind disguises her "woman's fear" with "A boar-spear in my hand" (I,iii,114). See I.532n. and II.474n. for the sexual and creative significance of the spear.

175-9. Ford[3] (42) explains Endymion's "countenance" in terms of the "two anthithetical aspects of Endymion's recent experience: his incomparably felicitious love-dream of Cynthia . . . and his grievous loss of that felicity when the dream faded." This is Endymion's response to a contrary dream-goddess who is both wanton and virginal. K. may have his actual audience in mind when he distinguishes between a "common" reader and a "fit audience though few" "who feelingly could scan" the lines of Endymion's pleasure-pain paradox. Cf. *Ode on Melancholy* 25-8.

177. *groves Elysian:* The inversion suggest a reminiscence of *The Excursion* Prospectus 47-9: "Paradise, and groves / Elysian, Fortunate fields like those of old / sought in the Atlantic Main." In his early verse K. developed an Elysium of immortal poets located in the Western Isles (a favorite location for English poets) and presided over by Apollo.

178-84. Another intimation of the dying god, whose loss of

virility corresponds to nature's "yellow leaves." Cf. the pale knight and withered nature of *La Belle Dame.* See also Shelley's *Alastor* 52-4: "But the charmed eddies of autumnal winds / Built o'er his mouldering bones a pyramid / Of mouldering leaves in the waste wilderness."

178. *feelingly:* Cf. *King Lear* IV,vi,146, where the eyeless Gloucester claims to see "feelingly" "how this world goes."

187. *meek:* mild and gentle. Allott remarks on K.'s frequent use of the word in describing women. Cf. III.46.

191. *wan, and pale:* Anticipates the knight of *La Belle Dame.*

199. *overtop:* crown.

204. Spurgeon (10) cites *The Tempest* IV,i,62 & 69: "Thy turfy mountains, where live nibbling sheep." "And thy sea-marge, sterile and rocky hard."

205-6. *sounds forlorn . . . Triton's horn:* Cf. Wordsworth's echo ("The world is too much with us" 14) of Spenser's *Colin Clout Comes Home Again* 245. Unlike Wordsworth's, K.'s "horn" is the expression of, and not an antidote for, the "forlorn."

208. *scrip with needments:* satchel with food. Allott cites *F. Q.* I,vi,35: "eke behind, / His scrip did hang, in which his needments he did bind. . ." The reference is to St. George's dwarf, who represents the shrunken form of waking reality that follows behind (or is left behind by) the quester, as Endymion leaves behind this community in his quest.

210. *Udderless:* motherless; but may also be viewed as a typical Keatsian imagined presence (cf. the "full grown limbs" of *To Autumn*), suggesting the on-going process of a life-cycle. It also contains a note of dumb pathos ("utterless") and, in its association with "girls," of fragile virginity and innocence.

213. Notcutt (10) sees an allusion here to the neo-classical separation of man and nature, against which the Romantic movement (the avid worshippers of Pan) is rebelling.

214. *lowing heifers sleeker:* Anticipates *Ode on a Grecian Urn* 33-4.

219. *Great bounty . . . lord.* Nature's bounty is a stock theme in earthly paradise literature, such as Spenser's *Gardens of Adonis.* K. was probably aware through Lemprière that Adonis is the Greek word for "lord."

223-7. *Thus . . . drinking it:* Knight (268) notes here "how the living earth is one with the ritual."

229. *gummy:* Ricks (139) finds it "attractive and yet tacky; its meltingness is both checked and accentuated by the very different physicalities with which Keats surrounds it: the porous earth drinking the sheer liquidity of the wine, the crisp crackling of the bay leaves, and the intangible fragrance and fire of the pile. . ." Cf. the "gummed leaves" burnt in the "sacrificial fire" in *The Fall of Hyperion* I,116.

232-306. *Hymn to Pan:* Frye[6] (19-20) notes that although "Wordsworth shook his head over the Hymn to Pan . . . and called it 'a very pretty piece of paganism' . . . Wordsworth had done much, was probably the decisive influence in making the Hymn to Pan possible. . ." For his "huge and mighty forms" are "the 'pagan' or latent numinous powers in nature that man turns to." For Haydon's account of Wordsworth's remark see Rollins (II,143-4) and Bate (264-7). Colvin (225-6), citing general sources in Chapman's Homeric *Hymn to Pan* and Jonson's *Pan's Anniversary,* feels "the Elizabethan pastoral spirit . . . emerged after near two centuries of occultation to reappear . . . wonderfully strengthened in imaginative reach and grasp, richer and more romantic both in the delighted sense of nature's blessings and activities and in the awed apprehension of a vast mystery behind them." For other Elizabethan sources and the influence of Wordsworth see Finney (260-72). Most critics agree on the poetic quality of the hymn. For Bate (179) "The Hymn and the lines that precede it . . . anticipate, as does nothing else Keats has thus far written, the great odes. . ." And Bush (48) calls it "the first of Keats's great odes . . . the finest piece of sustained writing he had yet done."

232-46. Knight (268) comments on a "trick" K. uses both here and in the Hymn to Bacchus (IV.182f), "involving rhymed half-line interspersions, often conclusions to swaying movements of other variously chosen rhyme-schemes, that seem to make the verse circle back and dance, sway, with a light ritualistic abandon before the deity concerned."

232-41. Dickstein (72-3) notes the dominant motif of the mystery of nature here (introduced at I.67-8): "Here the richness of nature becomes strange and exotic, not quite sinister, but pregnant with a significance that seems just beyond human reach."

235. Foreshadows, according to Finney (262), the 5th stanza of *Ode to a Nightingale.* Cf. II.285-6.

236-7. Ricks (87) answers a charge of voyeurism directed by a prurient reviewer (see Matthews 92) who failed to see the ambiguity: "with cunning humour and decorum, Keats did intimate a glimpse of nakedness before rounding the corner into the perfectly proper thing." Ricks is one of the few critics who addresses the poem's good humor.

236. *hamadryads:* According to Lemprière, "nymphs who lived in the country, and presided over the trees, with which they are said to live and die." K. calls the nightingale of the ode a "light-winged Dryad of the trees," presumably because of its empathic identification with the tree it inhabits.

238. *And . . . sit:* Anticipates, according to Bate (180), *To Autumn* where "autumn is seen sitting through the long day at the cider press, watching 'hours by hours.' "

240. *desolate:* sad and alone. Cf. *Ode on a Grecian Urn* 40.

241-6. For the story of Pan and Syrinx see Ovid, *Met.* I,689-712. Finney (260-1) compares K.'s earlier reference to the story ("I stood tip-toe" 157-62) and concludes that K. "converted the sentimental sighing of the wind among the reeds, 'a half heard strain, / Full of sweet desolation, balmy pain,' into the intensely imaginative verse, 'The dreary melody of bedded reeds.' " Dickstein (73) notes that Pan here, like Endymion at this point, is "a melancholy and disappointed lover." He sees the story as a "pregnant analogue to the main action of the poem. Like Arethusa Syrinx is a nymph of Diana who (as Ovid stresses) intently imitates her mistress' supposed chastity. Her metamorphosis turns Pan into a kind of poet, who makes music on a pipe fashioned out of her reeds, and even (foolishly) challenges Apollo himself."

241. *pipy:* of tubular shape; but in the context probably a pun.

247-8. *turtles . . . myrtles:* Both sacred to Venus. See Milton's *Nativity Ode* 150-2.

248. *Passion:* to imbue with deep feeling; Elizabethan. For a relevant but darker use see Venus's response ("Dumbly she passions. . .") to nature's "solemn sympathy" in *Venus and Adonis* 1057.

251-60. *O thou . . . near:* Comparing Pan to the nightingale of the ode, Wasserman (187) remarks: "Pan is one with the heart of nature, and nature belongs to him, not in its becoming, its spring, but in its full and changelessly vital being, its 'completions'–its summer." Here nature appears to be offering her "completions" to Pan in language suggestive of a Fortunate Fall. Cf. I.606.

261. The pine was traditionally consecrated to Pan. See Sandys's (267) commentary on *Met.* IV: "The browes of Pan are crowned with Pine branches, because those trees adorne the tops of the Mountains."

279-81. *O . . . bleating:* See *Lycidas* 75 and *Colin Clouts Come Home Again* 258, where Phoebus and Cynthia respectively represent the divine consolation of fame for the shorn sheep (i.e. prematurely dead poet). See III.580n.

285-7. Allott cites Baldwin (105): "All the strange, mysterious and unaccountable sounds which were heard in solitary places, were attributed to Pan." K. may have been thinking of Shakespeare's Ariel here.

287. *wither:* Jones (176) notes that "there are no 'withers' in the 1817 volume; they arrive in strength in *Endymion*'" Cf.

the refrain of *La Belle Dame.*

288-9. An abrupt transition from pastoral to higher truth, from local deity or genius of the place to universal nature or God, reminiscent of "the dread voice" of heaven's gate-keeper in *Lycidas* 133. Dickstein (74) notes that it is "only to the Latmians that Pan" is "dread." "They are satisfied to leave him an 'unknown,' " whereas "The quest of Endymion leads him to explore that unknown, to enter those doors." See K.'s letter to Reynolds of May 3, 1818: "This Chamber of Maiden Thought becomes gradually darken'd and at the same time on all sides of it many doors are set open—but all dark. . . We are now in that state—We feel the 'burden of the Mystery' " (I, 581). See also *Sleep and Poetry* 101-54.

288. *doors:* For the symbolic value of doors for K. see Wasserman (116-7). Cf. I.581-2 and III.959.

290. In Chapman's *Hymn to Pan,* Pan is represented as the son of Dryope and Hermes.

291. Dickstein (74) comments that "The Latmians are content with a static, sacramental relation to Pan . . . they seek him through ritual, perform a homage which leaves his mystery and their innocence intact."

293-302. Bush (48) regards Pan here as "the symbol of the romantic imagination." For Wasserman (16) he is the limit of what can be imagined, for were he more, "he would be unknowable, outside man's range, beyond the bourne, and therefore in the realm of pure immortality, which, in Keats's religion, can never be the home of man either in this life or in the next. Instead, Pan is the concurrence of the mortal and immortal, and hence a knowable unknown without being any the less unknown; he invests the physical with the ethereal. . ."

293-5. Several critics have noted the Wordsworthian nature of the lines. Hartman[3] (200) regards the conscious paradox here as stemming, like Wordsworth's nature, from the "mixed imaginative essence of the ancient gods—the fact that human and non-human co-existed in them—and the beautiful thought that some of them fell into nature and might revive from that base. . ." Hartman sees analogies to "this lodge or middle ground" in Wordsworth's "boundary images," such as the Leech-gatherer, and in Blake's Beulah. James (179), commenting on the "obscure sense of possible sublimity," compares *The Excursion* IV,136-7: "That 'tis a thing impossible to frame / Conceptions equal to the soul's desires." He finds that K. is similarly expressing "the bafflement which the imagination knows in its pursuit of vision. . ."

294-6. *such . . . brain:* "For the bourne of heaven is the outermost limit of the imagination after it has left naked the materialistic brain, which tries to seize everything in a clear, and therefore merely earthly, conception" Wasserman (16).

295. *bourne:* boundary. Finney (267-8) cites *Hamlet* III,i,79-80: "The undiscovered country from whose bourne / No traveller returns," which is the source of the modern usage. On the mythic concept of boundary or threshold of sacred space see Fletcher (45-9). The earthly paradise, like the moon which Endymion seeks, is the boundary between earth and heaven. Cf. III.31 and IV.461.

296-8. *be still . . . birth:* Cf. *King John* III,i,77-80:

> To solemnize this day the glorious sun
> Stays in his course and plays the alchemist,
> Turning with splendor of his precious eye
> The meagre cloddy earth to glittering gold.

298. *ethereal:* A highly significant word associated with "essence." See K.'s letter to Haydon of May 10-11, 1817: "the looking upon the Sun the Moon the Stars, the Earth and its contents as materials to form greater things—that is to say ethereal things—but here I am talking like a Madman greater things than our Creator himself made!!" (I,143).

299. Pan is literally "all."

302-3. *we . . . foreheads:* Brisman[2] (76) believes that Latmians screen "their foreheads so as not to see, not to think, the epiphany of the god."

306. *Mount Lycean:* A mountain in Arcadia sacred to Pan.

310-11. *when . . . brine:* Brisman[2] (76) notes that "Unlike Yeats's dolphins which transport to eternity, Keats's are so colloquially and sensually realized that we are drawn back to nature."

315-21. *those . . . first-fruits:* Dickstein (75) comments: "The Latmians are not so much men as 'fair living forms' upon which old marbles have conferred a timeless immortality. We see them here as stylized fantasy, in slow-motion, not dancing but, rather, swimming heavenly to tunes forgotten. They represent a mythic 'golden age' (II,896), 'unconscious' of the imminent onset of time and history (e.g. Thermopylae), yet they are the 'genitors' of that history."

320. *genitors:* progenitors. For other examples of aphaerisis see I.571, 808, and 850.

326-31. The Spartan youth Hyacinthus was beloved of Apollo, who accidentally slew him while playing at quoits and in his grief transformed him into that flower "inscribed with woe." See Ovid, *Met.* X,162-219. K. follows Lemprière in making the jealous Zephyr the cause of the accident, and there is at least a suggestion that he is the cause of the metamorphosis as well. See Abrams on the metaphorical significance of the west wind for the Romantics. See IV.66-75n. for the Indian Maid's attempt to revive Hyacinthus.

331. *Fondles:* Lends a sexual connotation to the pathos, suggesting that Zephyr here is Flora's lover—a mild, temperate wind bringing warm rain and morning dew (Cf. IV.570). *sobbing rain:* A good example of the pathetic fallacy. Cf. the "weeping cloud" in *Ode on Melancholy* 12, "That fosters the droop-headed flowers all. . ."

334. *raft:* torn away; Spenserian.

335. *Branch:* According to de Selincourt, K., like Chaucer, often has a single syllable do duty for the initial foot.

337-43. *Perhaps . . . cheeks.* Niobe was turned to dumb stone out of grief for her children, who were killed by Apollo and Diana at Latona's (I.862) command. See Ovid, *Met.* VI,165-312. Ricks (9) feels that "The power and humanity of these lines is not simply and solely a matter of their presenting a real anguish . . . what animates the lines is a particular recognition . . . that a great impediment to our full sympathy with frantic grief is its being embarrassing to contemplate, especially in its physical distortion. . ." They "not only do not avert their eyes from the mere gape (always fascinating in its way) . . . they embody a generosity that can accommodate a truthful recognition (and not be mesmerized), evoked through the repetitions which are like those of grief itself . . . evoked too in the simple dignity of 'Her motherly cheeks.' "

338. *frantic gape:* Cf. *Venus and Adonis* 1059: "Dumbly she passions, franticly she doteth." The exaggerated kinetic and grotesque nature of Venus's grief, as well as her dumb female animal ("milch doe") associations, may have influenced K. here, though he has created a more deeply human image of his own.

341. *paly:* According to Allott, a recently revived Elizabethan poeticism.

347-54. De Selincourt notes that the only account of the Argonauts in which Apollo appears is Rhodius's *Argonautica,* which K. may have heard Shelley recite. Although Apollo appears as a destructive deity in the other stories of the shepherds, here his "golden bow" is a vision of hope and guidance.

358. *eld:* old age.

360. *fragile bar:* Suggest that mortal life is fugacious and that, as Ford[3] (44) says, "a gifted spirit, perhaps even during mortality, can pass beyond the pale." Cf. II.124 and 185.

363. *Vesper:* Hesperus or the evening star. Rising before the moon (Cf. III.78n., IV.458, and 965-7), it shines through the night becoming the morning star or Lucifer (I.531); hence a symbol of post-mortal continuity. See Hartman (147-78) for an analysis of its literary history.

371-93. Ford[3] (44) finds "The significant expressions in the present passage—'heart certain,' 'anticipated bliss' and 'fond (i.e. loving) imaginations' are exactly echoed in Letter 31 [to Bailey of Nov. 22, 1817] where Keats argued that 'the truth of imagination' is inseparable from 'the holiness of the heart's affections.' that imagination is 'a shadow of reality to come,' and that this reality to come (=elysium) is 'happiness on earth repeated in a finer tone.' "

372. *Elysium:* Though variously used, here, as Frye[6] (134) notes, it is conceived as a pagan analogue to the Christian heaven, "the place of the presence of Pan [the "Dread opener" of "its mysterious doors"] . . . an 'eternal spring' of final reunion and happiness. The old men of Endymion's society are on the verge of entering it and it is also described in New Testament language as a world where lost lambs are found again. It is ordinarily reached by contemplation, to which Endymion proposes to devote himself at the end of the first book, but Endymion's real wish, and his destiny, is to enter it through his love for Diana (i.e. Phoebe) as the moon."

380. *eye-earnestly:* with earnest eyes; a coinage.

392. *famished:* scantly supplied.

394. De Selincourt notes the combined influence of *The Tempest* I,ii,408: "The fringed curtains of thine eye advance . . ." and *Pericles* III,ii,99-101:

> Her eyelids, cases to those heavenly jewels
> Which Pericles hath lost,
> Begin to part their fringes of bright gold. . .

395-406. Frye[6] (131), speaking of Endymion's "deep melancholy" here, "the same state of helpless pining grief in which we first meet Romeo," can explain the Courtly Love convention in so vigorous a poet only by the fact "that Endymion's world is the imprisoning, paralyzing world of dream, the dream being partly about a great achievement in the future, and so accompanied by all the anxieties that go with the dislocation of time. . . Endymion is not literally unborn, but his achievement is, and his world has the fragility that goes with something that is only potentially alive." See I.95-103n. Patterson (28), on the other hand, interprets Endymion's peculiar instability as a "daemonic trance": "His consciousness has gone out of himself and his immediate world but has not gone into any other. . ."

397. *fainting recollections:* Cf. Wordsworth's *Intimations Ode* 152-5:

> But for those first affections,
> Those shadowy recollections,
> Which, be they what they may,
> Are yet the fountain-light of all our day. . .

405-6. A conspicuous allusion to "The History of the Young King of the Black Isles" in *The Arabian Nights,* where a melancholy young king is paralyzed from the waist down, his legs turned to black marble by a beautiful enchantress. The "marble man" motif in the poem is discussed by Van Ghent (10-11), who associates it with embalming and sleep-healing, and believes it can have a beneficent or Apollonian significance (see II.392-406n.) as well as a sinister or deathly one (see II.200, III.136-8). The latter is associated with the Medusa myth (IV.754n.), the Circean or "Belle Dame" muse, and the "dumb enchantment" of dream. As a poetic motif it appears to have originated in the Niobe legend (I.337-43n.) employed in an epitaph by Browne (294). Milton uses it to represent a kind of imaginative transport or enthrallment (cf. *On Shakespeare* 14 and *Il Penseroso* 42).

408. *Peona, his sweet sister:* Perhaps derived from Paean, the physician of the gods, who is associated with Apollo; or from the peony, one species of which the ancients revered for its powers of staunching blood, and another (the "globed" variety) K. uses as a homeopathic cure for melancholy. For the healing power of flowers see II.482-3. Blackstone (124) believes that, as Endymion's sister, "She incarnates the maternal, the limited, the unspeculative. . . In Peona, Keats dramatizes the 'homely nurse' of Wordsworth's great Ode." Cf. I.411-3 and 705-6. Frye[6] (130-1) interprets Peona as representing the "youthful and presexual aspect of life. . ." "It is the state we work from, not the place we return to: in his letters Keats calls it the

'chamber of maiden thought.' " As the representative of an idyllic society, or the sisterly intimate familiarity of nature, Peona functions like Homer's Nausikaa, to revive the hero from the pains of experience, placing him in a comfortable bower so he can tell his story, but one he must escape from if he is to finish his quest.

412-52. Beautifully expatiates on the opening lines of the poem, evoking what Frye[6] (130-1) calls "the world of the pastoral myth in which poetic creation begins, a world still present and potential."

416-7. *Guarding . . . branches:* An odd image of the protective function of Peona. She protects Endymion from the branches of the material world and shades his flushing forehead from the heat of poetic fancy and teeming thought. For the forehead (the place of conception) as the locus of embarrassment, erotic feeling, and poetic creativity in K., see Ricks (162-5). Cf. I.302-3, II.138, and IV.837-8. See II.378-9 for Endymion's awakening into the material world by brushing against branches.

422. *crystal mocking:* reflections in the water.

423. *shallop:* a light skiff. Cf. *F. Q.* III,vii,27 and *Alastor* 299.

425-6. *dipped . . . dipped:* A sexual rhythm, though here the innocent or diffused sexuality of dream. K. continues to associate the verb with bowers and streams. Cf. I.663-5, II.58, and II.182.

428. *bowery island:* An innocent version of the bowery islands of Spenser's Phaedria and Acrasia. Though more ambivalent, it too is something of a prison-paradise. Its Biblical analogue is the *hortus conclusus* of the *Song of Songs* 4.12: "A garden enclosed is my sister, my spouse." Dickstein (76) views it as "the bower of the 1817 *Poems,* a world of soothing nature and refreshing sleep, which provide antidotes for excessive reflection."

432. *fingering:* the elaboration of natural growth. Allott compares the spider's web in Spenser's *Muipotmos* 366: "loupes of fingering fine. . ." But "silent" suggests that K. may be hinting

at its Shakespearean musical-sexual meaning as well. See *Cymbeline* II,iii,13-4: "If you can penetrate her with your fingering so; we'll try with tongue too." Cf. II.54. This reinforces the suggestion that Peona's bower, like Acrasia's, is her own creation, the fingering or sublimated sexuality of both needle and lute. For a more sinister web of natural beauty see IV.427-8.

450. *wailful gnat:* Allott cites *To Autumn* 27.

453-63. Knight (261-2) notes that here "sleep is (i) an introduction to the paradise symbols of the *Kubla Khan* sort, and (ii) at once a magic release and an outpouring of health for daylight living." D'Avanzo (60) regards sleep as "the first stage of the release of the poetic imagination" while "dreaming signifies the imaginative process unfolding." In commenting on the oxymorons here as "both the license and restriction of the poetic imagination," D'Avanzo (65) finds a useful analogy in Freud's concept of "dream work" and "censor."

453-4. *O comfortable . . . mind:* Perhaps a confluence of the halycon of Milton's *Nativity Ode* 66-8, and the dove of *P. L.* I.20-2.

453. *comfortable:* consoling. Cf. *King Lear* I,iv,296-7: "I have another daughter, / Who I am sure is kind and comfortable."

466-72. Although ending on a Wordsworthian note, it is remarkably parallel in thought and image to the *Song of Songs* 5.2.

495. *Dryope:* A nymph who bore a child to Apollo, who, out of compassion for her grief, transformed her into a lotus. See Ovid, *Met.* IX,371-9.

510. *Paphian dove:* From Venus's temple in Paphos.

512-4. *haply . . . death.* The Actaeon myth is associated with the listless melancholy lover in *Twelth Night* I,i,22-4. According to Frye[6] (134), it is functionally important, for it tells us that Endymion cannot approach Diana directly, and so must go in the opposite direction, must descend to reach her starry heights. Shelley (*Adonais* XXXI) associates K. with Actaeon, or his own

Alastor figure, who once having "gazed on Nature's naked loveliness," is pursued by his thoughts "like raging hounds."

529-38. Dickstein (76-7) views as Endymion's account "of a fall that seems radical and irrevocable. . ." According to Dickstein, the sun here "becomes a cosmic analogue for Endymion's heroic stature," suggesting "a world in which man and the cosmos were one. . ." But now "Endymion can no longer play the hunter's and the hero's part: he has fallen from legend to man, from health to despondency, above all, from activity to self-consciousness."

529. *horizontal sun:* Cf. Satan's faded glory in *P. L.* 594-6: "as when the sun new-risen / Looks through the horizontal misty air / Shorn of his beams."

530. See Clarke (126) for an account of K. hoisting himself up to dramatize Spenser's "sea-shouldering Whales" (*F. Q.* II,xii,23). K. associated the image with heroic stature (see *Letters* I,265). See IV.441-3n. for the fall of a "bare shouldered creature."

531. *Out-facing:* stare down, defy, with perhaps a sense of false bravado as in *As You Like It* I,iii,116-8. *Lucifer:* the morning star; Satan's pre-lapsarian glory.

532. *My spear:* In his letter to Hunt of May 10, 1817, K., brooding over poetic aspiration and death, says "it requires a thousand bodkins to make a spear bright enough to throw any light to posterity" (I,139). In associating lines of poetry with Hamlet's "bare bodkin," K. is perhaps expressing his anxiety in the face of the thousand little deaths he is heir to before becoming negatively capable of the "Loftiest Muse." See I.174n. for the self-destructive aspect of the spear, and II.294, where it is more explicitly associated with the poet's pen.

536. *progress silverly:* Stillinger[2] notes the conscious echo of *King John* V,ii,46: "Let me wipe off the honorable dew / That silverly doth progress on thy cheeks."

551-7. Evert (107) finds it significant that flowers sacred to

Diana are here blossoming in the light of the setting sun (see I.608-10n.).

552. *his snorting four:* Apollo's four horses are referred to in Ovid, *Met.* II,153-5. But see I *Henry IV* II,iv,503: "Fast asleep behind the arras, and snorting like a horse." The Shakespearean meaning (snoring) suggests that these horses, like those in IV.364-6, are sleeping.

555. *sacred ditamy . . . poppies red:* According to Lemprière, plants sacred to Diana. Frye[6] (136-7) views them as emblems of the "Eros-Thanatos world of the gods of sexual love and death," and analogous to the "little western flower" called "love-in-idleness" in *A Midsummer Night's Dream* II,i,155-68. That flower is turned red by the arrow Cupid aims at a Diana figure ("a fair vestal throned by the west"), its trajectory symbolizing for Frye "the cycle of life and death under the moon." As the juice of Cupid's flower creates love-visions, so here the flowers are a prelude to Endymion's love-vision of Diana. Cf. I.889-94.

559. *Morpheus:* The god of sleep, often associated with "poppies" (see *Met.* XI,605); also a supreme artist and counterfeiter of form. In Spenser (*F. Q.* I,i,39f.), Morpheus provides Archimago a false dream of an enchantress to delude the Red Cross Knight. Cf. I.747-9. Here the word is a disyllable.

562-3. *young Mercury . . . rod in it:* The god of eloquence, inventor of the lyre, and messenger of Apollo. He uses his caduceus as the white magician, such as Prospero, uses his staff—it may become an "opiate rod," as in the story of Argus (II.875-7), or serve to bring about a metamorphosis of ascent (cf. IV.67-8).

566-72. Dickstein (77) notes that "Characteristically, Endymion speaks less of passion and desire than of imaginative afflatus. He describes a visionary experience that Keats will repeatedly associate either with sleep and dreams or with the moon." Dickstein compares the language of the passage with the earlier invocation to Sleep (I.456-61).

567-8. Allott cites a correspondent breeze in Coleridge's "Dejection Ode" 86: "My shaping spirit of Imagination. . ." See I.681 where the breeze is laid asleep and the vision ends.

570. The polysyndeton retards the movement of the line, enacting the gradual fading out of consciousness.

582-8. *Ah . . . felt.* Dickstein (78) compares the distinction Endymion makes here with the one Coleridge makes in *Kubla Khan,* where the "whole poem, he tells us, must be heard as the partial echo of some much grander symphony and song of which we can only have a faint surmise (whose revival would transfigure the poet into a magical and godlike state)."

573-8. Ford[3] (17-8), comparing Adam's dream of Eve (*P. L.* VIII,460-78), finds that the "content of the two dreams (love) and their function (prefiguration) are the same. But most significant, so far as the problem of defining Keats's usage of 'truth' is concerned, Endymion shows the same relation between the hero's prefigurative dream and his value judgment" or "pleasure thermometer" as does *Paradise Lost.* "In a word, both judgments are ex post facto defenses of the prefigurative veracity of erotic dreams." But although both dreams reveal a scale of values, the truth Endymion's dream prefigures, unlike Adam's, must be postponed until the recognition scene at the end of the poem.

574-8. The wording suggests a reminiscence of Bottom's bottomless dream (*A Midsummer Night's Dream* IV,i,208-17). Like Endymion, Bottom is an innocent initiated into a new world of wonder governed by a Diana figure who promises to spiritualize him.

579. *milky way:* "according to Pythagoras, the people of dreams are souls, which are reported to be collected in the milky way; the appelation of which is derived from souls, nourished with milk after their lapse into the whirls of generation" (Porphyry 290-1). Blackstone (408) feels Porphyry may have influenced K. See II.758-9.

592-3. *moon . . . shell:* Eliade (156) notes that shells were originally believed to be created by the moon's rays. They are found in water and are a symbol of the vulva, both of which are governed by the moon. See III.761n.

594. *my dazzled soul:* See *P. L.* VIII,456-8, where Adam, "Dazzled and spent" from his colloquy with God, sinks into his dream of Eve.

598-9. *lidless-eyed . . . planets:* Allott suggests that planets do not wink as do stars. Later, in the "Bright star" sonnet and in the letter to Tom of June 25-7, 1818 (I.299), K. associates open-lidedness with the steadfastness of the North Star. See I.47n. where the "Polar Star" is identified with "Invention."

606-7. Dickstein (79) interprets as "partly the idealizing rhetoric of love," but believes "Endymion is also trying to describe an experience closer to transcendence than to ordinary love."

608-10. Evert (108-10), noting that the silver-moon goddess is here reflecting her twin brother's "golden hair" (associated with harvest and the western light of his setting), claims that Endymion's "special devotion to natural beauty (the sun) has earned a special revelation" that "includes both a more extreme perception of natural beauty and a closer communion with the divine presence" of Diana. Evert believes K. is here transferring the symbolic function of Apollo on to Diana.

614. *gordian'd:* One of several instances of hybrid participles generated of epithets. Cf. the serpent's "Gordian twine" of *P. L.* IV,348.

620-2. On other instances of post-visionary disillusionment in K. see Wasserman (170). Cf. *The Fall of Hyperion* I,175: "Only the dreamer venoms all his days."

624-32. A commonplace image in Renaissance literature and painting. Bush[3] (102-3) cites a number of possible sources, and comments: "Keats's eye is in a sense on the object, and in his fresh enjoyment of physical beauty he forgets his symbolic theme; his goddess is soft white flesh." Yet the hyperbolic "more" here suggests Enydmion, like Raphael, is "likening spiritual to corporeal forms" (*P. L.* V,573). In K., as in Milton, the spiritual realm is not without senses, it simply has more, and of greater intensity.

629-30. *over-spangled . . . eyes:* Bush[4] compares *P. L.* XI,130-1: "Spangled with eyes more numerous than those / Of Argus. . ."

633. *Dream within dream:* Bush[4] suggests that Peona refers here to the goddess' appearing (601f.) within the dream that began at 572.

638-52. The dream prefigures Endymion's adventures in earth, water and air (or fire) of Books II, III, and IV respectively.

639-40. *Who . . . coral:* Cf. Ariel's song (*The Tempest* I,ii,394-5): "Full fathom five thy father lies / Of his bones are coral made. . ."

642. *artillery:* shower of arrows.

653-60. *madly . . . blessedness.* The "give" and "take" works itself out in the language of Spenser's *Cave of Mammon* (cf. *F. Q.* II,vii,17-8). Dickstein (80) notes that "the 'full draught' foreshadows the 'domineering potion' that the poet drinks at the outset of *The Fall of Hyperion,* and the whole passage prefigures the theme important in both *Hyperion* poems of life and rebirth achieved through some sort of death." Ende (63-4) compares the poet's sacrifice to Apollo in *Sleep and Poetry* (see I.95n.), and notes that Endymion cannot finish his "draught" of "immortal drink," for his "ecstasy is halted by the presence of 'A second self' that holds his recollection and redeems the moments . . . to assure him of future remembrance."

658. *greedy help:* "The greedy self recalls the 'greediest eye' of *I Stood Tip-toe*, which needed the reassurance of natural plenitude when faced with the gentle shock of a spectral landscape" Ende (64).

675-8. *like . . . sleep.* Dickstein (81) feels the image "finely embodies both the beauty of vision and its fragility and transience."

677. *diamond:* Associated with the sun at II.245-6, and with the moon at IV.497.

678. *stupid:* stupified. See *P. L.* IX,465, where Satan, overawed by Eve's "heavenly form," remains for a moment "stupidly good."

683. *ouzel:* a European blackbird.

686. *solitary breeze:* The breeze that had brought on the vision at 567 is now waning, leaving Endymion in a state of solitude. In Bloom's (16) terms, he is overcome, like Shelley's Alastor-figure, by "the avenging diamon who is a baffled residue of the self, determined to be compensated for its loss of natural assurance. . ."

691-705. Evert (123) believes (contra Finney) that the waning of natural beauty for Endymion, as well as nature's sinister opposition to his divine aspirations, is "the condition that the poem exists to explore."

691-2. Bush[4] cites *Alastor* 196-7: "Whither have fled / The hues of heaven?"

696-7. *the vermeil rose . . . thorns out-grown:* Thorns were one of the results of the Fall (cf. *P. L.* IV,256), which, according to another legend, pierced Venus's flesh, turning the rose "scarlet" with her blood.

701-3. The mood and diction seems to owe something to *Alastor.* Patterson (33) sees here Endymion's postdaemonic condition in which he is "so disenchanted with actuality that he wanted the 'innocent bird' to be a 'disguised demon' leading him even to destruction if necessary for escape."

702. *under darkness:* the darkness of the underworld.

715-60. Belongs to the genre of dream-interpretation, as in Pertelote's realistic interpretation of Chauntecleer's foreboding dream in *The Nun's Priest's Tale.* Brown (633) interprets Peona's argument against Endymion following the quest as K. "forecasting the evil which will befall Endymion if he denies the human world for the vision—an end which *Alastor* demonstrated to Keats. . ." Dickstein (82) believes "Peona recalls Endymion to the heroic, active life that he himself had so vividly described to her."

723. *this middle earth:* Between heaven and the underworld.

744. *horses prancing:* D'Avanzo (85) regards as a metaphor of "metrical regularity that brings order to the flights of the imagination," the horse being "the most regular of pacing animals" and, as Pegasus, a dynamic image of imaginative flight.

747-60. *The Morphean fount . . . dream?* Dickstein (84-5) compares *Romeo and Juliet* I,iv,95-105, noting that "Peona borrows the language of Mercutio but the attitude of Benvolio: 'The wind you talk of blows us from ourselves.' " He adds that "Peona, like the chorus of Greek tragedy, defends safety and stability, the traditional wisdom of the community, warning the hero against overreaching his proper sphere."

748-9. *dreams . . . are made of:* Spurgeon (11) cites *The Tempest* IV,i,156-8: "We are such stuff / As dreams are made of, and our little life / Is rounded by a sleep." Peona wants Endymion to bury his staff and drown his book.

759. *high-fronted:* of noble bearing; a common Elizabethanism.

763-6. *Zephyr . . . manna-dew:* D'Avanzo (98-9) notes the union here of "Endymion's inspiration from 'manna-dew' with the literal inspiration provided by Zephyr's 'little breeze.' "

764. *fans:* A poeticism for "wings" frequently used by K.

765. *careless:* free from care. Cf. II.463.

766. *manna-dew:* Apparently coined, perhaps after Coleridge's "honey-dew" (*Kubla Khan* 53). Traditionally, dew, like manna, was believed to fall from heaven. See Marvell's *On a Drop of Dew.*

777-842. The controversial "pleasure thermometer," which measures "happiness" by means of intensity and selfless absorption. Its four gradations are 1) *nature,* represented by "A rose leaf" (782); 2) *art,* represented by "music" (783-94); 3) *friendship,* (803-5); and 4) *love* (805-42). K. added the passage while revising the poem, and explained its significance in his letter to Taylor of Jan. 30, 1818:

> The whole thing must I think have appeared to you, who are a consequitive Man, as a thing almost of mere words—but I assure you that when I wrote it, it was a regular stepping of the Imagination towards a Truth. My having written that Argument will perhaps be of the greatest Service to me of any thing I ever did—It set before me at once the gradations of Happiness even like a kind of Pleasure Thermometer—and is my first Step towards the chief Attempt in the Drama—the playing of different Natures with Joy and Sorrow (I,218-9).

The "pleasure thermometer" is the crux of Finney's (298-9) Neoplatonic interpretation of the poem: for him the four gradations are embodied successively in the four books and represent stages of a Neoplatonic ascent from substantial to essential beauty. Evert (118-22) refutes this rather theoretically reductive interpretation, arguing that the steps in the "ladder" do not exist in any necessary relationship nor correspond to the four books: "Keats does not, in good neo-Platonic style, assert that each stage in the process prepares one for experience of the next and higher stage. On the contrary, there are various essences to be in fellowship with. . . The 'degrees' of which the poet speaks are levels of experiential intensity, not prerequisites to be first achieved and then abandoned as the subject spirit becomes progressively more refined. . ." Although disagreeing with Finney, Evert does not fall into the other extreme, as does Ford[3] (14), who (exploiting K.'s unfortunate choice of words) calls the "pleasure thermometer" a "hedonistic hierarchy," the criterion of which is "the degree of pleasure in any category." Evert would agree in general with Wasserman (27 & 54-5) that the "pleasure thermometer" is both a "chronological progress of becoming" and "a scale of ethereal things," the values of which are determined by the intensity of the percipient. However, unlike Wasserman, Evert (116, n.1) does not consider it a key to K.'s "poetic metaphysics" or even (unlike most critics) a key to the poem. He even questions the appropriateness of its being spoken by a character who has still to learn the truths it expresses. Dickstein (87) assumes a middle position, regarding it as a "momentary peak, significant but not definitive, neither the 'key' to the poem nor a précis of its action. . ." It expresses rather "an ideal possibility that must be measured against the limiting conditions that so frequently reassert themselves along the way."

777-80. Wherein lies happiness? In that which becks
Our ready minds to blendings pleasurable
And that delight is the most treasurable
That makes the richest Alchymy." *FC*

Brisman[2] (71-2) notes that K. alchemized or sublimated some of the naturalism of the first version—replacing the solid "blendings pleasurable" with the gaseous "fellowship with essence." Frye[6] (162) regards the revised version as "the great vision which is at the heart of *Endymion,* the upper world that Endymion finally attains."

777. *happiness:* Something of a technical term K. will continue to use in his later poetry (cf. *Ode to a Nightingale* and *Ode on a Grecian Urn*). Wasserman (23) defines as "no cheap gaiety, but the *summum bonum,* the opposite of the weariness, the fever, and the fret that are the inherent attributes of the unhappy mortal world. It lies . . . in that which *beckons* us until we are free of the spatial, that extension which is the opposite of essence, and freedom from space begins at heaven's bourne, the point of mystic blending." See K.'s letter to Bailey of Nov. 22, 1817: "another favorite speculation of mine, that we shall enjoy ourselves here after by having what we called happiness on earth repeated in a finer tone and so repeated. . ." (I,185).

781. *The clear religion of heaven!* Dickstein (87) claims that, "in spite of the religious vocabulary," the unity of which K. speaks does not seem to be "a unity with anything supernatural."

781-97. *Fold . . . spirits.* A dense, difficult passage that has not been adequately explicated. Evert (120) parenthetically mentions that the forms of art here "represent the imaginative activity of the person inspired to creative dreaming by the sound of nature's voices." But a more specific analysis of the art-nature relation is needed. Are we, for instance, to take "music" literally or as a synecdoche for the potential creative spirit in man and nature? Are the "ditties" of "no tone?" Nature (both the "rose leaf" and the "free winds") appears to be the feminine beloved, while "music" is both lover and midwife, impregnating and unbinding and thereby freeing the spiritual essence (which includes the "old songs" of the cultural past) imprisoned, like Ariel, in the tomb-like objectivity of nature. Perhaps implicit here is an analogy between the poet's powers of articulating the language of "symbol-essences" (cf. III.700) and the magician's control of the spirits of nature. Cf. *Hyperion* III,62-6, *P. L.* IV,264-6, and see II.827-53n. for another instance of the translation of natural sound into human song.

783-6. *hist . . . wombs:* According to Spurgeon (12-3), an example of Shakespeare's deep influence on K.—a perfect description of the "essence of Ariel's being, spirit of ethereal music, 'free as mountain winds.' " For K.'s conviction that poetry must be free as the air see II.1-44n.

786. *Aeolian magic:* Abrams (38) notes that "the lyre of Apollo was often replaced in Romantic poetry by the Aeolian lyre, whose music is evoked not by art, human or divine, but by a force of nature. . . The wind harp has become a persistent Romantic analogue of the poetic mind, the figurative mediator between outer motion and inner emotion." Cf. II.866.

787-94. De Man (37) believes the "passage refers to the discovery and study of the world of art and learning" (Keats in his formative years "discovering Shakespeare, Homer, and the Elgin marbles") and feels it "is of some importance that it does not refer to the practice of art as a creative poet."

788. Spurgeon (56) cites *The Tempest* I,ii,402: "The ditty does remember my drown'd father."

789-90. "The poet Lucan said that Apollo founded the Delphic oracle at a huge chasm where 'the earth breathed forth divine truth, and . . . gave out a wind that spoke' " Abrams (46).

791. *bruit:* proclaim.

797-800. *our state . . . chief intensity:* Dickstein (89-90) believes that, unlike the notion of Negative Capability K. describes in his letters and which he imputes to drama, here "Endymion is describing a willed and total self-annihilation more serious than what the dramatist undergoes in creating his characters. It is an annihilation of the man as well as the poet, and it leads not to creativity but to stasis, to 'ardent listlessness' (I,825) on the part of those who can willingly 'let occasion die' and 'sleep in love's elysium.' "

798. *entanglements:* Connotes for D'Avanzo (43) "physical involvement and verbal union" (cf. Coleridge's "mingled measure"), as well as the psychic perplexity of "enthrallments." "Both words point to the spellbound state into which love and imaginative creativity cast the poet. . ."

800. *intensity:* Degrees of which are measured by the "pleasure thermometer." See K.'s letter to his brothers of Dec. 21, 1817: "the excellence of every Art is its intensity, capable of making all disagreeables evaporate, from their being in close relationship with Beauty and Truth—Examine *King Lear*. . ." (I,192).

801. *love and friendship:* Ford[3] (16) compares Adam's desire for "Collateral love and dearest amity" (*P. L.* VIII,426).

804. *friendship:* Perhaps should be viewed in the context of K.'s ideal society where individuals interpenetrate or "interassimulate." In his letter to Reynolds of Feb. 19, 1818, K. says "Man should not dispute or assert but whisper results to his neighbor. . ." (I,232). Bloom[3] (393) believes friendship is illustrated in Book III in the form of "an alchemized sharing of essence between two equal partners." See III.801-2n. K. links friendship with art in *Sleep and Poetry* 245-7, where he speaks of "the great end / Of poesy, that it should be a friend / To sooth the cares, and lift the thoughts of man." Hence the Grecian Urn is "a friend to man."

805-7. *but . . . love:* Evert (111-2), discovering in Lemprière that Cupid and Diana, love and light, extend their influence over the same four spheres of nature, sees here a concentrated image of their interfusion: "love is expressed as the distillation of light. And light is the symbol-essence . . . of human understanding carried to the threshold of divine intuition, to the point at which . . . true poetry becomes possible." Cf. Milton's "unseen" spiritual light: "So thick a drop serene hath quenched their orbs" (*P. L.* III,25).

807-8. *its influence . . . eyes:* Cf. Cupid's influence condensed in the love-charm Puck throws in the eyes of Lysander in *A Midsummer Night's Dream* II,ii,77-8: "Churl, upon thy eyes I throw / All the power this charm doth owe." See I.555n.

815. *pelican brood.* The Medieval bestiary served up pelicans as an allegory of the Eucharistic meal. Mother pelicans were said to kill their young and restore them after three days with the blood from a self-inflicted wound. K. may have been drawn to the image by its cannabilistic parody in Lear's "pelican daughters" (III,iv,73). Wasserman (32) comments: "Just as the legendary pelican partakes of the blood (essence) of its mother . . . so through increasing intensities and enthrallments human life may ultimately be nourished in spirit by partaking of the nature of heaven's bourne. . ." Dickstein (95-6), however, feels K.'s conception is less Eucharistic than "a return of experience to its own vital sources, a breakdown of encrusted layers of selfhood." He believes that "in seeking to return not simply to the mother but to that ultimate and self-limiting mother who nourishes with her own blood, Keats also expresses a wish to destroy the mother, a wish that he will begin to realize in his portrait of the malicious Circe. . ."

816. *unsating food:* Traditionally said of divine knowledge, but K. may have in mind, as Godfrey (28) suggests, *Antony and Cleopatra* II,ii,241-3: "other women cloy / The Appetities they feed, but she makes hungry / Where most she satisfies. . ."

820-1. *wipe away all slime . . . serpentry:* Ricks (138) cites *Antony and Cleopatra* II,viii,20-3: "The higher Nilus swells, / The more it promises; as it ebbs, the seedsman / Upon the slime and ooze scatters his grain, / And shortly comes to harvest." But he finds K. more convincing when using such imagery in a less negative, more charactistic way.

825. *ardent listlessness:* A typical Keatsian love-oxymoron. Wasserman (200) compares the "vibrant repose" of the heaven of which the nightingale sings in "Ode to a Nightingale."

828-31. As an expression of love's power, Dickstein (66) finds that while in "one respect this is a benign reciprocity between individual love and the natural order . . . it is also true the love song, while apparently personal, bewitches a cosmic power and causes a temporary suspension of the natural order."

828. *the nightingale:* Evert (61) remarks that, like Apollo or the wind, the nightingale is invariably an invisible presence in K.'s poetry. Van Ghent (23) feels it is here a symbol of fertility.

831. A recurring image in K. (cf. II.261), where, as Knight (272) remarks, "motion and stillness seem to meet" and "where sleep meets waking life and the inanimate takes its own deep unheard breaths. . ." Allott cites *Romeo and Juliet* III,vi,9-10: "jocund day / Stands tiptoe on the misty mountain tops."

839.42. What Puttenham (217) calls a marching or climbing figure, "for after the first steppe all the rest proceede by double the space . . . and goeth as it were by strides or paces; it may as well be called the clyming figure, for climax is as much to say as a ladder. . ." Climbing a ladder is a Freudian dream-symbol for sexual intercourse; the verse moves with an accelerating pulse, reaching a climax with "kiss and greet." Knight (275) beautifully refers to the idea conveyed as human love "feeling the outer universe. . ." Its analogy to the sympathetic magic of fertility rites seems clear enough.

843-4. *Now . . . mortal, immortal:* Wasserman (40) notes the "the adjacing of 'mortal' and 'immortal' brought about by the inversion 'being mortal' is designed to deny the dichotomy of mortal and immortal and to convey instead the sense that although men's being is made immortal by love, it thereby loses none of its mortal attributes except its mortality, its existence in a context of mutability and decay."

849. Ford[3] (125) translates as "A love everlasting, the love of an immortal." The immortal is Cynthia.

851. *atomies:* mites. Allott cites *Romeo and Juliet* I,iv,58-9: "Drawn with a team of little atomies / Athwart men's noses as they lie asleep."

855. *luxury:* Trilling (81) notes the particular charm the word had for K., and claims that he is "on the point of reviving its Middle English meaning, which is specifically erotic . . . for Chaucer *luxures* were lusts and *luxurie* was licentiousness. . . Women present themselves to Keats's imagination as luxuries . . . and poetry itself is defined by reference to objects of luxury." For a survey of the important instances of the word in K., see Guy.

857. The hope evidently refers to a truth the dream prefigures. Ford[3] (48) compares K.'s letter to Bailey of Nov. 22, 1817, where he speaks of a "life of Sensations" as "a Shadow of reality to come" (I,185). The truth or "reality," according to Dickstein (85), transcends "the dichotomy between imagination and reality. . ."

862. *Latona:* The mother of Apollo and Cynthia, to whom she gave birth on the island of Delos (I.966). Cf. *Hyperion* III,24f.

864-8. Cf. Venus's mount in Spenser's *Gardens of Adonis* (*F. Q.* III,vi,44). As in Spenser, here we find a temperate enclosed space that satisfies an atavistic urge and is protected from the vulture-sun of mutability and decay.

870-3. The "well" here is a "crystal eye" through which Endymion views the heavens. Cf. *I Stood Tip-toe* 163-70 and IV.394-7n.

889. *cloudy Cupid:* Eros as fertility god, who, like Zephyr, brings "plenteous showers" (899) of natural luxuries.

893-4. *behold / A wonder:* Technically, a thaumasmus. Cf. Aeneas's "mirabile dictu" (*The Aeneid* I,439), echoed in Milton's *"Behold a wonder!"* (*P. L.* I,777).

895-905. Allott compares the vision in the well in Shelley's *Alastor* 479-92. The legend of Narcissus seems to be behind both contexts.

895. *tasted:* See I.816 for love as an 'unsating food." The sense-transference, common in K., adds a sense of sexual-physical contact to what would otherwise be merely a visual image.

896. *My heart did leap:* Cf. Wordsworth's "My heart leaps up." K.'s, however, leaps down, not to leap up till IV.445. The image serves to complete a rather clever identification of up and down, for Cynthia is both above Endymion and below him reflected in the "cool depth."

898-902. For another shower of floral luxuries see II.424-7.

898. *refreshfully:* a coinage.

903. *breathless honey-feel of bliss:* Ricks (133-4) defends the immaturity of the line, arguing that "it is only because of Keats's ability to retain a sense of the truth accessible to the 'juvenile' and not to the self-conscious adult, that he is able to create the astonishing candour. . . What we really want to do with honey is feel it, and not necessarily in our mouths and throats where it can indeed be perilous in its clinging ('breathless'). . ."

907-8. *Clings . . . haunches:* K. probably chose "sloth" for its slow, heavy, clinging sound, without considering that it might prefer leaves to "haunches."

924. *amber studs:* Allott notes the echo of Marlowe's *The Passionate Shepherd to his Love* 18: "With coral clasps and amber studs. . ."

932. *bedded pebbles:* See II.17n. K. was evidently attracted to the smooth volubility of bilabials, as in "Billiard-Balls."

939. *sweet grief at parting.* Allott cites *Romeo and Juliet* II,ii,184: "parting is such sweet sorrow."

943-4. *the grot / Of Proserpine:* In Spenser (*F. Q.* II,vii,51f.), Proserpine avoids the heat of "Hell" by retreating to her garden located in the Cave of Mammon. Proserpine, the female counterpart to Adonis, prepares us for the Proserpine figures of Bk.II (see II.27-32n.) and for Endymion's descent underground.

944. *Hell, obscure and hot:* The place and its sovereign are here interfused. In relation to the legend of Pluto raping Proserpine (cf. *P. L.* IV,268-72), "obscure and hot" takes on the figurative meaning of sexual passion.

947. *cell of Echo:* Complements the previous vision associated with Narcissus. There is a suggestion in these reflections of eye and ear of the dangerous and self-destructive subjectivity of dream. Cf. "Echoing grottoes" (I.459) and the "elfin grot" of *La Belle Dame.* For K.'s earlier use of the Narcissus and Echo legend, see *I Stood Tip-toe* 163-80.

955. *dyingly:* Connotes for D'Avanzo (162) "the spending of the poet in the difficult act of creating. . ." Also relevant is Knight's (273) remark that K.'s "sensory perception is throughout so acute and thirsting that love becomes almost synonymous with swooning, if not death."

970-1. *where . . . fled?* Cf. Wordsworth's *Intimations Ode* IV: "Whither is fled the visionary gleam? / Where is it now, the glory and the dream."

972-7. Frye[6] (133-4) remarks that "Endymion's resolution though unconvincing appears to involve a sense of guilt, a responsibility not yet assumed which pushes him out into a lower world, resolves him 'for the world's dusky brink.' " Though he vows here to lead a life of contemplation in preparation for Pan's "Elysium," "his real wish and his destiny is to enter it through his love of Diana." Cf. K.'s farewell to the simple "joys" for "the agonies, the strive / Of human hearts" in *Sleep and Poetry* 122-5.

975. De Selincourt cites Milton's *Il Penseroso* 31-2: "Come pensive Nun, devout and pure, / Sober, stedfast, and demure. . ."

977. *dusky:* A word rich in associations. Knight (261) associates it with the underworld of sleep (cf. II.224 and IV.384), and finds it "characteristic of Keats's liking for darkness as a positive luxury." Frye[6] (33) speaks of the word "dark" as thematically important in Romanticism, usually referring "to the seeping of an identity with nature into the hidden and inner parts of the mind." He finds it associated with such Wandering Jew figures as Byron's Cain and Shelley's Alastor. See IV.60n.

988. *sun is setting:* Cf. *Intimations Ode* XI: "The clouds that gather round the setting sun / Do take a sober colouring. . ." Another image of descent, the light of which Endymion will

follow beneath the horizon into the underworld of Bk.II. It may also suggest, since it served as the setting of Endymion's dream-visions, that Endymion is to continue his quest for the realization of his dreams, even as he appears to renounce them.

990-2. The dramatic frame-effect of the closing lines of *Lycidas.*

Notes to Book II

1-43. A prologue in defense of love against history. K. rejects history, as Bloom[3] (389) says, "because it cannot affect poetic consciousness, which depends altogether on love." Frye[6] (37) points out that what K. and the Romantics reject is not so much "history as the social process of which actual history is the record. The rejection of history in this sense is an anti-mimetic tendency, a rejecting of social reality in favor of a social ideal." Frye[6] (142-3) speaks of the two sense of "identity" in K. ("identity-as" and "identity-with") as representing "the two poles of Endymion's cosmos, the worlds of Circe and Phoebe. . ." Circe's domineering, ego-centered world of action and history is precisely the opposite of Phoebe's world of "poets and lovers, who identify themselves with what they make or love." Wasserman (57) emphasizes K.'s sense of historical events imprisoned "in a context of space and time. They belong to mutability and have not been lifted by a giant into an immortality, or pursued with an ardor until they are 'unconfined' by space, time and identity; they are 'real things,' not ethereal things, symbols." Wasserman supports his statement with an important quotation from K.'s essay "On Kean in 'Richard Duke of York,' " where K. speaks of the poetry of Shakespeare's historical plays as

> for the most part ironed and manacled with a chain of facts, and cannot get free; it cannot escape from the prison house of history, nor often move without our being disturbed with the clanking of its fetters. The

> The poetry of Shakespeare is generally free as is the wind—a perfect thing of the elements, winged and sweetly coloured. Poetry must be free! It is of the air, not of the earth; and the higher it soars the nearer it gets to its home. The poetry of "Romeo and Juliet," of "Hamlet," of "Macbeth," is the poetry of Shakespeare's soul—full of love and divine romance. It knows no stop in its delight, but "goeth where it listeth"—remaining, however, in all men's hearts a perpetual and golden dream. The poetry of "Lear," "Othello," "Cymbeline," &c., is the poetry of human passions and affections, made almost ethereal by the power of the poet.

6. *pine:* cause to pine.

11. *some backward corner of the brain:* Cf. *The Tempest* I,ii,50: "In the dark backward and abysm of time." See II.376 for another echo of the line.

12. *amain:* with full force; an Elizabethanism.

13. *close:* embrace. De Selincourt cites *Troilus and Cressida* III,ii,51: "an 'twere dark you'ld close sooner."

14. Cf. the prologue of Bk. III where K. attacks the Circean charm or "gilded masks" of temporal pomp and power.

15. *Swart:* dark, black. Allot cites "Lycidas" 138: "On whose fresh lap the swart Star sparely looks. . ."

17. *pebbled shore of memory:* Cf. Shakespeare's sonnet IX 1-2: "Like as the waves make towards the pebbled shore, / So do our minutes hasten to their end. . ." In K. the shore acts as an echo chamber for the waves of historical deeds, which echo in the memory as "one continuous murmur."

22-3. *owl . . . mast?* The allusion is to Themistocles and the owl.

27-32. *Juliet . . . Hero . . . Imogen . . . Pastorella:* Romance heroines from *Romeo and Juliet, Much Ado About Nothing, Cymbeline,* and *F. Q.* VI,xi respectively. Besides illustrating "love and divine romance," each is what Frye would call a

Proserpine figure. Having suffered a real or ritual death and descent, they comprise an appropriate prologue to Endymion's underworld descent in search of his beloved.

47-51. For D'Avanzo (176) "The regular noise of the axe suggests not only the monotony of the poet's existence in the real world but also the cutting pain of the despondency he feels."

54. *elbow-deep:* Cf. the fertility rite in *Julius Caesar* III,i,107, where the conspirators dip their arms "up to the elbows" in Caesar's blood.

57. *A bud:* The beginning of a chain of metamorphoses involving a rose, a butterfly, and a nymph, and hence for Finney (305) symbolic "of the fleeting beauty of this ever-changing world of matter, which, despite its imperfect and evanescent nature, is the only guide by which man can be led into the region of ideal beauty." See *Sleep and Poetry* 343-5.

60. *pight:* placed, fixed; a common poeticism.

61. *A golden butterfly:* Frye[6] (132-3 & 135-6) finds a curious parallel in the rose-garden scene of Eliot's *Burnt Norton,* "a private and unshared vision, like sentimentalized childhood memories and other nostalgic pastoral themes." For "the butterfly leads Endymion, like Eliot's thrush, to a fountain, where the butterfly, whose name is presumably Psyche, turns into a nymph, and tells him he must descend lower, down through the worlds of earth and water, to accomplish his quest." Frye's naming is felicitous not only because Psyche or the soul was traditionally represented as a butterfly, but also because she was, in Apuleius's story, forced by Venus to descend into the Stygian waters and Proserpine's underworld before she could be reunited with Cupid. It is appropriate that a butterfly leads Endymion out of his chrysallis world of "pent up butterflies" (I.258).

62-3. Endymion is here the watcher watched, as K. distances himself from his character so to experience natural beauty vicariously. See the letter to Fanny Brawne of August 16, 1819: "I am getting a great dislike of the picturesque; and can only relish it over again by seeing you enjoy it" (II,142).

62. *character'd:* inscribed. Cf. *As You Like It* III,ii,6: "O Rosalind! these trees shall be my books / And in their barks my thoughts I'll character. . ." See III.762n. and, for a more obvious use of his source, IV.789-90.

66-7. *Onward . . . on he hies:* Cf. II.352-5 and Satan's ineluctable approach to Eden (*P. L.* IV,131f.).

74. *unseams:* divides.

80-2. *when . . . Delphi.* Like the pilgrims to Delphi, Endymion is headed toward an oracular cave.

91. *mealy gold:* The fine dust on a butterfly's wing. De Selincourt cites *Troilus and Cressida* III,iii,78-9: "Men like butterflies / Show not their mealy wings but to the summer."

98-103. K.'s water nymphs are generally Spenserian in nature (cf. *F. Q.* II,xii,62-8). See II.939n.

102. *anxiously . . . twist:* carelessly . . . twine *D*. K.'s revision appears to reflect a change of intention from Spenserian temptress to sympathetic guide pointing the way. Cf. Sabrina in *Comus* 860-2.

109. *Amphitrite:* A sea goddess who is the wife of Neptune.

124. *scanty bar:* Cf. I.360 and II.185-6.

132. *brooded o'er the water:* Cf. Genesis 1.2 and *P. L.* I,21.

136. *dimpling:* Ripples made by fish as they rise to feed.

138. *burr:* indistinct profusion. Visually, the moon's nebulous nimbus; but see *As You Like It* I,iii,14, where Rosalind's amorous fancies are "burrs" "in my heart!"

159-61. *Where soil . . . strike in:* Endymion is still in the realm of innocence, the Gardens of Adonis or place of seed, where, as Frye[6] (135) says, he "can feel no roots. . . The purpose of his quest is to strike these roots into experience." Since his descent into experience is primarily sexual, the image has phallic associations. Cf. II.904-9.

164-8. *and . . . love:* K. is possibly comparing "the soft shadow of my thrice-seen love" to the shadow of Euridice fading back into Hades. Like Orpheus, Endymion is looking back on his visions, but has yet to descend into the underworld to redeem them. See IV.506-10n.

170-4. Endymion is not aware that his "thrice-seen love" is Cynthia. His ignorance of her identity can be traced in the invocations of II.302-32 and III.142-87, reaching a crisis at IV.92-7.

172-4. Spurgeon (92) cites *A Midsummer Night's Dream* II,i,161-2: "young Cupid's fiery shaft / Quenched in the chaste beams of the watery moon."

177-8. *but . . . shoulders:* The allusion is to Icarus (io-carius, 'dedicated to the Moon-goddess Car'), who wished to escape the labyrinth of earthly existence with tragic consequences. K.'s frequent allusions to Icarus and Phaeton express his sense of the youthful audacity of his poetic enterprise. See IV.441-3n.

197-8. *Deucalion . . . Orion:* Deucalion, the Ovidian Noah, longed for the flood to recede as he waited on the summit of Mt. Parnassus (Ovid, *Met.* I,316-29). Orion longed for the dawn, which was to give him back his sight. De Selincourt cites *The Odyssey* V,121, where Orion marries Aurora and is as a result killed by Diana. De Selincourt also speculates on K. having seen Poussin's "Landscape with Orion," which shows blind Orion facing the dawn with Diana watching from the sky.

199-200. Ende (77-8) views as a foreshadowing of the substitution of voice and hearing for eyes and sight in Bk. IV: "The voice that rises form the cavern to save the natural man is the voice of the other, heard in the calm of thought . . . or in the Keatsean moment of breathless anticipation. It augurs a future that breaks with the past, a moment of origin that is authentically revitalizing. . ."

202-14. Evert (127-8) claims the chief function here is "to guide not so much Endymion as the reader, who sees that the shepherd prince who scorns the earth and yearns for heaven has sought his immortality too precipately. He must learn that it is to be achieved not by direct assault on heaven . . . but by submission and descent. . . If the underworld reveals the barrenness of beauty divorced from common life, the submission to experience it represents spiritual descent."

204. *sparry:* rich in crystalline metals; a common epithet of the time. Its phonetic and alchemical relation to "starry" suggests K.'s identification of the way up with the way down.

205-10. *Oft . . . being:* Refers to Endymion's mountain home.

210-11. *as deep . . . descent!* The way down is the mirror image of the way up.

221-5. Patterson (49) finds the effect reminiscent of the "darkness visible" of Milton's hell.

224-6. Finney (252) notes the influence of Spenser's Cave of Mammon (*F. Q.* II,vii,17)–an influence Ford[3] (41) believes is pictorial rather than allegorical.

230. *vast antre:* De Selincourt cites *Othello* I,iii,140: "of antres vast and deserts idle."

230-1. *the metal woof, / Like Vulcan's rainbow:* Interwoven with colors like a rainbow. Cf. *Lamia* II,237: "Unweave a rainbow. . ."

239-43. *On a ridge . . . surge.* While at the Isle of Wight and under the influence of *King Lear*, K. appears to have associated the sound of the sea with that of a waterfall. See his letter to Reynolds of April 17, 1817: "But the sea, Jack, the sea–the little waterfall–then the white cliff–then St. Catherine's Hill" (I,131). See also his letter to Haydon of May 10, 11, 1817, where K. views himself as hanging like " 'one that gathers Samphire dreadful trade' " as "the Cliff of Poesy Towers above me" (I,141).

240. *vast:* a noun. Cf. *The Tempest* I,ii,327: "at vast of night."

243. *the murmuring surge.* Cf. *King Lear* IV,vi,20-2: "The murmuring surge / That on th'unnumb'red idle pebble chafes, / Cannot be heard so high." See I.120-1n.

245. *orbed diamond:* Frye[6] (138) regards as an image "whose illumination proceeds from a hard center" and thus central to the world of Bk. II, where subject and object are mutually enclosed, the object withdrawing or rolling away from human approach. Cf. Blake's "Crystal Cabinet" where there is a similar withdrawal and where external or material form is considered "translucent all within." Bate (184) interprets the image in the context of poetic influence as "one of the great poets of the past. . ." See III.628n.

245. *fray:* frighten; an archaism common in Spenser.

277-80. Refers to will-o'-the-wisp or *ignis fatuus.* De Selincourt cites *A Midsummer Night's Dream* II,i,39 and *P. L.* IX,634-42, and Spurgeon (13) suggests Ariel. See K.'s letter to Bailey of March 13, 1818: "I am sometimes so very skeptical as to think Poetry itself a mere Jack a lanthern to amuse whoever may choose to be struck with its brilliance" (I,242). Cf. *Ode to a Nightingale* 23-4. See IV.653-6 for Endymion's renunciation of deceiving "fancy."

281. *drowningly:* A coinage perhaps inspired by Shakespeare's profound use of "smilingly" (*King Lear* V,iii,200).

282. *raught:* reached; an archaism common in Spenser.

284-95. Patterson (50) thinks Endymion here "experiences for the first time the anti-daemonic. There surges up in him, now cut off from sensory contact with his usual world, an extraordinary powerful longing to feel sensation, to revel in the normal, pleasing, wholesome ordinary world of natural phenomena."

288. *cloudy rack:* a light cloud or bank of clouds. Cf. *The Tempest* IV,i,155-6: "And, like this insubstantial pageant faded / Leave not a rack behind."

292. *surcharg'd:* weighed down; an Elizabethanism.

294. Evert (125, n.34) notes as the only instance of Endymion "in the act of artistic creation for its own sake."

298. *chief:* upper end, head; an Elizabethanism.

302. *Haunter:* "We are implicitly asked to ponder the relation of haunting to hunting" Ricks (71).

306. *smoothest . . . smoother:* A use of polyptoton for the sake of hyperbole.

308. *disparted:* separated; cf. *F. Q.* V,iii,7.

317-32. K. appears to be imitating the stichomythia in *A Midsummer Night's Dream* I,i,194-201. Thus Endymion is required to speak in two voices: vocative and plaintive. Colvin (211) feels the result happily sacrifices rhetorical effect for a suspended or delayed rime echo.

333-4. *o'erleap / His destiny:* Typically Romantic, suggesting the daemonically driven poet whose desire recognizes no bounds in man or nature. Possibly derived from Satan's unaccommodating manner of jumping over the wall of Paradise: "high overleaped all bound" (*P. L.* IV,181). Cf. *Alastor* 207: "He overleaps the bounds."

339-50. Frye[6] (137) compares this "rhythm of vegetable life reviving from death" with Adonis's revival from winter sleep at II.495f.

341. *sallows:* willows.

345-50. "Slow, even movement joins in the first line with a hint of strangeness in 'enchanted.' In 'heaved' commences a rhythmical rising and falling. The repeated 'o' sounds in 'Old ocean rolls' unite with 'lengthen'd' to heighten the feeling of motion, which becomes a curving dizzying glide. All this prepares for the effect of the wave itself within which there are two places of movement. Within the motion of its green body is contained the steady, 'gradual' bursting of the foam, which takes on a wavering, dancing swirl from 'wayward'. . ." Fogle (165).

345-7. *floral pride . . . footsteps:* Cf. I.789-90.

359-63. An apparent reference to the progress of poesy from east to west (see IV.1-29n.), with the suggestion that the west is now capable of reversing the influence.

360. *Arion's magic:* See III.1002n.

382-3. Fogle (108-9) notes how K. here "synaesthetically endows light with breathing, throbbing sentience. It pulsates in regular bursts, and to this organic pulsation is added the further sensuous attribute of sound. . . The general impression of sunlight resolves itself into living, breathing forms. . ."

387. De Selincourt notes the classical construction as a Miltonic influence. Cf. *Comus* 48: "after the Tuscan mariners transformed."

389-533. *The Garden of Adonis:* Sources include Ovid's *Met.* X, Shakespeare's *Venus and Adonis* and, most significantly, Spenser's *Gardens of Adonis* (*F. Q.* III,vi,29-50). Frye[6] (136) notes that, like Spenser's *Gardens of Adonis,* K.'s is the place of seed "where Adonis sleeps and dreams through the winter and revives to life in summer." It is the driving force behind the "sexual love that makes the cycle of nature go round." Frye thinks it more than coincidence that Endymion arrives at the turn of the seasons when Adonis is reviving. Van Ghent (9) finds condensed here on a "miniature scale the familiar archaic motifs of the underground journey, death and symbolic burial, the foetal sleep-healing, the rebirth, and the mystic marriage, which does not occur once but repetitively and always." Dickstein (102-4) regards it as a summation of all the indolent, sensual bowers of K.'s early poems, and sees a suggestion of the effeminate or infantile, as though it "were a cradle rather than a bed of love" and a bier as well. To support his sense of it anticipating Circe's bower, he cites Frye[6] (139-40): "The love of Venus for Adonis is already much more possessive than the love of Phoebe for Endymion, much more of a Blakean 'female will' who keeps the lover bound to a cycle of possession and loss." For Venus's possessiveness see II.459-60.

392-415. A marvelously delicate passage. Fogle (62) analyzes its "sensuous luxuriance," attained "by suggestions of soft, silky surfaces, of light but sensuous pressures, of tender but tenacious clingings. . . The attitude of Adonis is described in terms which reproduce the actual pressures of his body." Van Ghent (11) emphasizes the sculptural effect, noting that Venus transforms Adonis into a statue, as "the embalmed dead are statues of themselves and live the affective death-life meant by Keats's 'identity.' " Van Ghent sees Adonis as the "Apollonian" ideal that the Dionysian Endymion is striving after.

397. Perkins (201) sees here an instance of K.'s "mature" style, where "faded" is part of a process which also permits October to become "ripe." The "marigold" was perhaps chosen because of its Apollonian golden bloom and because it "goes to bed wi' th' sun" (*The Winter's Tale* IV,iv,105).

399-401. *Apollonian . . . knee:* Possibly influenced by the Belvedere Apollo, which K. greatly admired. K. alters the image in *The Eve of St. Agnes* XXXIII: "Upon his knees he sank, pale as smooth-sculptured stone."

400. *tenting:* like the top of a tent. Cf. *Hero and Leander* II,263-4: "And as her silver body downward went, / With both her hands she made the bed a tent."

403-7. *Sideway . . . rose.* See Ricks (12-4) for a subtle analysis of the "intimations of embarrassment" here. Knight (222) compares Shelley's "Spirit of the Earth" (*Prometheus Unbound* IV,261-8), which is represented as a sleeping child "Pillow'd upon its alabaster arms" with his lips moving "like one who talks of what he loves in dream."

412-5. Knight (265) cites as an example of K.'s "heavy rounded perception."

430. *embarrassment:* Surprisingly K.'s only use of the word. Ricks (13) feels this is something which the reader has to share with Endymion as the effect of having watched Adonis's

"slumbery pout" (406): "What is embarrassing about watching somebody asleep is their no longer having command of their features; we feel an unfair advantage in seeing them so."

436-9. "The 'ethereal donor' is an immortal (Cynthia or Venus?) and has signalized the human shepherd's fidelity in love by permitting him a glimpse of heaven. Manifestly this honor is not an end in itself: it promises ultimate happiness to the wanderer and is then a kind of equivalent in direct experience of a prefigurative vision. It serves the same function, on a smaller scale, as the Glaucus-Scylla episode in Book III, where the legions of dead lovers are resurrected" Ford[3] (53). Wasserman (70) regards as the top rung of a ladder of intensities that Endymion ascends through his appreciation of nature's beauty (345-7), of music (357-8), and now of "the love-visitation of Venus and Adonis." This final intensity enables him to be released from "the prison house of his mortal self."

441-55. The wine, fruit, and cream is each associated with a well-known love story and with a figure, like Adonis, from the seasonal and dying god mythology. Evert (129) calls these refreshments "not essences but substances, rare enough, as their description attests, for the delectation of gods, but the produce of that very nature which Endymion had come mistakenly to despise."

443. *Ariadne:* Consoled by Bacchus after being abandoned by Theseus (see III.755-6n.), a fate similar to that of the Indian Maid. See *Sleep and Poetry* 335-6.

444. *So cool a purple:* Fogle (111) feels that "pleasure in its chill is synaesthetically allied to delight in its rich coloring."

445-6. *Vertumnus . . . Pomona:* Vertumnus, a deity of spring and orchard, courted Pomona, an elusive wood-nymph of gardens and fruit trees. Cf. Ovid, *Met.* XIV,623-771 and *P. L.* V,378; IX,393-5.

448. *Amalthea:* A Cretan princess who brought up the infant Jove on goat's milk, and was rewarded with one of the horns of the goat, known as the horn of plenty. De Selincourt notes that the allusion to Amalthea's horn in *Paradise Regained* II,256

is followed significantly, as here, by a reference to the Hesperides.

450-1. *a bunch . . . gums:* Another instance of K.'s love of bilabials. The lines have been frequently scorned as infantile; but Ricks (101-3), while recognizing the mixed feelings evoked by the "pink wet physicality" and "toothlessness" of "gums," presents a subtle defense: "What makes Keats's lines something more than a relapse into the infantile or babyish is their combining the full feeling of undifferentiated sensation (for the baby, everything concentering in the mouth) with the adept little differentiations that make 'blooming' a complicated part of the whole."

450. *blooming plums:* K. playfully revises the "blooming gold" (*Comus* 393) of Milton's Hesperidean apples. Contrast *Venus and Adonis* 547-8, where Adonis protests he is too green for Venus to pluck: "the mellow plum doth fall; the green sticks fast / Or being early plucked is sour to taste." Cf. II.908-9.

452. *manna:* K. sometimes associates with "dew" (cf. "manna-dew" at I.766), and hence with that which falls gratuitously from heaven, like the grace of poetic inspiration. Here, however, it refers to the apples of the Hesperides.

459-60. *how . . . self:* For Venus's possessiveness see *Venus and Adonis* 539-813, and *F. Q.* III,vi,46: "But she her selfe, when ever that she will / Possesseth him, and of his sweetness takes her fill."

460. *all in all:* Although Biblical (cf. 1Cor.15-28 and *P. L.* III,341), it refers here to a pagan fertility marriage. In earthly paradise literature Venus often takes on some of God's duties.

461. *fond elf: fond:* foolish: *elf:* a word K. associates with Spenser's knights and Shakespeare's fairies. For an elaborate discussion see D'Avanzo (74-80).

466. *love, lovelorn:* Allott cites *Venus and Adonis* 328: "love-sick love."

468-70. Evokes the deeply passionate nature and almost animal physicality of Shakespeare's Venus.

468. *diverse passion:* Allott cites *Venus and Adonis* 967-8: "Variable passions throng her constant woe, / As striving who should best become her grief. . ."

470. *nostrils:* Ricks (110) compares its "disturbing and magnetic physicality" with Chapman's use in *The Odyssey* much admired by K. (cf. Clarke 130): "all with froth / His cheeks and nostrils flowing." Cf. also *Venus and Adonis* 273-4.

474. *When the boar tusk'd him.* See I.174n. and *Venus and Adonis* 1111-6, where the sexual overtones of Adonis's death suggest a maiden's loss of virginity.

475-6. De Selincourt compares *Il Penseroso* 107: "Drew iron tears down Pluto's cheek. . ." K. is implicitly comparing the "plainings" of Venus for Adonis with those of Orpheus for Euridice.

477-86. Ford[3] (54) believes the passage functions "to renew Endymion's faith in the veracity of his dream."

483-4. Possibly a conflation of the creation of Adam with that of Eve. Cf. *P. L.* VIII,254-5: "Soft on the flowery herb I found me laid, / In balmy sweat." and *P. L.* VIII,467-8: "wide was the wound, / But suddenly with flesh filled up and healed." The second quote prefigures Christ's "passionate" intervention on behalf of Adam, the Christian analogue to Venus's intervention for Adonis.

483. *balming power:* Van Ghent (10) remarks on the "obsessive usage in which much of the death-sleep-healing-rebirth configuration is secreted." See II.392-415n.

484. Van Ghent (8) refers to the medicining of Endymion and Adonis as "sleep-healing," a formula of archaic ritual which is part of an initiation into immortality. Endymion's is postponed until the "Cave of Quietude" (see IV.548n.). She feels Endymion must "learn to sleep permanently, like Adonis, in order to achieve the permanent love-union which is the affective aspect of his immortality." She neglects to explain, however,

the meaning of Adonis's awakening.

500-6. *Then . . . begin!* Brisman[2] (67) notes "the natural continuity of iambic pace" (Adonis is "attuned to the season") in contrast to the opening lines of *Lycidas,* which accelerate beyond iambic pace, expressing a tension between poetic inspiration and nature.

530-1. *Who . . . minutes?* Brisman[2] (68-9) sees as an instance of the poet's embarrassment in confronting "poetic origins" or "sexual begettings." He compares *P. L.* VII,250-1: "For Man to tell how human life began / Is hard: for who himself beginning knew?" noting that while Adam looks back to his creation, K. glances at Adonis's re-creation becoming sexual recreation.

532-3. *The unchariest muse . . . coy excuse.* Cf. *Hamlet* I,iii, 36-7. "The chariest maid is prodigal enough / If she unmask her beauty to the moon." and *Lycidas* 18: "Hence with denial vain and coy excuse. . ." Ricks (61) refers to both in commenting on the good-humored tension "between the words of Milton's 'Lycidas' and Keats's right to rule them with the word 'unchariest.' "

537. *quell:* the power or means to destroy; here referring to Cupid's bow and arrow.

548-79. See III.903-21 where Venus again encourages Endymion.

563. *full fringed lids:* See I.394n.

573-8. As in Homer, Virgil, and Dante, the reward of descent is the oracular knowledge of the future.

579-81. *Upflew . . . uprose . . . upwent:* The upward thrust of eros, as in the awakening of newborn life in the spring. Cf. the creation of vegetable life in *P. L.* VII,320-6.

593-626. "You can see how, without any rigid oppositions at all, the close mesh of impressions present (i) nature, (ii) the architectural and geometric or circular, (iii) the specifically ritualistic and religious; the last being the fusing medium of the other two" Knight (270).

612-26. Knight (270-1) notes how "liquidity forms into solids of human artistry from line to line" ("lattices," etc.) "then becomes heavier—'wrought oaken beams' . . . ending with the religious suggestion of 'cathedral.' "

639-48. "It is to be noted that this image is a picture in a frame, appearing momentarily in the open space between two rocky arches" Fogle (166). On the magic casement effect in K. see Hartman[2] (129-30).

640. *mother Cybele!* The Magna Mater, mother of the gods and of all things, and hence the ultimate vision, as Blackstone (143) says, of the chthonic world, "the supreme dispenser of mysteries." She represents the nadir of Endymion's descent, and because she is the ultimate mystery, he catches only a glimpse of her. Van Ghent (10) compares Moneta of *The Fall of Hyperion* ("pictorially a duplicate"), Ops of *Hyperion*, and "veil'd Melancholy" of the ode, and notes that K.'s poetry intensifies whenever the earth-mother appears. Possible sources include *The Aeneid* III,111-14, Lempriere, and especially Ovid, *Met.* X, 697-706 (Sandys 191), the influence of which is discussed in detail by de Selincourt.

643-6. *Four maned lions . . . drowsily:* Cf. K.'s definition of poesy as "might half slumbering on its own right arm" (*Sleep and Poetry* 237).

661-9. Possibly influenced by *P. L.* I,740-6. Evert (130) interprets as Endymion no longer opposing his will to his experience but submitting to circumstance, and thereby carried down to a paradise of natural beauty.

662. Spurgeon (58-9) cites *The Tempest* III,iii,101 and V,i,54.

668. *airs:* Cf. Milton's pun in *P. L.* IV,264-6: "airs, vernal airs, / Breathing the smell of field and grove, attune / The trembling leaves." K.'s use contributes a strong sense of the tactual.

674. *Hesperean:* westward; from Hesperus, the evening star. Bush[4], however, interprets as Hesperidean, referring to the garden of Hesperides. The usual spelling ("Hesperian") is the 1848 variant, considered corrupt by Garrod and Stillinger.

In K.'s only other use of the word (*To Haydon* 13), it seems to refer to the Hesperidean apples, which reflect (Hesperus's?) starlight.

687-94. Although ignorant of Cynthia's identity, Endymion has intimations of her influence on the various realms (or elements) of nature.

688. An allusion to the Horae, or seasons, who open the gates of heaven at the first sign of morning. See IV.421-5n.

689-90. *starry seven, / Old Atlas' children?* The Pleiades, daughters of Atlas by Pleione.

693. *scions:* branches, twigs; an archaism.

707-873. Endymion's apparently sexual encounter with Cynthia. Finney (296) calls it a "nympholeptic dream," "a crude imitation of that in *Alastor,*" objecting, as have other critics, to the vulgarity of K.'s Cockney diction. Thorpe (58), conceding its sentimentality, feels it is "a necessary step to a higher plane," a "communion with, a complete penetration into, the spirit of the sensuous." Evert (131), more openly disagreeing with Finney, claims that K., like Milton's Raphael, is "lik'ning spiritual to corporal forms," and thus Cynthia here is "the ideal 'essence' with which the receptive soul wishes to be in fellowship." Frye[6] (137) speaks of the scene as Endymion's "initiation into the world of Eros," "both a fall (loss of innocence) and an advance to a greater maturity." Since Cynthia is here incarnate, Frye identifies her as the Indian Maid.

724. *scroll:* K.'s poetic version of the Book of Life, containing the names of the immortal poets living in Apollo's "western" Elysium. Cf. III.747.

729. K.'s sense of belatedness.

738. Prefigures Alpheus and Arethusa (II.912f).

739-45. Ford[3] (56) compares the "Bright Star" sonnet, where the breast of the beloved becomes a luxurious pillow for the male head and where the lover attempts to "prolong the ecstasy of physical love through all eternity." For Wasserman (114-5) the scene is more than an extended luxury, it is the "mystic oxymoron" of the "chief intensity," immortal vision made palpable through an intensity of passion. He implicitly compares Endymion, in his passionate awakening of Cynthia to physical reality, with Porphyro, who, by means of the sensuous and imaginative entrances into "essence" (rich foods and music respectively), attempts to awaken Madeline "to physical reality so that she is not longer . . . locked in the self-sufficiency of her vision, no longer the unknown but . . . a 'known Unknown' . . . an ideal now accessible to Porphyro so that he may melt into her vision."

741-4. *Be ever . . . for ever? ever . . . for ever . . . for ever:* Cf. *Ode on a Grecian Urn* 22-7.

742. *Pillow my chin:* Milton coins the verb in a Keatsian line, in which the sun "Pillows his chin upon an orient wave" (*Nativity Ode* 231). Cf. III.234-5.

756-70. Fogle (63-4) interprets as K. attempting, through the use of tactual imagery and heavy consonantal sounds, "the impossible task of transferring sensations as it were bodily into literature, of expressing sexual ecstasy directly in words."

757. *completion:* Suggests "complexion." Cf. I.260.

758. *Those lips, O slippery blisses:* A much quoted touchstone for the vulgarity of K.'s immature diction. Ricks (104), however, bravely defends it, interpreting the scorn of the critics as "the recourse of embarrassment and of a timorous imagination finding itself ardently, even improperly moved. . ." He thinks "the effortlessness, naturalness, and yet surprize with which 'lips' slips into 'slippery' is a bliss to experience." Its effect is a "morally apt and percipient one: of demanding that we recognize salivation" and admit being disconcerted by it.

758-9. *twinkling eyes . . . milky sovereignties:* Liquidities (the eyes "twinkle" with moisture) that serve as a context for "slippery" (see Ricks 105). As "twinkling" stars and the Milky Way (or the milky moon on which the western sun pillows his head), they suggest the descent of Cynthia's transcendent "starry sphere" into a human and sensuous realm.

761-824. Cynthia's longest speech, in which she reveals her passion to be that of the all-too-human Venus, and her chastity, traditionally her essence, merely a social form.

774-815. Patterson (53) notes that Cynthia "voices the same consuming passion for Endymion that Venus had voiced for Adonis."

793. *vailed:* lowered.

804-8. Ford[3] (57) compares Juliet's (cf. II.28-9) sense of the supreme experience of a woman as "the transition from the state of maidenhood to that of passionate love."

808. According to Ford[3] (39), this is the ideal Endymion seeks.

823-4. *is grief . . . deeps of pleasure:* Anticipates a central motif of the Indian Maid in Bk. IV, as well as *Ode on Melancholy.*

827-53. *Ye who . . . gusty deep.* A beautiful account of the natural origin of myth, the translation of natural sound into human song. Despite the Spenserian magic, the conception was probably influenced by *The Excursion* IV,347-87.

829-35. Knight (266) acutely notes that "poetry, sleep, and dream, and a certain human, if sleepy, consciousness in nature are all intertwined."

840-1. *those ears . . . glowing hot.* Allott suggests they are glowing with passion and thus sensitively attuned to the poet's song. She compares "Lycidas" 77: "Phoebus replied and touched my trembling ears. . ."

856. *paining:* Suggests "plaining."

868-9. *Oh . . . pleasure's nipple:* Knight (260) claims there is nothing decadent in Keats's sensuous imagery: here it "suggests a typical blend of intoxication with health-giving nourishment." Ricks (105-6) elaborates on Knight, viewing the image as an accurate representation of a baby's sensations and (drawing on on Freud) a felicitious metaphor for adult love.

875. *Alecto:* The serpent-haired daughter of Nox, and considered to be the most terrible of the furies. Cf. II *Henry IV* V,v,37: "fell Alecto's snake."

875-7. *ravishments . . . eclipsing eyes:* Hermes lulled to sleep with his music the hundred-eyed monster Argus. Cf. *P. L.* XI,129-33 and K.'s sonnet "As Hermes once."

885-96. *In this . . . clans:* Wigod (785) cites as an instance of "personal allegory" as K. is here recalling his decision to make poetry his life's work.

904-9. Perhaps suggested by *F. Q.* III,vi,35, where the forms or essences of the Gardens of Adonis are spoken of in the language of Ovid's "uncouth formes" spawned on the fertile bank of the Nile (cf. *Met.* I,423-8). Bloom (390) sees here Endymion's sexual adventure with Cynthia having "transvalued his vision of essences." Frye[6] (137-8) comments that Endymion's "initiation into the world of Eros" "gives him the roots in experience he lacked before. . ." See Intro.

907. *fertilize:* See III.747f. where Endymion uses a scroll as fertilizer to resurrect dead lovers, and I.296-8 for Pan as a fertilizing "leaven."

908. *golden fruit:* Possibly one of the golden apples of the Hesperides.

912. *Dark as the parentage of chaos.* Allott compares *P. L.* II,969-70: "Spirits of this nethermost Abyss, / Chaos and ancient Night. . ."

912-1009. *Alpheus and Arethusa:* In the Ovidian legend, the amorous river-god Alpheus pursued Arethusa, a nymph attending Diana, under the sea to Sicily, where she sprang up as a fountain and eventually mingled with his waters. See Ovid, *Met.* V,572-641 and "Lycidas" 85 & 132. Most of the critical commentary has been oriented toward the growth of human sympathy in Endymion (see de Selincourt XI and Finney 309-10). But Evert (133-6), while conceding the humanitarian element, believes the immediate function of the episode is rather "the illustrating of an aesthetic truth." Under "the influence of his fellowship with the highest essence [his recent union with Cynthia], Endymion is entering sympathetically into fellowship with a lower one, terrestrial rather than celestial nature, and is interpreting the natural sound [of the streams of water] in the light of his own governing preoccupation. The result is . . . the creation, from natural sound, of a humanly articulated poetic myth." Frye[6] (137) differs from Evert in viewing the scene as an analogue to Endymion's sexual experience with the terrestrial Cynthia (essentially the Indian Maid) rather than a descent from his union with the "highest essence" or celestial Cynthia (see II.707-873n.). Frye seems to imply that the structure of the Alpheus-Arethusa myth, involving a metamorphosis of descent and subsequent fulfillment and watery resurrection, outlines Endymion's "initiation into the world of Eros," which "is both a fall (loss of innocence) and an advance to a greater maturity. Arethusa is a nymph of Diana, who on this level is the elusive virgin huntress, occasionally glimpsed but never possessed, and Arethusa's complaints tell us how sexual union brings about a desire for a still more complete union which it cannot satisfy, hence it is as much a frustration and an upsetting of balance as it is a satisfaction. And yet the reality of the experience as an incarnation of love is unanswerable: Endymion's possession of the Indian maid is for him . . . a new life. . ." Dickstein (68-9) develops Frye's notion of the scene as a description of Endymion's sexual awakening and fall from innocence. For Dickstein "Arethusa's consciousness of desire is . . . the beginning of self-consciousness." He goes on to draw a personal analogy in K.'s own sexual awakening, which K. refers to in the Preface of the poem as "a space of life between, in which the soul is in a ferment. . ." Bloom[3] (390) notes that Diana here, as the elusive huntress of the Actaeon myth, brings on a watery metamorphosis of Alpheus and Arethusa. This arouses an instinctive sympathy in Endymion for the lovers and he plunges into the underwater world of Bk. III in pursuit of them. Since Diana is also, as Bloom goes on to say, the goddess of Endymion's pilgrimage, he prays to her for the fulfillment of Alpheus and Arethusa locked in their watery prisons. Presumably, she enables Endymion to resurrect the drowned lovers of Bk. III, but then resurrection from the sea, as "Lycidas" shows, is inherent in the myth of Alpheus and Arethusa.

937-8. *Great Dian . . . prayer?* Diana answered Arethusa's prayer for protection by transforming her into a river.

939. *dainty:* delicately or enticingly beautiful; Spenserian. Cf. *F. Q.* II,xii,63, where the word is used to describe the sexual parts of Spenser's teasing water nymphs: "ne cared to hyde, / Their dainty parts from vew of any, which they eyde." See III.408, where K. uses the word to describe another water nymph (Scylla).

945. *rillets:* rivulets; an Elizabethanism.

961. *Oread-Queen!* Diana. See I.671n.

963-74. *Alas . . . Avaunt!* Patterson (55-6) sees Arethusa "in precisely the same situation as Endymion himself–torn between the daemonic lure of the river god and the quiet appeal of the satisfaction of her ordinary life before she knew any other . . . here is expressed for the first time the idea that daemonic ecstasy may not be worth its price."

984-5. *Dian's self . . . very pangs.* Possibly a certain ironic humor in the understatement.

994. *Saturn in his exile:* Saturn's banishment by the usurping Jupiter marked the end of the Golden Age. Some say his place of exile was one of the western "islands"; others, the "pleasant darkness" of the underground Elysian fields or the less pleasant Tartarus. De Selincourt cites the opening of *Hyperion.*

996-7. *mealy sweets . . . honied wings:* See II.91n.

999. *incense-pillow'd:* Fogle (113) finds that the synaesthesia "gives body, weight, and softness to an olfactory image. . ."

1018. *a whelming sound:* The sound of the "giant sea above his head." Cf. *Lycidas* 157-8: "Where thou perhaps under the whelming tide / Visit'st the bottom of the monstrous world."

1019. *cooler light:* Fogle (114) suggests "the feel of the water on his body and . . . the sun's rays . . . filtered through the sea above him." But the obvious reference is to Diana's cooler moon-light, which governs the tides and which Endymion is following under the sea.

1023. Gittings (146) claims the line "has the sudden sharp isolated echo of the great single lines with which Dante finishes each canto" and "does for Endymion what the last line of *Inferno,* Canto 26, in Cary's version, did for Ulysses, 'And over us the booming billow clos'd.' "

Notes to Book III

1-21. K.'s attack on the reactionary regimes of the day. Evert (140) regards "the distinctive characteristic here as the inward-turning of self-love. Those whose high positions lay upon the obligation of service to their fellow men too often gratify their own desires through exploitation of their fellows." As Bloom[3] (388) remarks, K. here is invoking the regality of the four elements while denouncing all political regalities. Later in the book Circe's self-absorbed tyranny is renounced in favor of Neptune's regality of the sea.

7-8. *Fire-branded foxes . . . ripe-eared hopes.* Refers to one of Samson's practical jokes (see *Judges* 15.4-5). But in the present context of tyranny destroying "ripe-eared hopes," K. may have had in mind *King Lear* V,iii,22-3: "He that parts us shall bring a brand from heaven / And fire us hence like foxes."

10. *delight:* clothed; an archaism.

20-1. The Chaldean storm-god Rammon was worshipped as a god of oracles.

23-39. Wasserman (50) interprets in the context of the silent "Grecian Urn" as "forces outside the range of mutability which are nevertheless perceptible in the texture of sensory things. These powers do not obtrude their meaning upon us," but communicate silently. "When through the ecstatic and visionary loss of his self one can mount the ladder of 'ethereal things' and thereby participate in these silent sessions, his every sense is filled 'with spiritual sweets to plentitude. . .' "

25-8. Wasserman (55) notes that like the progression in *Ode on a Grecian Urn,* "These 'ethereal things' which lead to the abysm-birth of elements—the mystery—are obviously also a pleasure thermometer of real things and semireal things and no things transfigured by the intensity with which they are experienced . . . they are unconfined, abstracted from time by the ardor of pursuit."

31. *bourne:* domain; an incorrect usage according to the *OED.* But the correct meaning, "boundary" (see I.295n.) is implied, since air forms a boundary between water and fire.

38. *Ceres:* The mother of Proserpine and fertility goddess of ripening corn. Cf. *The Tempest* IV,i,60f.

40-1. *And . . . Creation:* Cf. Ovid's account of the Creation in *Met.* I,7-21.

42-4. See I.608-10n.

43. *gentlier:* A coinage.

54. *a holier din:* de Selincourt believes the elevation of the commonplace word here is influenced by the "fervent din" of Wordsworth's *White Doe of Rhylstone.* For the commonplace usage see "city's din" (I.40).

56-69. See Eliade (180) on the multiple influences of the moon: "The rhythms of the moon weave together harmonies, symmetries, analogies, and participations which make up an endless 'fabric,' a 'net' of invisible threads which 'binds' together at once mankind, rain, vegetation, fertility, health, animals, death, regeneration, after-life, and more."

56-7. *Thou . . . life:* Knight (258-9) speaks here of "the mysterious levelling alteration irrespective of objects that moonlight performs; its strange ability to create a sacred and romantic glamour, rendering the inanimate mysteriously significant and vital; the use of 'kissing' to saturate the statement with specifically romantic and erotic feeling; personification in 'lip'; and concrete, sculptural weight in 'silver.' " Knight (266) likens K.'s poetry to the moon, for it "passes across the world of nature or sleep, miraculously 'kissing dead things to life.' " The lines perhaps also suggest that Cynthia is instrumental in Endymion's resurrection of the drowned lovers. See *Romeo and Juliet* V,i,6-9, for the resurrectional power of a kiss.

69. *monstrous:* inhabited by monsters. Cf. *Lycidas* 157-8, quoted in II.1018n. The monsters can be friendly, however, as in III.350.

70-1. De Selincourt argues that "his" refers to "Ocean" rather than to "Tellus," the feminine Earth. Ocean's forehead "bows" under the "cumbrous load" of the incoming tide, and Tellus feels its weight. *spooming:* foaming; the first use of the word with this meaning, developed by association with "spume."

75-6. *Thy cheek . . . is pale.* See I.191n.

78. *Vesper's eye:* Vesper, or Venus as the evening star, heralds the rising moon (Cynthia). Her eye, in the traditional courtly love conceit, radiates a light of "amorous influence" (85).

80. Cf. *P. L.* I,84-5: "If thou beest he; but O how fallen! how changed / From him, who in the happy realms of light. . ." which K. uses again in *The Eve of St. Agnes* 311: "How changed thou art! How pallid, chill, and drear. . ."

97-9. *Leander . . . Orpheus . . . Pluto:* Each was plucked out of his element by the power of love. Leander braved the sea for Hero; Orpheus descended into the underworld for Euridice; and Pluto ascended into the upper air for Proserpine. The three have an obvious structural significance in the poem.

99. *thin:* Cf. "too thin breathing" (IV.650).

100. *winged chieftain:* Cupid.

106-7. *a warm / Of his heart's blood.* Cf. K.'s letter to Reynolds of Sept. 22, 1818: "This morning Poetry has conquered. . . There is a warmth about my heart like a load of Immortality" (I,370).

113. *peering:* peeping or (just) appearing. Cf. *The Nativity Ode* 139-40: "And hell itself will pass away, / And leave her mansions to the peering day."

123-36. *Old . . . monster.* What might be called the sea-salvage topos, here representing the historical memory. Cf. II.16. Colvin (239) compares Clarence's dream of drowning in *Richard III* I,iv,24-8, to which Bush[3] (103) adds *The Aeneid* VII,183f.

129. *mouldering scrolls:* Cf. III.747f.

130. *those souls:* the Titans?

133. *ancient Nox:* See II.912n.

134. *behemoth . . . leviathan:* Biblical monsters of tyranny and chaos. Cf. *Job* 40.15 and *P. L.* VII,412 & 471.

142-87. Endymion's apostrophe to the moon. Besides the general Wordsworthian influence, Colvin (216) cites Drayton's *Endimion and Phoebe* 569-78, and de Selincourt compares Coleridge's "Nightingale" 98-105, where he describes the effect of the moon on his child. Bush[4], however, believes that K.'s "ardent conception, which embraces nature, art, friendship, heroic action, and sensuous pleasure, is his own." Cf. I.1-35 and 777f.

145. *Hand in hand:* Cf. *P. L.* IV,689-90: "Thus talking, hand in hand alone they passed / On to their blissful bower."

157. *mesh:* entwine.

158. *spright:* A close relative of Shakespeare's Puck and Ariel. It suggests for D'Avanzo (74-5) not only "spirit," but also "vital essence," "elf," "fairy," "goblin," "the mind," and "mental faculties," all of which apply to the imagination. It is that which "would achieve supreme poetic happiness in 'fellow-

ship with essence.' "

163-73. *Thou wast . . . immortality.* An effective use of zeugma and anaphora for dramatic condensation. Evert (171) regards it as "an abbreviated anthology of Keatsian symbols, at the same time that it crisply recapitulates the process of natural inspiration leading to imaginative ideality, which was expressed in so much of the previous poetry and which furnished the conceptual basis of *Endymion.*"

175-84. Another dramatic instance of Endymion's ignorance of Cynthia's identity, as he fails to identify her with his first love, the moon. See II.170-4n.

179. *under-passion:* The subliminal source of all his feelings. Cf. "under-darkness" at I.702.

192. *An old man:* Glaucus bears some resemblance to Wordsworth's solitary leech-gatherer, who is likened to a "sea-beast." Frye[6] (139-40) sees analogies in "the bound Prometheus," "Eliot's aged fisher king," and "Blake's Albion sleeping on the Couch of Death in Atlantic under the sea." Glaucus anticipates the fallen Saturn of *Hyperion,* whose fall marks the end of the Golden Age of his Identity: "I have left / My strong identity, my real self" (I,114).

196-203. *winding-sheet . . . woof:* Cf. Gray's *The Bard* 49-52: "Weave the warp, and weave the woof, / The winding sheet of Edward's race. / Give ample room, and verge enough / The characters of hell to trace."

197-212. Colvin (170) believes the cinematographic quality of Glaucus's robe was inspired by Phoebe's cloak in Drayton's *The Man in the Moone* 145-220.

202. *Quicksand and whirlpool:* Cf. the marine world surrounding Spenser's Bower of Bliss (*F. Q.* II,xii,18).

204. *That skims, or dives, or sleeps:* The polysyndeton may have been suggested by Satan's precarious journey through Chaos in *P. L.* II,949-50: ". . . pursues his way / And swims, or sinks, or wades, or creeps, or flies." Satan is a "shape-

shifter" in the radically metamorphic environment of Chaos; hence the experiment in shifting perspectives (205f.) may also owe something to him.

230. *stole:* a long robe.

234. *Thou art the man:* Allott compares 2 *Samuel* 12.7: "And Nathan said to David, Thou art the man."

238-50. Bears a remarkable similarity in tone and imagery to Blake's *America* 2.7-17, where Orc has newly cast off his "serpent-skin of woe." Glaucus has been, like a bound Orc or Prometheus, imprisoned in a water world of subjectivity, but is here liberated by the symbolic hope (represented by Endymion) that activates his sympathy for others. In Freudian terms, Orc and Glaucus (or Glaucus-Endymion) represent the libido newly risen or liberated from the chaotic id.

243. *that giant:* Typhon or Enceladus chained under Mt. Etna; a bound Prometheus figure.

251. *Sisters three:* The Fates; cf. the Hecate sisters in *Macbeth.*

254. Bush[4] compares the first witch in *Macbeth* I,iii,22-3: "Weary sev'nights nine times nine / Shall he dwindle, peak, and pine." Glaucus is under the spell of the witch Circe.

265. *magian:* magical.

271. Bush[4] compares *Cymbeline* V,v,263-4, where Posthumus says to Imogen: "Hang there like fruit, my soul, / Till the tree die."

272-3. *Her lips . . . Of happiness!* Cf. *King Lear* IV,iii,19-22: "those happy smilets / That played on her ripe lip seemed not to know / What guests were in her eyes, which parted thence / As pearls from diamonds dropped." The lines are echoed again in IV.717-8.

272-4. *ripe sheaves . . . garnered:* Anticipates "When I have fears" 3-4.

282. *Look'd high defiance:* De Selincourt compares *P. L.* IV,873: "Stand firm, for in his look defiance lours."

299. *weep no more:* Cf. *Lycidas* 165: "Weep no more, woeful shepherd, weep no more. . ." which K. may have taken as a consoling echo of Lear's "I will weep no more" (III,iv,17).

314f. *Glaucus and Scylla:* K.'s free adaptation of Ovid's version of the myth in *Met.* XIII,898-968; XIV,1-74. Several critics have noted the parallel between Glaucus's story and Endymion's. Bloom[3] (391) points up the similarities with a succinct paraphrase: "Glaucus is a kind of shepherd of the ocean, a follower of Neptune as Endymion was of Pan. But he is not contented, and feels 'distemper'd longings.' He plunges into the sea, 'for life or death,' and learns to live beneath the waves, where he falls in love with a timid sea nymph, Scylla, who flees from him. After he vows to seek help from Circe, he is seduced in a deceptive bower by an 'arbitrary queen of sense.' One day he discovers his seductress presiding over a witch's sabbath and calls on Circe to break his bondage, but Circe is revealed to be his mistress, and he is cursed by her to a watery death-in-life."

314-5. *My soul . . . mortality:* Chatterjee (23) compares the first line of Cary's Dante: "In the midway of this our mortal life."

318. Cf. Wordsworth's *Resolution and Independence* 15: "I was a Traveller then upon the moor." Wordsworth's poem also tells of a fall from innocence.

322. An obvious allusion to Lear.

326. *one thousand years:* Although a typical Spenserian hyperbole, it could be regarded as a pagan millenium, the length of time seeds are preserved in the Garden of Adonis before they "are clad with other hew, / Or sent into the chaungefull world againe" (*F. Q.* III,vi,33).

329. *with backward glance sublime:* See II.11n.

330. Cf. I.820.

341. *sea-mew's plaintive cry:* Cf. *P. L.* XI,835: "The haunt of seals, and orcs, and sea-mews' clang." Milton's fallen Eden referred to here is located, like Spenser's Bower of Bliss, in a marine world of "yelling Meawes" (*F. Q.* II,xii,8).

364. *Aethon:* One of Apollo's horses.

370. *bounty:* Glaucus, like Endymion, acts as a fertility god, bestowing nature's bounty on the community. Cf. I.219.

380-91. *To interknit . . . 'Twas freedom.* Frye[6] (140) comments: "Like Milton's Satan after he separates himself from the community of God, Glaucus finds the new feeling of individuality exhilarating at first. . . But of course it quickly becomes, as with Satan, an imprisonment which reduces him to the narrowest of all prisons, the one he carries around with him as his own subjectivity." See I.812, where the soul is said to "interknit" completely only with the "light" of love.

406. Hercules's "last labour" took place at Taenarum (see III.1001n.). Here he descended into the underworld, freeing Theseus from the Chain of Forgetfulness, as Endymion frees Glaucus from his "trance." *wound up:* Suggests Theseus's own device for escaping from an underground labyrinth (see III.755-6n.). The story of Theseus and the Circean Medea (*Met.* VII,405f.) may have linked Theseus and Glaucus in K.'s mind.

407. *Egyptian Nile:* The serpentine home of another enchantress, Cleopatra.

412-76. *Glaucus's thralldom to Circe:* Evert (143-4) notes the rich use here of the central image-complex (Cynthia-Apollo-evening-west-gold-lyre-nightingale) of the poem; K. even goes out of his way to mention that Circe is "Phoebus's daughter." Evert then offers two possible interpretations: 1) K. "draws upon his most potent images in his arsenal in order to represent the enormous power of a temptation sufficient to make Glaucus forget his passion for Scylla": or 2) he is "counterpointing the elevated implications of his imagery to the debased and selfish response of Glaucus, in order to imply a comparison between right and wrong responses to sensations. . ." i.e.

sensations must be used as a means toward attaining a "fellowship with essence" rather than as an end in themselves.

412. *Circe:* Glaucus's "Belle Dame"; the false muse or enchantress who, like Spenser's Acrasia, is an "arbitrary queen of sense" (459). She functions here as the Hecate of the *diva triformis.*

414. *Phoebus' daughter:* Circe is the daughter of Helios and Perses (Sandys 475). Cf. *Comus* 50-1: "who knows not Circe / The daughter of the Sun. . ." D'Avanzo (49) considers Circe the perverse use of the divine power of poetry and hence "Apollo's bad seed."

415. *Aeaea's isle:* An isle off the coast of Italy where Circe lived after she was expelled from Colchis.

427-8. *A net . . . Elysium.* The initial illusory charm of the prison-paradise, such as the Bower of Bliss, is spellbinding. The "net" is a common image of enthrallment, especially in Blake, whose "nets of beauty and delusion" represent the sinister charm of nature's beauty. See also Acrasia's "veil of silk" which is likened to a "net" in which to catch lovers (*F. Q.* II,xii,77). Glaucus is a "fisher" (317) caught in his own net.

440-5. The archetypal temptation scene with Circe playing the role of Satan, wishing to pluck the sensuous fruit of desire for the innocent Glaucus. It may serve to call into question Endymion's own excesses, his own "dalliance with a demon thing."

453-63. Patterson (60) notes that Glaucus here is "in precisely the condition of the knight in 'La Belle Dame' at the end of that poem. . ."

456. D'Avanzo (51) feels that the "metaphor used here is especially appropriate in suggesting that Circe provides the teat of inspiration whose nourishment is as life-giving to Glaucus' imaginative powers as real milk is to the life of the child." Frye[6] (140) refers to Circe as a Jungian "terrible mother." She is the sinister aspect of the maternal Venus of the Garden

of Adonis in Bk. II, keeping her victim in a state of foetal dependency.

459. *arbitrary queen of sense:* Evert (145) interprets as "a purposeless stimulator of sensation, leading it nowhere."

461. *Amphion's harp:* Actually, a three-stringed lyre made to celebrate Diana as *diva triformis.* As at III.1001-2, K. appears to be identifying Amphion with Arion. See III.1002n. for an explanation.

476. Frye[6] (140) refers to the "specious heaven" as "pure subjective consciousness."

477-82. D'Avanzo (51) notes that "Glaucus' grim realization of his enslavement to her occurs only after she withdraws her sexual favors."

488. *complain:* complaint.

498. *The banquet of my arms:* Appropriate, since all Glaucus's sensual pleasure comes from Circe. It is a parody of love as "unsating food" (see I.816n.) and, as in *Comus,* of the sacramental meal.

504. *penny pelf:* The obolus; Charon's charge for ferrying souls across the Styx.

511. *grapes:* Van Ghent (9) regards as a parody of the initiatory food motif (cf. II.442f.). Only when burst by the "strenuous tongue" do they become the communion wine of III.801-2.

521. *sooty oil:* A direct parody of the drop of light which is love (cf. I.807-8), which is thrown in the eyes of the poet-lover.

530. *one huge Python:* Knight (276) groups with the other animal and snake images in this book, symbolizing "an objective sense of potential hell within physical love . . . pointing to 'La Belle Dame' and *Lamia.*" Python was spawned out of the ooze deposited by the flood of Deucalion, and later slain by Apollo.

545-6. De Selincourt compares *Julius Caesar* II,i,288-90: "my true and honourable wife, / As dear to me as are the ruddy drops / That visit my sad heart. . ."

565. De Selincourt compares a similar use of "dungeon" in *Comus* 349: "In this close dungeon of innumerous boughs. . ."

567-8. *O Dis . . . brow:* Chatterjee cites Cary's Dante (*Hell,* III): "This said, the gloomy region trembling shook / So terribly, that yet with clammy dews / Fear chills my brow."

570-7. Sperry (51) sees in this coarse mockery a "parody of the whole conception of the love-nest." See also Trilling (83) on K.'s sense of the perverse in eroticism.

580. *gentle shears:* See I.279-80n.

590-9. Allott cites Lyly's *Endymion* II,iii,29-36, which describes Endymion's transformation resulting from Tellus's jealous anger at his fidelity to Cynthia.

604-6. *A hand . . . finger.* The expulsion of Glaucus from his false paradise. The vivid iconographic detail may have been influenced by Italian paintings of the expulsion of Adam and Eve.

615-6. *Young . . . tell?* De Selincourt cites *P. L.* XI,494-5: "Sight so deform what heart of rock could long / Dry-eyed behold?"

621-5. *Could . . . hair.* A trembling pathos reminiscent of Niobe's at I.337-43.

628. *fabric crystalline:* Suggests for Frye[6] (140), "like the 'orbed diamond' of the previous book [II.245], a world which is visible but not approachable. Its poetic relatives include the crystal cabinet of Blake's poem in which the narrator struggles unsuccessfully to reach an 'inmost Form,' and the self-enclosed world of the unproductive and narcissistic beautiful youth of Shakespeare's sonnets, a 'liquid prisoner pent in walls of glass.' " Bloom[3] (342) interprets it as "an illusion of mercy until its unreal structure is startled into life by the engendering of

a relationship of sympathy between Endymion and himself [Glaucus]."

638. Cf. IV.764 and *Hyperion* I,18.

646-68. Spurgeon (62-3) compares Miranda's first speech (*The Tempest* I,ii,1-9) where she voices an instinctive sympathy for the "noble creatures" drowned at sea.

689-711. Frye[6] (143-4) remarks that "the scroll they find informs them they have to learn magic, like Prospero, and this magic is an act of releasing the 'symbol-essences' of nature delivering the spirits in the prisons of subject and object alike." This is the white magic (Hermes's moly) needed to counteract Circe's black magic. Cf. "Nature's universal scroll" (*Hyperion* II,151).

700. *symbol-essences:* Frye[6] (147-8) claims "The poet can escape from the spectral world by his power of being able to articulate the language of 'symbol-essences,' a language which expresses the identity of the real subject and the real object. In Keats, as in Shelley and Shakespeare, this poetic power is symbolized by the magician who can command the spirits of the elements."

710-11. *The youth . . . destroyed:* Bate (188) notes the return of this warning in the powerful lines of *The Fall of Hyperion* 107-8: "If thou canst not ascend / These steps, die on that marble where thou art."

713. *twin brothers:* For the twin destinies of Glaucus and Endymion see the note on III.314f. Frye[4] (78), discussing the twins in Shakespeare's comedies, says that "identical twins are not really identical (the same person) but merely similar, and when they meet they are delivered, in comic fashion, from the fear of the loss of identity. . ." He also notes that twins sometimes function as bisexual Eros figures, who "crystallize a comic society" (83). In *Twelth Night,* for instance, Viola as Cesario redeems a society of melancholy lovers after revealing her true identity to her twin brother, who has escaped from the sea "like Arion on a dolphin's back" (I,i,332). See III.1002n.

719-23. *Tis . . . bondage.* Cf. Old Genius's function of preserving "a thousand thousand naked babes" (*F. Q.* III,vi,32) in Spenser's *Gardens of Adonis.* There are also analogies in Shakespeare's romances: in *Pericles,* for instance, Thaisa is miraculously preserved in a coffin at sea, later to be revived in the temple of Diana during the festival of Neptune.

728-34. For another military metaphor used for lovers see II.41.

735. *in silent rows:* Cf. the orderliness of the pre-existent forms in Spenser's *Gardens of Adonis:* "And every sort is in a sundry bed / Set by it selfe, and ranckt in comely rew. . . In endless rancks along enraunged were, / That seemed the Ocean could not containe them there" (*F. Q.* II,vi,35).

739-40. Ford[3] (66) notes that "like Juliet in the tomb they seem to sleep in beauty." The implication for him is they are dreaming of a reunion of eternal felicity.

747-76. Frye[6] (144) comments: "during his descent Endymion has feared the total loss of his identity, and that he would suffer the traditional *sparagmos* fate of the god in the underworld and be torn 'piece-meal' cf. III.263. But instead it is the scroll that is torn up and that fertilizes the sunken world with new life." Frye compares "the image of the torn-up fertilizing scroll with the almost identical image in the speech of Orc in Blake's *America* plate 8." Cf. I.296 and II.905-9.

753. *This wand:* Cf. Mercury's caduceus, the necessary antidote (or antibody) to Circean charm. See IV.331-44n.

755-6. *first . . . clue.* Lemprière speaks of a "clew of thread" Ariadne gave to Theseus as a clue for escaping from Minos's labyrinth. Frye[6] (144) finds in this book "a good deal of imagery suggesting a version of the Theseus story in which all the previous sacrifices to Minos were delivered from the labyrinth." *clue:* nail.

760. Suggests the harrowing of hell.

761. *a shell:* A recurring image in the poem, associated with the silvery moon (I.593) and Cynthia (II.103); the "sea-born

Venus" (I.626-7) and Neptune (I.593, III.238 & 965)—both of whom are "shell-borne"; water nymphs (II.115, 921); and in general with fairyland, magic grottos (note the frequent use of the image in Bk. II), and the magic healing of fairy lore (see *On Receiving a Curious Shell* 20f. and its source in *F. Q.* IV,xi,6).

762. *charactery:* writing. Cf. *On Receiving a Curious Shell* 21 and "When I have fears" 3. Also see II.62, where the character'd" butterfly leads Endymion into a metamorphosis of descent. Here it augurs a counter-metamorphosis.

769. *minced:* cut up finely.

785-806. Ford[3] (67) notes that with the exception of Glaucus, for whom Endymion has atoned, only the "devout and true" lovers are immediately saved.

798-800. A remarkable kind of incremental synaesthesia.

801-2. Communion follows the vicarious sparagmos, wine being the essence of natural fruition as well as the dying god's blood. In his letter to Reynolds of May 3, 1818, K. speaks of the "third Chamber of Life . . . stored with the wine of love—and the Bread of Friendship. . ." (I,282-3).

806f. Bush[4] believes the festival at Neptune's palace may owe something to Jonson's masque, *Neptune's Triumph.*

812. *emerald:* Frye[6] (144) interprets as "a reunion of the sphere of water with that of the green earth."

816. Cf. *To Autumn* 33. Like the Adonis of Bk. II, the lovers revive in the summer. Cf. I.502.

835. *shouldered:* See I.530n.

836-43. *At every . . . blush of coral.* Cf. *Hero and Leander* 25-34.

850-3. *the bow . . . arch:* In *The Tempest* IV,i,70-1, Iris is the goddess of the "wat'ry arch" and messenger of Juno. Frye[6]

(144) points out the traditional appearance of the rainbow following the deluge.

853. *Paphian army:* army of lovers. The isle of Paphos was sacred to Venus.

856. *raught:* reached.

861. *Ripe from hue-golden swoons:* Ford[3] (67) remarks that the "dead lovers were not precisely dead. . . Evidently death was, in virtue of their amorous fidelity converted into a kind of swoon or sleep full of pleasant (and prefigurative?) visions. Such had been Adonis's reward, his death being medicined . . . to a lengthened drowsiness filled with prefigurative love-dreams. The implication is that death, like dreamful sleep, thus becomes for faithful lovers a prefiguration of eternal felicity." It is the poet, here Glaucus and Endymion, who, as Frye[6] (143) says, "awakens the dream into his world, and releases it from its subjective prison."

865. *Beauty's paragon:* Venus.

866-87. According to Knight (266-7), K. in his "mythological treatment" never "loses sense of the natural object, however precisely it be personified. . ." He "is always seeing the *eternal dimension* of the *lower elements themselves.* The sea-palace, in becoming a palace, does not at all cease to be the sea."

879. *lucid death:* Cf. "lucid wombs" at I.786.

880-2. *As . . . air:* A startling, if not incongruent, image, perhaps influenced by *The Excursion* IV,1277-82. The Indian returns in the opening lines of *Hyperion.*

888. *Triton blew his horn.* See I.206n.

890. Knight (267-8), noting the vivid use of "dripping," claims "There is no facile anthropomorphism, nor any overstress of the human. The personification is, as it were—quite apart from the water suggestion—technically fluid." Cf. *F. Q.* IV,xi,12: "His dewy locks did drop with brine apace / Under his Diadem imperiall."

893. *ooze-born goddess:* Venus. Ricks (139) finds the epithet "profoundly disconcerting and truthful, a possibility of distaste not at all permitted to overcome awe and sensual pleasure. . ." He believes the "ooze" is from Cleopatra's Nile in the Shakespearean passage quoted in I.820-1n.

899. *Nais:* The mother of Glaucus by Neptune. According to Lempriere, she has the Circean power to turn young men into dumb fish.

918. *Cytherea:* Cythera, the island sacred to Venus.

927. *pleached:* interwove. Cf. *Much Ado About Nothing* III,i,7: "the pleached bower."

930. *coverture:* shelter. Cf. *Much Ado About Nothing* III,i,30: "couched in the woodbine coverture."

943-90. *Hymn to Neptune:* Bush[3] (92, n.16) believes K. is linking here some obvious reminiscences of Virgil's picture of Neptune calming the storm with a recollection of Milton's "At a Vacation Exercise" 34f.

944-5. *co-inheritor / Of elements!* Jove, Neptune, and Pluto inherited the heaven, the sea, and the underground respectively.

956. *Gulfs:* Rushes forward like a gulf.

961. *front:* brow or forehead.

978. Cupid.

979. Cf. III.144.

993. *On oozy throne:* Cf. *The Tempest* V,i,150-1: "I wish / Myself were mudded in that oozy bed." Also, *Lycidas* 175: "With nectar pure his oozy locks he laves. . ."

994-1004. A mythological pageant de Selincourt believes to have been influenced by the somewhat parallel scene of the marriage of the Thames and the Medway in Spenser (cf. *F. Q.* IV,xi,11,12, & 18). Comparing the two pageants, de Selincourt concludes that "Keats rises in places to a higher plane of emotion, and where Spenser is content with presenting a picture of serene beauty, Keats is more dramatic, and realizes more fully the human significance in which the legends took their rise."

1000. *Doris:* Wife of Nereus and mother of the sea-nymphs. Cf. *F. Q.* IV,xi,48.

1002. *Amphion:* Niobe's (I.337-43) husband, whose music resurrected his marble wife and built Thebes–as here Neptune's palace rises to music. As at III.461, he is identified with Arion, the son of Neptune, whose music charmed a school of dolphins into carrying him to Neptune's temple at Taenarum.

1004. *Amphitrite:* See II.109n. and *F. Q.* IV,xi,11.

1022-7. The voice of Cynthia heard in Endymion's inner consciousness in the midst of his "hue-golden swoon."

1024. Cf. II.808. Evert (150) feels this may be more than "the expression of a goddess's happiness over her impending fulfillment in love. . ." for it "implies a conception of reciprocal action and complementary relationship between heaven and earth . . . [that] imposes upon mankind the necessity of acting *as* man. . ." Endymion "has won eternal felicity for the goddess not by a ritual act of devotion, but by cooperating with another mortal in alleviating the evil of death so to make possible for others the enjoyment of love."

Notes to Book IV

1-29. The invocation is composed, according to Finney (228), in the "lofty and artificial style of Milton's *Paradise Lost.*" On K.'s attempt for an effect of lofty generality see his letter to Bailey of Oct. 28, 1817: "you will see from the Manner I had not an opportunity of mentioning any Poets, for fear of spoiling the effect of the passage by particularizing them" (I,172-3). De Selincourt compares *Sleep and Poetry* 163-312, where there is also a "deep recognition of the greatness of the past, mingled with a feeling of despondency at the present" and "the same ambition for himself blended with the humility which naturally accompanies his abiding reverence for 'the eternal principle of Beauty and the Memory of great Men.' " He also compares Gray's *Progress of Poesy* for the idea of tracing the genius of poetry through Greece, Rome and Italy to England. On the belatedness of the invocation see Bloom[3] (393): "The invocation to the British Muse salutes that sub-deity for its patience, with unintentional irony. Underlying this glad hailing is an intimation of mortality, with an implied reminder that this poem is dedicated to Chatterton and a hint of Keats's lack of time."

2-3. *first born . . . begot:* Ende (86) cites *P. L.* III,1: "Hail, holy Light, offspring of Heav'n first-born."

10. *eastern:* hebrew D. An allusion to the Bible.

15. *Ausonia:* the ancient name for Italy, apparently represented here by Virgil and Dante.

20-2. *Great Muse . . . wings:* Cf. *The Excursion* IV,179-83: "Too, too contracted are these walls of flesh, / This vital warmth too cold, these visual orbs, / Though inconceivably endowed, too dim / For any passion of the soul that leads / To ecstasy . . ."

23-5. *and . . . lives.* Cf. *Richard III* IV,iii,51: "Delay leads impotent and snail-paced beggary." Evert (173) interprets the wasted morning light as K.'s sense of failure and the failure of most of his generation. See IV.927-33n.

26. *shrives:* confesses.

27-8. *But then . . . I now.* Similar in tone to Wordsworth's allusion to Chatterton in *Resolution and Independence* VII.

29. Ende (86-7) cites Wordsworth's *Lines, Left upon the Seat of a Yew-tree:* "True dignity abides with him alone / Who, in the silent hour of inward though, / Can still suspect, and still

revere himself, / In lowliness of heart."

30f. *The Indian Maid:* As the problematic core of Bk. IV, she has given rise to a variety of interpretations. Colvin (197) sees her as evidence of the lesson Endymion must learn, that "all transient and secondary loves, which may seem to come between him and his great ideal . . . are really . . . visitations and condescensions to him of his celestial love. . ." De Selincourt believes she "typifies intense human love, which is keenest when brought into being in sorrow," though he fails to indicate how this identity relates to the other Cynthia-identity. Thorpe (60-1) identifies her with "the spirit of sorrow and suffering in the world," for K. believed that "the poet must find in the tragedy of the world his poetic salvation. . ." Finney (319) relates her to Cynthia as particular to general, actual to ideal: "The beauty of a particular woman is a manifestation of ideal or essential beauty . . . and the love of a particular woman is the highest means by which man can attain a fellowship with essence." Ford (70-2) attempts to avoid allegorical meaning by considering the Indian Maid as Cynthia assuming a disguise both in order to visit her earthly lover without the embarrassment of detection in heaven and to test his constancy—an interpretation suggested by Drayton's *Endimion and Phoebe.* Pettet (192-200) offers a psychological interpretation of the Cynthia-Indian Maid complex as the dark and light, actual and ideal aspects of erotic adolescent day-dreaming. Evert (153-5), rejecting Pettet's search for psychological causes and Ford's "test of constancy" thesis, interprets her in light of Endymion's qualification for the immortal world through the acute awareness of "purely human existence." "In Book I, the cause of his other defections was the love of a goddess met in a dream. For the completion of his re-education, then, he must love another human being . . . a mortal as weak, limited, and wretched as himself, and one upon whom he can himself confer a benefit." The Indian Maid provides the opportunity for him to act as a god, "and (on the model of Apollo and Cynthia provided at the beginning of Book III), manifest toward one weaker than himself an outgoing, giving love . . . and the revelation that she and Cynthia are one confirms the whole point of Endymion's journeyings, the lesson that only by full sensitivity to and appreciation of the mundane can we come to apprehension of the divine. . ." Patterson (87) feels she has some of the aura of Hecate, and Bradley (230) suggests she is Cynthia veiled, "the shaded half of the moon." Brown (646-8) sees an analogy in the Arab Maiden of *Alastor,* who falls in love with Shelley's poet-hero, but, as human love, is ignored in favor of the elusive and fair dream-maiden representing ideal love. K., Brown claims, regarded the theme of human love of immense importance and thus rewrote Shelley, making the Indian Maid Endymion's true bride. In the context of Shakespeare's comedies, the Indian Maid is analogous to the dark heroine (e.g. Juliet, Hermia, Rosaline), who Frye[4] (85) calls "the black bride"—a "disappearing and returning heroine" who "revolves cyclically around a male love, and is usually the efficient cause of the conclusion." She is the opposite of the elusive "white goddess," who the male hero revolves around. "The ordeal of the heroine [Frye says] who seeks her lover through darkness, disguise, humiliation, or even death until she finds him brings her close to the folklore figure of the loathly lady, who must remove some handicap of slander, ugliness, or captivity before her identity is recognized." Cf. Psyche, referred to in II.61n.

32-3. *myriads . . . pleasant fields!* While "myriads" suggests Milton's Fallen Angels (cf. *P. L.* I,87,622), K. may be conflating two other Miltonic contexts: Satan's first speech where he bids adieu to his lost heavenly home: "Farewell happy fields. . ." (*P. L.* I,249), and the simile associating "Ganges" with the rivers of Paradise toward which Satan is flying: "flies toward the springs / Of Ganges or Hydaspes, Indian streams" (*P. L.* III,436-7). Cf. IV.143 and *Cap and Bells* 1. K. uses Milton, in effect, to identify earthly with heavenly paradise in describing the Indian Maid's home—possibly a subtle hint of her heavenly origin as Cynthia.

48-9. *eyelids . . . twinkle:* Plays on the traditional eye-star conceit; fluttering eyelids cause the star's "twinkling." By contrast, the "lidless-eyed" "planets" (I.593-4) do not twinkle.

60. *curls of glossy jet:* Connects the Indian Maid with the various displaced forms of the "black, but comely" bride of the *Song of Songs* discussed in the note on IV.30f. Originally the black bride was associated with the dark fertility of the soil; "curls" suggests here a sexual fertility or potency. See I.977n. on "dusky."

66-70. *O . . . crown!* Ende (79) believes that unlike Glaucus and Endymion, who sought to escape their "green prison" through the sublime, the Indian Maid seeks to escape it through human existence itself; she wants to humanize nature rather than transcend it, to transform the fallen god into "human shape." Comparing the account of Hyacinthus's death at I.326-31, one could view the Indian Maid here giving a human voice to the dumb pathos of Zephyr, while her "tears" humanize his "sobbing rain."

95. *triple soul:* Generally interpreted as Endymion's simultaneous love for the Moon (cf. III.142f), the unknown dream-goddess, and the Indian Maid. Patterson (89-90) argues convincingly that it suggests Endymion's growing awareness of the *diva triformis* aspect of the unknown dream-goddess. He claims that as yet Endymion "does not know the Indian Maid's relationship to this triad and therefore now considers her an entirely separate entity in opposition to the goddess. . ." He feels that "triple soul" cannot possibly refer to "Endymion's three loves in the narrative," as this makes the immediately following change to two ("for both. . .") utterly inexplicable. For the *diva triformis* see K.'s sonnet "To Homer" 14, where he refers to her as "Dian, Queen of Earth and Heaven and Hell."

103-4. *her eyes . . . alive.* Cf. *Venus and Adonis* 1033-8, which K. quotes in his letter to Reynolds of Nov. 22, 1817:

> Or as the snail, whose tender horns being hit,
> Shrinks backward in his shelly cave with pain,
> And there, all smother'd up, in shade doth sit,
> Long after fearing to creep forth again;
> So at his bloody view her eyes are fled
> Into the deep dark cabins of her head. . .

According to Eliade (164), the snail has primitive associations with the moon. Like the moon, for instance, its horns withdraw into a dark "inter-lunar cave."

111. *Thou . . . my executioner:* De Selincourt compares Phoebe's words to her lover Silvius in *As You Like It* III,v,8: "I would not be thy executioner."

121. *Erebus:* Hades.

124-5. *As her heart . . . replied:* Evert (156) comments: "In the light of our after-knowledge of the Indian Maid's true identity, we can understand why, at this point, she falls to weeping . . . for Endymion, in believing that mortal love cuts him off from heaven, has in a single moment unlearned all that was to fit him for union with her immortality."

143. *Indian streams:* Cf. *P. L.* III,437 quoted in IV.32-3n.

145. *roundelay:* The song resembles a roundelay only in that the opening measures are repeated at the close.

146-290. *The Song of the Indian Maid:* Frye[6] (153) sees it as a song of joy, the Hymn to Bacchus (182-272), enclosed in a song to sorrow (146-8 & 273-90), representing the union of joy and sorrow "at the point of the greatest intensity of both." The Song evokes for Colvin (229) a "mood of tender irony and wistful pathos like that of the best Elizabethan Love-songs . . . a power like that of Coleridge, perhaps partly caught from him, of evoking the remotest weird and beautiful associations almost with a wand. . ." Knight (274) senses here a melancholy that is "sincerely felt and luxuriantly enjoyed," as well as a "delicate humour . . . felt within the lilting, yet also sad, rhymes." For Knight's comment on the rhythm see I.232-46n. Evert (157) regards the function of the Song as an attempt to convince Endymion of the beneficence of nature and thus elicit another declaration from him grounded on the poem's naturalistic teaching.

146-63. Excerpted in letters to Jane Reynolds of Oct. 31, 1817 and to Bailey of Nov. 3, 1817 (I,176-7 & 181-2), perhaps indicating that K. considered these stanzas separable and complete in themselves. Ford[3] (75-6) interprets the thought as "a kind of law of aesthetic compensation in the universe, specifically: the natural world becomes more beautiful as a consequence of the sorrows of lovers." Ford regards this "law" as the prefigurative truth ("What the Imagination seizes as Beauty must be truth. . .") that K. in his letter to Bailey of Nov. 22, 1817 sees this "little song" illustrating. Ford goes on to compare *Hyperion,* where he believes there is a more explicit identification of the "law" with "truth": "Oceanus can foresee this 'law' of aesthetic compensation, but to his mind it comes as a vision of 'eternal truth' (II,187); throughout the universe it operates as an 'eternal law' (II,228)."

157. *spry:* An Elizabethan variant of "spray."

167-8. De Selincourt cites Sabrina's song in *Comus* 898-900: "Thus I set my printless feet / O'er the cowslip's velvet head / That bends not as I tread."

182-272. *The Hymn to Bacchus:* Finney (276) believes K. is following Sandys's commentary on *Met.* IV in fusing the Medieval *Lay of Aristotle,* which tells of Alexander's conquest of India and love of an Indian maid, with the Greek myth of Bacchus–his encounter with the deserted Ariadne (see II.443n.) and his conquest of India. See Finney (272-91) for a further discussion of sources and see de Selincourt for the influence of Titian's *Bacchus and Ariadne.* Fyre[6] (144-5) feels it "balances the hymn to Pan in Book I, but is a product, not simply of a state of innocence, but of a new energy that has returned to that world from experience."

182-3. *Beneath . . . a weeping.* Deeply resonant. Cf. *The Tempest* I,ii,390-1: "Sitting on a bank, / Weeping again the King my father's wrack."

186. De Selincourt notes the echo of *Lycidas* 150: "And daffodillies fill their cups with tears."

198. *a merry din:* Cf. "the merry din" of the marriage in Coleridge's *Ancient Mariner* 8; here appropriately introduced by "kissing cymbals."

200. *a moving vintage:* Finney (282) compares *Macbeth* V,v,37: "a moving grove," which represents the celebratory conquest of the melancholy Macbeth. The moving grove is a traditional masque motif. Fogle (168) speaks of "empathy bursting into life embodied by the remarkable "moving vintage" in which landscape and figures dissolve into delirious motion, so that animate and inanimate, sentient and insentient, are fused in a dance."

201. *Crown'd with green leaves:* Bacchus was traditionally crowned with ivy berries and wreathed with ivy. *faces all on flame:* Cf. "sunburnt looks" at I.139.

203. Cf. Milton's *L'Allegro* 1: "Hence, loathed Melancholy."

213-4. Finney (285) cites Marlowe's *Hero and Leander* 63-5:

> Even as delicious meat is to the taste,
> So was his necke in touching, and surpast
> The white of Pelops' shoulder.

215. *Silenus:* An attendant of Bacchus Lempriere describes as "a jolly fat old man riding on an ass crowned with flowers and generally intoxicated."

235. Here "Pan's own satyrs are lured out of their 'forest haunts' by the odour of wine" Blackstone (181). Cf. I.263.

245-9. Bush[4] compares *Antony and Cleopatra* II,ii,199-214, and Landor's *Gebir* IV,157-8: "Crown'd were tame crocodiles, and boys white-robed / Guided their creaking crests across the stream." The image can be found in Blake and Shelley as well. It appears to represent the "new energy" that has returned to the world of innocence from experience.

247. *coil:* noisy bustle; an Elizabethanism.

263. *vail:* lower. Cf. *Pericles* II,iii,42: "Did vail their crowns to his supremacy."

265-7. De Selincourt compares the infant Christ's triumph over the pagan deities in Milton's *Nativity Ode* xix-xxv, where "Lars and Lemurs moan with midnight plaint." De Selincourt believes the irregular stanzas here also reflect the influence of Milton's poem.

273-90. Patterson (69) views as "a choral commentary on the events . . . in Endymion's story at the moment, for he is learning to accept the limitations of mortality; and one of them is that mortal joy, unlike daemonic joy, is inseparable from sorrow, as Keats later set forth in 'Ode on Melancholy. . .' "

274-6. Wasserman (189-90) compares the "self-forgetting pleasure" induced by the wine in *Ode to a Nightingale* II, as opposed to the "happiness" resulting from "self-annihilation through the projection of self into essence." When the "Indian Maiden followed Bacchus and his crew she experienced the entire range of earthly pleasures and yet was 'Sick-hearted, weary.' "

279-84. Knight (275) notes that "The lamentations of Constance in *King John* and Cleopatra's death-scene present a similar association of tragic sorrow and maternal possession."

294-5. Cf. Coleridge's *Dejection: An Ode* 96-7: "I turn from you, and listen to the wind, / Which long has raved unnoticed."

311-20. Evert (159) believes it is Endymion's decisive commitment here "to the substantial beauty of the real world which brings Mercury and the feathered steeds, upon which the lovers are then borne into the Empyrean."

311-4. Ricks (157) comments: "In so far as a blush is the blood moving involuntarily and markedly, it can be a type of metaphor for erection; in so far as it glows out and spends itself, a type of or metaphor for orgasm. For the poet it can offer a glimpse . . . of life stayed for ever in an eternal intensity of erect desire which is also an eternal intensity of sexual fulfillment. . ." Jones (144) contrasts this sort of blushing with the "cowardly blushes" (II.788) that Cynthia expresses to atone for sexual pleasure.

320-6. *Woe . . . thunder cloud.* An enigmatic warning perhaps reflecting Endymion's fear of the awesome force of nature, the power of fate or circumstance. See 989-90n. for the analogous taboo on the Indian Maid. As a natural phenomenon, it is the thunder of the approaching "hail storm."

331-44. Mercury's caduceus, the beatific counterpart to Circe's "gnarled staff" (III.508), brings about a metamorphosis of ascent. Here the winged horses enable the mortals to ascend from their "green prison." Cf. IV.66-70.

343. *steeds jet-black:* Suggests that Endymion and the dusky

Indian Maid are not leaving behind the dark underworld, but rather ascending by means of its "splenetic fire" or Promethean libido. See IV.60n.

349-50. See IV.1002n.

355-8. *This . . . Precipitous:* Perhaps influenced by Satan's defiance of Chaos where "chance" rules all (cf. *P. L.* II,927f). On the Miltonic nature of the polysyndeton see III.204n.

365. *Snuff:* De Selincourt compares *P. L.* X,272: "He snuffed the smell of Mortal change on earth." Cf. *Hyperion* I,167.

366. *native fire:* Perhaps the imaginative fire K. derives from the Muse of his "native land," whom, in his letter to Taylor of Feb. 27, 1818, he appears to identify with Shakespeare: "O for a Muse of fire to ascend!" (I,239).

368-9. *as when . . . willow:* See IV.391-7n.

370. De Selincourt compares *Comus* 553-4: "Gave respite to the drowsy frighted steeds / That draw the litter of close-curtained Sleep."

374. *aloof:* aloof from. Satan in his flight to Eden remains "Aloof the vulgar constellations thick" (*P. L.* III,577).

376-80. The dream prefigures the climax of Endymion's quest as well as of K.'s career. Frye[6] (128) sees the passage as connecting "the wish-fulfillment element in dreams with the ambition of the poet which drives him to realize his aims." Cf. "When I have fears," where dream deepens into Apollonian foresight.

377. The "bat," which one would expect to find in a "depth Cimmerian," is evidently "lean" after its "wintery" sleep. For another instance of K.'s use of "plump" as a verb see *To Autumn* 7: "plump the hazel-shells."

380. *Jove's daughter:* Phoebe was the daughter of Latona by Jove.

385. *litter:* See IV.370n.

391-7. *as one . . . far.* The first simile here seems remote and fanciful but nonetheless grows out of the one at IV.368-9. In the earlier simile one catches silvery glimpses of the "new moon" through the "clouds" (drooping like a "weeping willow"), so here one glimpses the "silver-throated eels" through the "sallows" (i.e. willows). In the third simile of the sequence (394-7), "fog" replaces "clouds" and "sallows," and "hamlet faint and far" replaces the "moon" and "eels." The three similes serve to characterize the "Cimmerian" nature of "Sleep," as well as the elusive moon-lit dream within him.

394. *old Skiddaw's top:* Wordsworthian, e.g. *To Joanna* 62.

399. *earth's splenetic fire:* The Promethean fire of earth, the energy needed to reach the fiery spheres above.

407-38. Endymion's dream of deity and its realization: Evert (160) claims that each stage of Endymion's "growth back toward spiritual health is climaxed by a revelation of deity, and each revelation is more impressive than the last. In the underworld, after desiring to see living nature again, Endymion is permitted to watch the awakening of the nature-deity Adonis. Later, after submitting his senses wholly to mastery by nature's beauty, he is visited by Cynthia herself. In the sea, having enlarged his sympathy to include human life once more, he is permitted to see Cupid and Venus, the god and goddess of love, together with Jove's own brother Neptune. . . Now, after declaring his love for the 'mortal' Indian Maid, he is carried to heaven itself. . ."

411-2. *golden bow . . . golden apples:* An implicit identification of Apollo's western Elysium with the garden of the Hesperides. Cf. I.347-54, where the Golden Fleece is associated with Apollo's "golden bow."

415. *Hebe:* Jove's daughter and Hercules's wife; Goddess of youth and cupbearer to the gods, here closely associated with Phoebe. Cf. Milton's *At a Vacation Exercise* 38-9: "While Hebe brings / Immortal nectar to her kingly sire." See I.170n.

418-9. "The interplay of sight and touch is very swift. There is a trace of 'wit,' of conscious ingenuity, which lends to the image a certain flavour of modernity. The lips of Endymion are 'dazzled,' of course, because the hand which they touch is 'starlight' . . . and also because he is dreaming that he is among the Gods on Olympus. . ." Fogle (112).

421-5. Bush[4] compares Ovid's description of the palace of the Sun in *Met.* II,1f. (Sandys 25). Cf. also the procession of the Seasons in Spenser's *Mutabilitie Cantos* (*F. Q.* VII,vii,28-31).

426. *morris:* dance. Allott cites *Comus* 116: "Now to the moon in wavering morris move."

430-1. *She rises . . . goddess.* Endymion solves the riddle of the unknown dream-goddess. It now remains for him to identify Diana with the Indian Maid.

433-8. Cf. K.'s letter to Bailey of Nov. 22, 1817: "The Imagination may be compared to Adam's dream—he awoke and found it truth" (I,185). Ford[3] (77) believes that since his love dreams have proved their prefigurative veracity, "the poem should have ended at this point with a simple account of the transformation of the Indian girl to her original self, Cynthia." For an ironic use of the theme, see Madeline's awakening into Imagination's truth, which she finds "pallid, chill, and drear!" (*The Eve of St. Agnes* XXXV).

437. *merry Hebe laughs and nods:* Cf. *L'Allegro* 28-9: "Nods and becks and wreathed smiles, / Such as hang on Hebe's cheek."

441-3. The allusion is to Icarus, who, trying to escape from Daedalus's labyrinth, flew too close to the sun, losing his wings. Left bare-shouldered, he fell into the sea—a premonition of Endymion's fall back to earth. See II.177-8n. and *Sleep and Poetry* 302-3. In relation to Satan's flight in Chaos (see IV.355-8n.) and Endymion's need of further knowledge, see K.'s letter to Reynolds of May 3, 1818: "The difference of high Sensations with and without knowledge appears to me this—in the latter case we are falling continually ten thousand fathoms deep and being blown up again without wings and with all [the] horror of a bare shouldered creature—in the former case, our shoulders are fledge[d], and we go thro' the same air and space without fear" (I,277). See I.530n. on K.'s fondness for Spenser's "sea-shouldering Whales."

445. *His heart lept up:* See I.896n.

459. *daedale:* labyrinthine, cunning; from the ingenious Daedalus.

475-7. *What . . . identity.* Frye[6] (142) sees here Endymion's realization of his Negative Capability, and compares the similar use of "identity" (selfhood or "identity-as") in *Hyperion* 113-4: "I have left / My strong identity, my real self."

485. *throe:* be in throes.

500. Bush[4] compares *Comus* 333: "Stoop thy pale visage through an amber cloud."

506-10. The language of Ovidian metamorphosis; perhaps the legend of Orpheus and Eurydice (cf. *Met.* X,56-9) as well as of Narcissus (cf. *Met.* III,428f.). The story of Orpheus and Euridice, as Frye[6] (148) points out, is a myth of the failure of ascent, which is the theme of the present episode. Endymion fails to liberate the bride (Indian Maid) from an imprisoning lower world, which results in his relapse into narcissistic subjectivity. Bloom[3] (394) compares Scylla's metamorphosis or death at the hands of Circe with the Indian Maid's fate here where "Diana seems to be another Circe" (cf. III.616-26). As this leaves Glaucus to "fall into a death-in-life beneath the surface, so Endymion falls into the Cave of Quietude. . ."

512-48. *There lies a den . . . Cave of Quietude.* K.'s paradoxical "Dark paradise" eludes confident interpretation. Murry (175) attempts to interpret it as a psychological state: "There is a sudden passing sorrow and joy which comes unsought for. If it is sought for, it is not found. It comes when misery has reached its extreme point; then the misery marvellously changes into a profound content. Then silence is the fullest utterence, a hope and sacrilege: then, in this calm ecstasy of despair, the whole being of the sufferer is bathed and renewed." Murry (176) sees "The importance of this strange experience" in "the fact that it is the psychological culmination of the poem, with it what we may call the experiential element of the poem ends." Though influenced by Murry, Bloom[3] (394-5) notes that the singular concentration of verbal figures and oxymorons suggests that "Keats's notion of this state is aesthetic, and only secondarily psychological." Bloom views it in Blakean terms as "a den of Ulro, a deathly isolation, yet with an unsuspected Eden in the heart of it" and feels it "is a prophecy of the lesson that Keats will read in the silent countenance of Moneta in the climactic passage of *The Fall of Hyperion. . .*" Knight (262) views the cave in terms of sleep as an "entry into final mysteries. . ." Van Ghent (8) believes it is sleep as a healer of mortality—a concept operating in K.'s Garden of Adonis (see II.484n.). Van Ghent also mentions its aerial location as indicating "the spiritual quality of the experience that must 'spiritualize' Endymion for marriage." See K.'s letter to Bailey of Oct. 29, 1817, where he speaks of becoming "self spiritualized into a kind of sublime Misery" (I,173). Frye[6] (146) stands back from the cave to note its structural significance, comparing it to Homer's Cave of Nymphs from whence Ulysses returned home in a deep sleep or swoon after his stay at the Garden of Alkinoos. He notes too that, like the "unlook'd for change" at the climax of the poem, the cave can be entered only involuntarily (cf. IV.531-2).

520-1. *And . . . flies:* Murry (173-4) suggests that the darts refer to "those thoughts of human misery which affect the unselfish man."

531. *death-watch:* "Any of various insects which make a noise like the ticking of a watch, supposed by the superstitious to portend death" (*OED*).

536. *Semele:* Pregnant with Bacchus by Jove, she asked for and received Jove's lethal lightning stroke. Bacchus later rescued her from the underworld and she joined the Immortals on Olympus (see *Met.* III,250-315).

558. *A skyey masque:* K. may have had in mind here the masque Prospero shows to Ferdinand and Miranda in honor of their approaching marriage.

563-611. A choric song in honor of the approaching marriage of Diana and Endymion. According to Evert (161), it tells us that Endymion has fulfilled his quest and thus the trials he confronts hereafter will not be determinative. Evert believes that K. may have used the fact of Endymion not having heard the song as a pretext for continuing the poem through another 400 lines. The song serves as a choric background for the rest of the book, though generally just out of Endymion's hearing.

570. *Zephyrus . . . Flora:* See I.331n.

581-614. Blackstone (410-11) cites as a parallel or possible source one of Taylor's footnotes to the *Cave of Nymphs* Porphyry (287), where he speaks of the soul's descent through the zodiac to the cave of genesis. De Selincourt claims, however, that K. here has "no other object than to present the signs of the Zodiac that are propitious to man as triumphing over those which were regarded as hostile. Thus Castor and Pollux (the Gemini) who are under the direction of Apollo are represented as subduing Leo and the Bear, both hostile, and the Centaur, another hostile planet, is also put to flight."

582. *Aquarius:* Sandys (196) associates with Ganymede.

599. *shent:* disgraced; an Elizabethanism.

606. *Danae's Son:* Perseus, the son of Jupiter and Danae, saved Andromeda from a sea-monster while returning home with the head of the Medusa (cf. IV.129;754).

611. *Daphne . . . Apollo:* Daphne, an elusive woodland nymph of Diana, escaped Apollo's amorous pursuit by turning into a laurel tree. Apollo continued to love her despite her metamorphosis (see *Met.* I.441-590). The fable marks the end of Endymion's pursuit of the elusive Phoebe and his return to the Indian Maid in her "green prison."

614. Bloom[3] (395) calls "a very great line," and comments: "It is the earth that he chooses, but he comes to it from a world beyond, and pain attends his rebirth into common things. Keats is imaginatively right in equating Endymion's first touch of earth, pain, and the pleasure of finding the Indian Maid lying by

his side again."

619-21. *to him . . . shadow:* Cf. Niamh's "dim" realm beyond earthly sorrow in Yeats's *The Wanderings* of Oisin.

636-48. Endymion's renunciation of his quest. Bloom[3] (395) notes that "Endymion comes out of the Cave sufficiently disinterested to disqualify him for more questing. He has passed from innocence to experience, touched the hell within experience, and is ready for a more organized innocence that may precede the vision of art." Patterson (43) claims that Endymion's emphatic rejection of his pursuit of Cynthia here is in line with her failure to come through as an effective symbol of the ideal all along. His "recantation of the daemonic is in favor of the claims of humanity and the beauty of the human world."

637. *nothing . . . a nothing . . . nothing:* The traditional pun on the word as grammatical negative and a positive that lacks essence (cf. *King Lear*). Endymion is ostensibly denying his idealistic notion that, as K. says in his letter to Bailey of March 13, 1818, "Nothings . . . are made Great and dignified by an ardent pursuit" (I,243). He now appears to have conceded to Peona's skepticism (cf. I.755-6), having returned to her mortal and naturalistic realm.

638-43. *O . . . gone!* Cf. I.13-24.

639. *Presumptuous:* The tragic fault of many of the mythic characters in the poem.

641. *each to each:* Cf. Wordsworth's compensation for the loss or renunciation of vision: "The Child is father of the man / And I would wish my days to be / Bound each to each by natural piety."

646-55. This could be viewed as K.'s deliberate rejection of Shelley's visionary idealism in *Alastor.* Bloom[3] (395) sees here Endymion's realization that "he has barely escaped the fate that Keats will later visualize as that of the knight of arms in 'La Belle Dame Sans Merci.' " Evert (162) finds the lines "out of keeping with the aesthetic vision that *Endymion* exists to propogate, and the narrative voice assures us that Endymion, 'by fancies vain and crude' (IV.722), is rationalizing. The narrative disclaimer is necessary because Endymion is already destined for immortality, and we must not be permitted to doubt that, in his heart, he still longs for it." Cf. *To Reynolds* 78f.

650. *too thin breathing:* Cf. I.751 and III.381. According to Ende (84), this refers to the recurring "breathless" stance before the sublime, which Endymion has come to fear: "What he wants is not to lose his breath to the voice of otherness . . . because loss of breath is also loss of self and the possibility of one's own voice."

650-3. *gone . . . seas!* De Selincourt compares *Comus* 205-9.

654. *airy voices:* Perhaps a reference to Ariel's Siren-like music.

655. *breathless:* In his letter to Taylor of Feb. 27, 1818, K. mentions as one of his "Axioms" on poetry that "Its touches of Beauty should never be half way thereby making the reader breathless instead of content: the rise, the progress, the setting of imagery should like the Sun come natural to him—shine over him and set soberly although in magnificence leaving him in the Luxury of twilight. . ." (I,238).

656. *Adieu, my daintiest Dream:* Cf. Prospero's adieu to Ariel: "my dainty Ariel! I shall miss thee" (*The Tempest* V,i,95).

667. *dew at ooze from living blood:* See Ricks (118) on this periphrasis for the Indian Maid's sweat, who notes K.'s characteristic use of "ooze" previously associated with Cleopatra's Nile (I.820-1n.) and the "ooze-born goddess" (III.893). Cf. *Hyperion* I,137: "His Druid locks to shake and ooze with sweat."

668. *Whither didst melt?* The dusky Indian Maid naturally faded with the rising moon at IV.496-508. At IV.982-6 she will be transfigured by it.

670-721. Bush[4] views in the tradition of the pastoral "invitation to love," as in Polyphemus's wooing of Galatea in *Met.*

XIII,789f. Colvin (201) calls it a "pastoral fantasia" and cites, besides Ovid, Marlowe's *The Passionate Shepherd to His Love.* Both Patterson (81) and Evert (173) note the return of golden naturalistic imagery here.

658. *dew-claw'd:* dappled with dew.

691-6. *The rill . . . wells.* Cf. II.109-16 for a similar offering.

694. *squirrel's barn:* Patterson (82) notes that the "image is quite appropriately the same as the much-improved 'squirrel's granary' in the anti-daemonic opening lines of 'La Belle Dame Sans Merci,' where all is well in the world of men and things, in contrast to that of the pale knight. . ." Cf. "The squirrel's hoard" in *A Midsummer Night's Dream* IV,i,39.

701. *Vesta:* The Roman goddess of the hearth, to whom virgins were consecrated to keep her altar fires burning.

713-4. According to D'Avanzo (95), the Delphic gift from Cynthia of "Laws" and "color," i.e. meter and frenzy, becomes apparent if the reader sees her as a Delphic priestess uttering oracles in hexameters. See II.80-1n.

717-8. Cf. *King Lear* IV,iii,19-21 quoted in III.272-3n.

730. *feathered tyrant:* Cupid.

752-7. Ford[3] (70-1), connecting the Indian Maid's words here with those of Cynthia at II.761-824, infers that she is revealing her identity to the reader. Her mysterious refusal of Endymion's love, then, can be seen as stemming from Cynthia's inner conflict in Bk. II—her inability to renounce her public dedication to chastity. Evert (163), evidently attempting to account for her sudden change of mind at the climax of the poem, regards the Indian Maid's refusal of Endymion as an unnecessarily cryptic way of informing him that "she, *as* Indian Maid, can never be his," since "she will be his in her own person, as Cynthia." For whatever reason the Indian Maid refuses, there appears to be a taboo ("gorgon wrath") that must be lifted before she can be united with Endymion.

754. *gorgon wrath:* Cf. *Comus* 446-9:

> What was that snaky-headed Gorgon shield
> That wise Minerva wore, unconquered virgin,
> Wherewith she freezed her foes to congealed stone?
> But rigid looks of chaste austerity. . .

For Minerva as Cynthia's superego see II.789-804.

757. *Nor may I be thy love:* The Indian Maid's reply (cf. Raleigh's *The Nymph's Reply to the Shepherd*) to Endymion's somewhat forced pastoral proposal of the "Come live with me and be my love" sort (623-721).

764. *lovelorn, silent, wan:* Allott cites a similar grouping of epithets in *Hyperion* I,18: "nerveless, listless, dead."

769. *cirque:* circle; Wordsworthian. Cf. *Hyperion* II,34-5.

770-3. Murry (178) feels K. is not being disengenuous here, but actually has some psychological conflict that must be resolved before the story can flow onward to its destined end. For Patterson's argument that Endymion is never "ensky'd" and that "truth" prevails all the way, see IV.993-4n.

772. *Ensky'd:* Allott cites Lucio's flattering speech to Isabella in *Measure for Measure* I,iv,34: "I hold you as a thing ensky'd and sainted. . ."

774. *Thy lute-voic'd brother:* Apollo, the new-born god of *Hyperion*. For other possible indications of the poem to come, See II.994, III.129, 993f., IV.943, 956-7.

776-80. *Yes . . . tale.* Ende (97) compares Milton's elegaic mythic allusions to Ceres and Calliope (*P. L.* IV,268-71; VII,32-8), where mythic possibility is abandoned for a mortal perspective: "Keats responds to Endymion as though he were as undefended a son as Orpheus, and as if the myth culminated in the defeat of the desire to be sublimed. As a consequence, the poet is able to assume a posture identical to that of the figures that remained to face mortality in the 'pathetic' scenes he admires: on those widening, human shores stand Ceres and Calliope, and like them he 'on the brink of tears' acknowledges the inability of ecstasy and the sublime—the 'felicity' of timelessness and discontinuity—to console a human audience."

782-97. K.'s version of Wordsworth's recollection in tranquility, recalling the "sportive wood run wild" of his boyhood past. See I.881f. and III.142f. for similar motifs.

786. *first soft poppy dream:* Cf. I.555-67.

789-90. *The . . . charactery:* See II.62n. for the Shakespearean source.

792. *feared:* frightened.

798-9. *Why . . . sorrowing?* Ford[3] (82) interprets the Indian Maid's enigmatic smile as her foreknowledge of the ultimate joy succeeding Endymion's sorrow. But ambivalence of response seems to be part of the Indian Maid's nature: earlier she had wept "tears of sorrow" (725) at hearing Endymion voice his hopes of living a blissful life with her.

804-46. Peona emerges in a Wordsworthian manner following Endymion's boyhood reminiscences to welcome him back to his former role of leader and benefactor of his people.

819-20. *Perhaps . . . common day:* De Selincourt cites the Prospectus to *The Excursion* 52-5 as a deep influence here: "For the discerning intellect of Man, / When wedded to this goodly universe / In love and holy passion, shall find these / A simple produce of the common day."

827-33. Ford[3] (82) regards the augury of the Golden Age as a prefigurative vision granted to the soothsayers by Cynthia herself, and connects it with the "anticipated bliss" of the "contemplative" shepherds (cf. I.360-90).

849-63. Bush[4] regards as Endymion reverting back to his earlier idealism. Evert (163) believes K.'s strategy in doing this is very sound, for "while Endymion's affection for the earthly, signified by his choice of the Indian Maid, is a necessary culmination of the poem's whole progress, it must not be achieved at the cost of heaven's rejection, for the poem's whole argument is that the ideal is perceived only through the full appreciation of the real." Endymion's idealism here takes the form not of his idealistic love of the unknown goddess, but of celibate contemplation—the life he had unconvincingly vowed to lead in compliance with Peona's objections to his fanciful love (cf. I.975).

854. Endymion's apparent rejection of the Wordsworthian "natural piety" he had appeared to accept earlier (see IV.641n.).

857-64. Endymion appears to be setting himself up as a Delphian Apollo with Peona as his priestess.

877-8. A pagan version of Matt. 10.29, possibly by way of *Hamlet* V,ii,208-11: "we defy augury. There's special providence in the fall of a sparrow. If it be now, 'tis not to come; if it be not to come it will be now; if it be not now yet it will come. The readiness is all."

880-6. *Behold . . . Dian's sisterhood:* The typical fate of the romance heroine. The Indian Maid's vow of chastity matches Endymion's and is made with a similar lack of conviction. If we regard the Indian Maid as Cynthia in disguise, as Ford suggests, then the vow reconciles her inner conflict, though as a rationalization it ignores the source of the conflict. See IV.752-7n.

889-90. The three are dreamers in the sense of being manipulated by a will greater than their own. Knight (264) notes the intuition here of "people meeting each other in a sleep-world possessing its own independent laws of existence."

906. *cypress grove:* Traditionally sacred to Diana and generally funereal. K. may be implicitly associating chastity with death or the death-wish. For the dark heroine, such as Hermia in *A Midsummer Night's Dream,* chastity is a fate worse than death.

915. As K. always assures that the spiritual event has its natural correlative, the evening will provide the necessary setting for the rising moon, the naturalistic counterpart to the Indian Maid's metamorphosis into Phoebe.

927-33. "*Why . . . the last time.* According to Evert (174), Endymion's abandonment of his quest is allegorically "Keats's abandonment of poetry and hence there is acute point in questioning the utility of a 'golden eve.' " Cf. IV.957-61. Later, of course, the point becomes bitterly acute when K.'s illness forces him to abandon Fanny Brawne and poetry.

931. *breath:* Having renounced enchantment, Endymion is no longer "breathless" (see IV.655n.). Cf. Prospero's Epilogue to *The Tempest*: "Now my charms are all o'erthrown, / And what strength I have's my own, / Which is most faint."

934. *myriads of lingering leaves:* Possibly an unconscious recollection of Milton's simile likening the Fallen Angels to fallen leaves (cf. *P. L.* I,302-3). For "myriads" see IV.32-3n.

937. *butterfly:* See II.61n.

940. *My kingdom's at its death:* As an Adonis figure, Endymion would naturally die with the death of his "kingdom," nature (see I.178-84n.). Autumn was expected to be, however, not the death of summer, but its golden fruition—the season in which K. had hoped to end his poem "With universal tinge of sober gold" (I.56).

943. *Titan's foe:* Jove, the repressive force Endymion seems to view as governing his fate.

945. *deathful glee:* Knight (264) sees this mysterious state as part of the "unguessed and resolving unity" of the poem that ends Endymion's "labyrinthine quest, his bright and dusky voyages alike. . ."

950. *seemlihed:* seemliness; Spenserian.

953. *Rhadamanthus:* One of the judges of Hades, who, according to Virgil, "hears and chastens fraud" (cf. *Aeneid* VI,566-9).

955. Prometheus created man by animating clay with the fire he stole from heaven. He is the archetypal artist "cast out," bound and tortured by Jove, or his own sense of divine trespass.

956-7. Cf. *Hyperion* I,89-94. The number of mythical themes referred to this late in the poem suggests for Frye[6] (146-7) K.'s impatience to begin again with the story of Apollo.

957-61. *I did wed . . . impious.* Evert (174) sees here "Keats's own bitterness over what he takes to be the failure of the poem."

959. *lorn:* forlorn.

964-7. *for the choir . . . vesper hymn:* The sound of the rising moon before it appears. Probably the hymeneal song of IV.563-611.

970-1. *Wan as . . . spring.* Allott cites *The Winter's Tale* IV,iv,122-5: "pale prime-roses, / That die unmarried ere they can behold / Bright Phoebus in his strength (a malady / Most incident to maids)."

971. *chilly finger'd spring.* De Selincourt compares Collins, *How Sleep The Brave* 3: "Spring with dewy fingers cold."

982-7. The recognition scene, which Knight (264) compares with the recognition conclusions of Shakespeare's final plays. According to Patterson (93), "Cynthia does not supplant the Indian Maid and take her place; the Indian Maid simply takes on the radiant blue eyes and blond hair of Cynthia right here on earth. This way of handling the matter seems to imply that the maid retains within her being what she already represents and adds to it what Cynthia represents. . ." Frye[6] (145-6), comparing Phoebe's assumption with Poe's Ligeia, believes "The world of this final assumption is still continuous with the physical and sexual world, but has transformed it into a metamorphosis which goes in the opposite direction from those celebrated by Ovid." See IV.506-10n. for the Indian Maid's Ovidian metamorphosis. In *Hyperion*, K. speaks of "Nature's law" that breeds forth Olympian "eagles golden-feather'd" from Titanic "forest trees."

989-90. *but foolish fear . . . decrees of fate:* The stigma or blocking agent (cf. III.1023; IV.90), still rather engimatic, has at any rate been removed—the necessary condition for the marital climax of comedy. See Frye (293) on the mythic theme of taboos.

992. *unlooked for change:* As in Endymion's entrance into the Cave of Quietude (see IV.512-48n.), here, Frye[6] (145) remarks, "Endymion's quest cannot be completed by an act of will. That was why the Courtly Love tradition, although it demanded the most strenuous efforts from the poet-lover, still made his ultimate success depend on the grace of his lady."

993-4. *Be spiritualiz'd . . . forests:* Patterson (92) argues that Endymion needn't be "ensky'd" (772) in order to be "spiritualiz'd." He can be "spiritualiz'd" in this world by "perceiving the essence of earthly love through his 'self-destroying' love of the Indian Maid. It appears he will haunt the 'forests' of Diana rather than the skies of Cynthia." But given the oxymoronic nature of the "bourne of heaven," there is no reason we have to choose between heaven and earth, skies and trees. The "fellowship divine" of Cynthia and Endymion acts, like Pan or the nightingale of the ode, as protective genius of the forests, and yet is "Full alchemized, and free of space."

1001. *three swiftest kisses:* Suggest Endymion's recognition of Cynthia as the *diva triformis.* Unlike the "Threefold kiss" that provokes the young man in Blake's *The Crystal Cabinet* to willfully grasp after the "inmost Form" of his vision, here the kisses are the grace accompanying the destruction of Endymion's will, sealing his consummate union with Cynthia's "inmost Form."

1002. *They vanish'd far away.* According to Evert (164), "By the end of the poem, Endymion ceases to have any strong, individual identity and disappears from our consciousness as effectively as he vanishes from the Latmian scene. What remains, or is intended to remain, is an understanding of the process by which he was spiritualized." Bloom[3] (396), however, speaks for a number of critics in calling this "a mechanical end to the luxuriant, natural overgrowth of the poem, and probably the least satisfactory episode in the entire structure. Keats had resolved none of his inner conflicts, and one wonders at the appropriateness of the derived mythical material to the very personal synthesis Keats hoped to achieve." Yet Brisman[2] (66) notes that "those who find the conclusion . . . weak are objecting not to Keats's final touches but to the standard stuff of romance—what comes 'after' the music of truth that is more authentically Keats's own." Cf. the climax of *The Eve of St. Agnes:* "And they are gone: ay, ages long ago / These lovers fled away into the storm."

1002-3. *Peona went . . . in wonderment.* De Selincourt compares the phrasing in *I Stood Tip-toe* 141-2: "Psyche went / On the smooth wind to realms of wonderment." Colvin (204) remarks that "The poem ends on no such note of joy and triumph over the attained consummation as we might have expected and such as we found at the end of the third book. . . The fourth book closes, as it began, in a minor key, leaving the reader, like Peona, in a mood rather musing than rejoicing." See Bailey's comment in his letter to Taylor of May 20, 1818 (Rollins I,25), where he likens the rather "abrupt" conclusion here to that of *Paradise Regained.*

The Original Dedication and Preface*

Endymion,
a Romance

by John Keats—

The stretched metre of an antique song—
Shakespeare's Sonnets

Inscribed,
with every feeling of pride and regret,
and with "a bowed mind,"
To the memory of
The most english of Poets except Shakespeare,
Thomas Chatterton—

Preface

In a great nation, the work of an individual is of so little importance; his pleadings and excuses are so uninteresting; his "way of life" such a nothing; that a preface seems a sort of impertinent bow to Strangers who care nothing about it—

A preface however should be down in so many words; and such a one that by an eye glance over the type, the Reader may catch an idea of an Author's modesty, and non opinion of himself—which I sincerely hope may be seen in the few lines I have to write, notwithstanding certain proverbs of many ages' old which men find a great pleasure in receiving for gospel.

About a twelvemonth since, I published a little book of verses; it was read by some dozen of my friends, who lik'd it; and some dozen whom I was unqcquainted with, who did not. Now when a dozen human beings, are at words with another dozen, it becomes a matter of anxiety to side with one's friends;—more especially when excited thereto by a great love of Poetry.

I fought under disadvantages. Before I began I had no inward feel of being able to finish; and as I procedded my steps where all uncertain. So this Poem must rather be consider'd as an endeavour than a thing accomplish'd; a poor prologue to what, if I live, I humbly hope to do. In duty to the Public I should have kept it back for a year or two, knowing it to be so faulty; but I really cannot do so: —by repetition my favorite Passages sound vapid in my ears, and I would rather redeem myself with a new Poem —should this one be found of any interest.

I have to apologise to the lovers of Simplicity for touching the spell of Loveliness that hung about Endymion: if any of my lines plead for me with such people I shall be proud.

It has been too much the fashion of late to consider men biggotted and addicted to every word that may chance to escape their lips: now I here declare that I have not any particular affection for any particular phrase, word or letter in the whole affair. I have written to please myself and in hopes to please others, and for a love of fame; if I neither please myself, nor others nor get fame, of what consequence is Phraseology?

I would fain escape the bickerings that all Works, not exactly in chime, bring upon their begetters:—but this is not fair to expect, there must be conversation of some sort and to object shows a Man's consequence. In case of a London drizzle or a scotch Mist, the following quotation from Marston may perhaps stead me as an umbrella for an hour or so: "let it be the Curtesy of my peruser rather to pity my self hindering labours than to malice me."

One word more:—for we cannot help seeing our own affairs in every point of view—. Should any one call my dedication to Chatterton affected I answer as followeth: "Were I dead Sir I should like a Book dedicated to me"—

Teignmouth March 19th 1818—

---

* Keats sent the Preface on March 21, 1818, to his publisher, who (apparently through Reynolds) asked him to revise it. Reynolds evidently felt the Preface savored of Huntian "affectation," and Keats, unsettled by this, reluctantly and defensively agreed to rewrite it (see *Letters,* I,253; 266-67). Keats's two quotations ("a bowed mind" and "way of life") are, as Stillinger[2] notes, from the 1796-97 text of Coleridge's *Ode to the Departing Year* 6 and *Macbeth* V,iii,22 respectively.

Review in the *Champion**

Although this poem has very lately appeared, the short delay between its publication and our notice, was intentional. We are sincerely anxious for its ultimate success: we were willing that the age should do honour to itself by its reception of it; and cared little for having been the first to notice it. We were fearful, that if we ventured to decide on it, and could induce *the few* to take its consideration into their own hands, our great critical authorities would choose, as usual, to maintain an obstinate silence, or to speak slightingly, perhaps contemptuously, to keep up the etiquette; for they have a spice of Cicero, and "never follow any thing that other men begin." Neither have we now altered our opinion, but having seen more than one public notice of the work, do not choose longer to delay it. That the consequences will be pretty nearly as we predict we have little doubt. If the reviews play the sure game and say nothing, to nothing can we object; but if they really notice it, let us have something like a fair and liberal criticism—something that can be subjected to examination itself. Let them refer to principles: let them show us the philosophic construction of poetry, and point out its errors by instance and application. To this we shall not object: but this we must think they owe to Mr. Keats himself, and all those who have written and spoken highly of his talent. If however, they follow their old course, and having lacked the introduction of the first book, to the fag end of the last, swear the whole is an unintelligible jumble, we will at least exert ourselves to stop their chuckling and self congratulation.

We cannot, however, disguise from ourselves that the conduct that may be pursued by these reviews will have its

* Unsigned review, *Champion*, June 8, 1818, 362-4. Both Reynolds and Woodhouse have been nominated as the possible author.

influence, and a great influence, on public opinion: but, excepting as to the effect that opinion may have on the poet himself, we care not two straws for it. Public opinion is not a comprehensive or comprehending thing: it is neither a wit nor a wise man: a poet nor a philosopher: it is the veriest "king of shadows:" it is nothing but the hollow echoing of some momentary oracle: and if we estimate the work of the reviews themselves, we have it, for they are the things now in authority: they are your only substantials: they give currency to our poets: and what chance has an original genius that differs from all our poets, when nearly all our poets write for one or other of them. These men have it in their own hands, to meet out praise and censure, for half the population. We only hope they do not flatter themselves on the general assent: if they really mistake their popularity for immortality, they trick out an idiot in motley, and having stuck a Bartholomew trumpet in his hand, persuade themselves it is fame. But we do fear even public opinion from our knowledge of human nature. No man ever lived but he had a consciousness of his own power, and if he chose to make a fair estimate was perhaps a better judge than any other of his own ability. If then with this consciousness he find nothing in unison with his own feeling, no fair and liberal estimate made of his worth, no concessions made, no deference paid to him by the opinion that for the time passes current, he is driven by necessity upon his self-love for satisfaction, his indignation lashes his pride, he is unsupported by others were he has an undoubted assurance of being right, and he maintains those errors that have been justly objected against him, because they have been urged too far, and refuses to concede any thing because too much has been demanded. This, however, is a speculation, and we trust, it will remain so.

It is ever hazardous to predict the fate of a great original work; and of Endymion, all we dare venture in this way is an opinion, that an inferior poem is likely to excite: a more general interest. The secret of the success of our modern poets, is their universal presence in their poems—they give to every thing the colouring of their own feeling; and what a man has felt intensely—the impressions of actual existance—he is likely to describe powerfully: what he has felt we can easily sympathize with. But Mr. Keats goes out of himself into a world of abstractions:—his passions, feelings are all as much imaginative as his situations. Neither is it the mere outward signs of passions that are given: there seems ever present some being that was equally conscious of its internal and most secret imaginings. There is another objection to its ever becoming popular that it is, as the Venus and Adonis of Shakespeare, a *representation* and not a *description* of passion. Both these poems would, we think, be more generally admired had the poets been only veiled instead of concealed from us. Mr. Keats conceives the scene before him, and represents it as it appears. This is the excellence of dramatic poetry; but to feel its truth and power in any other, we must abandon our ordinary feeling and common consciousness, and identify ourselves with the scene. Few people can do this. In representation, which is the ultimate purpose of dramatic poetry, we should feel something of sympathy though we could merely observe the scene, or the gesticulation, and no sound could reach us: but to make an ordinary *reader* sensible of the excellence of a poem, he must be told what the poet felt; and he is affected by him and not by the scene. Our modern poets are the showmen of their own pictures, and point out its beauties.

Mr. Keats' very excellence, we fear, will tell against him. Each scene bears so actually the immediate impress of truth and nature, that it may be said to be local and peculiar, and to require some extrinsic feeling for its full enjoyment:—perhaps we are not clear in what we say. Every man then, according to his particular habit of mind, not only gives a correspondent colouring to all that surrounds him, but seeks to surround himself with corresponding objects, in which he has more than other people's enjoyment. In every thing then that art or nature may present to man, though gratifying to all, each man's gratification and sympathy will be regulated by the disposition and bent of his mind. Look at Milton's Sonnets. With what a deep and bitter feeling would a persecuted religious enthusiast select and dwell "On the late Massacre in Preniout." Has a social man no particular enjoyment in those to Laurence and Skynner? or a patriot in those to Fairfax, Cromwell, and Vane? What is common to humanity we are all readily sensible of, and all men proportioned to their intelligence, will receive pleasure on reading that on his birth day:—it wants nothing exclusive either in persons or age:—but would not a young and fearful lover find a thousand beauties in his address to the nightingale that must for ever escape the majority. In further illustration, we would adduce the first meeting of Endymion and Cynthia in the poem before us; which, though wonderfully told, we do not think most likely to be generally liked. It is so true to imagination, that passion absorbs every thing. Now, as we have observed, to transfer the mind to the situation of another, to feel as he feels, requires an enthusiasm, and an abstraction, beyond the power or the habit of most people. It is in this way eloquence differs from poetry, and the same speech on delivery affects people, than, on an after reading would appear tame and unimpassioned. We have certain sympathies with the person addressing us, and what he feels, we feel in an inferior degree; but he is afterwards to describe to us his passion; to make us feel by *telling us what he felt:* and this is to be done by calculating on the effect on *others* feelings, and not by abandoning ourselves to our own. If Mr. Keats can do this, he has not done it. When he writes of passion, it seems to have possessed him. This, however, is what Shakespeare did, and if Endymion bears any general resemblance to any other poem in the language, it is to Venus and Adonis on this very account. In the necessarily abrupt breaking off of this scene of intense passion, however, we think he has exceeded even his ordinary power. It is scarcely possible to conceive any thing more poetically imaginative; and though it may be brought in rather abruptly, we cannot refuse ourselves the pleasure of immediately extracting it. [Quotes II.827-53].

The objection we have here stated is equally applicable to the proper and full appreciation of many other beautiful scenes in this poem: but having acknowledged this, we shall extract the hymn to Pan, that our readers may be satisfied there are others to which universal assent must be given as among the finest specimens of classic poetry in our language. [Quotes I.232-62; 279-306].

We shall trespass a little beyond the hymn itself, and must then postpone our further observations.

Even while they brought the burthen to a close,
A shout from the whole multitude arose,
That lingered in the air like dying rolls,
Of abrupt thunder, *when Jonian shoals*
Of dolphins bob their noses through the brine.
Meantime, on shady levels, mossy fine,
Young companies nimbly began dancing
To the swift treble pipe, and humming string.

Aye, those fair living forms swam heavenly
To tunes forgotten—out of memory:
Fair creatures! whose young children's children bred,
Thermopylce its heroes—not yet dead,
But in old marbles every beautiful.

This last line is as fine as that in Shakespeare's Sonnets,

And beauty making beautiful old rhyme:

and there are not a dozen finer in Shakespeare's poems.

Croker's Attack in the *Quarterly Review**

Reviewers have been sometimes accused of not reading the works in which they affected to criticise. On the present occasion we shall anticipate the author's complaint, and honestly confess that we have not read his work. Not that we have been wanting in our duty—far from it—indeed, we have made efforts almost as superhuman as the story itself appears to be, to get through it; but with the fullest stretch of our perseverance, we are forced to confess that we have not been able to struggle beyond the first of the four books of which this Poetic Romance consists. We should extremely lament this want of energy, or whatever it may be, on our parts, were it not for one consolation—namely, that we are no better acquainted with the meaning of the book through which we have so painfully toiled, than we are with that of the three which we have not looked into.

It is not that Mr. Keats, (if that be his real name, for we almost doubt that any man in his senses would put his real name to such a rhapsody,) it is not, we say, that the author has not powers of language, rays of fancy, and gleams of

* Unsigned review, *Quarterly Review*, April, 1818 (published Sept., 1818), 204-8.

genius—he has all these; but he is unhappily a disciple of the new school of what has been somewhere called Cockney poetry; which may be defined to consist of the most incongruous ideas in the most uncouth language.

Of this school, Mr. Leigh Hunt, as we observed in a former Number, aspires to be the hierophant. Our readers will recollect the pleasant recipes for harmonious and sublime poetry which he gave us in his preface to 'Rimini,' and the still more facetious instances of his harmony and sublimity in the verses themselves; and they will recollect above all the contempt of Pope, Johnson, and such like poetasters and pseudo-critics, which so forcibly contrasted itself with Mr. Leigh Hunt's self-complacent approbation of

——' all the things itself had wrote,
Of special merit though of little note.'

This author is a copyist of Mr. Hunt; but he is more unintelligible, almost as rugged, twice as diffuse, and ten times more tiresome and absurd than his prototype, who, though he impudently presumed to seat himself in the chair of criticism, and to measure his own poetry by his own standard, yet generally had a meaning. But Mr. Keats had advanced no dogmas which he was bound to support by examples; his nonsense therefore is quite gratuitous; he writes it for its own sake, and being bitten by Mr. Leigh Hunt's insane criticism, more than rivals the insanity of his poetry.

Mr. Keats's preface hints that his poem was produced under peculiar circumstances.

'Knowing within myself (he says) the manner in which this Poem has been produced, it is not without a feeling of regret that I make it public.—What manner I mean, will be *quite clear* to the reader, who must soon perceive great inexperience, immaturity, and every error denoting a feverish attempt, rather than a deed accomplished.'—*Preface,* p. vii.

We humbly beg his pardon, but this does not appear to us to be *quite so clear*—we really do not know what he means—but the next passage is more intelligible.

'The two first books, and indeed the two last, I feel sensible are not of such completion as to warrant their passing the press.'—*Preface,* p. vii.

Thus 'the two first books' are, even in his own judgment,

unfit to appear, and 'the two last' are, it seems, in the same condition—and as two and two make four, and as that is the whole number of books, we have a clear and, we believe, a very just estimate of the entire work.

Mr. Keats, however, deprecates criticism on this 'immature and feverish work' in terms which are themselves sufficiently feverish; and we confess that we should have abstained from inflicting upon him any of the tortures of the '*fierce hell*' of criticism, which terrify his imagination, if he had not begged to be spared in order that he might write more; if we had not observed in him a certain degree of talent which deserves to be put in the right way, or which, at least, ought to be warned of the wrong; and if, finally, he had not told us that he is of an age and temper which imperiously require mental discipline.

Of the story we have been able to make out but little; it seems to be mythological, and probably relates to the loves of Diana and Endymion; but of this, as the scope of the work has altogether escaped us, we cannot speak with any degree of certainty; and must therefore content ourselves with giving some instances of its diction and versification:—and here again we are perplexed and puzzled.—At first it appeared to us, that Mr. Keats had been amusing himself and wearying his readers with an immeasurable game at *boutsrimés;* but, if we recollect rightly, it is an indispensable condition at this play, that the rhymes when filled up shall have a meaning; and our author, as we have already hinted, has no meaning. He seems to us to write a line at random, and then he follows not the thought excited by this line, but that suggested by the *rhyme* with which it concludes. There is hardly a complete couplet inclosing a complete idea in the whole book. He wanders from one subject to another, from the association, not of ideas but of sounds, and the work is composed of hemistichs which, it is quite evident, have forced themselves upon the author by the mere force of the catchwords on which they turn.

We shall select, not as the most striking instance, but as that least liable to suspicion, a passage from the opening of the poem.

———' Such the sun, the moon,
Trees old and young, sprouting a shady boon
For simple sheep; and such are daffodils
With the green world they live in; and clear rills

That for themselves a cooling covert make
'Gainst the hot season; the mid forest brake,
Rich with a sprinkling of fair musk-rose blooms:
And such too is the grandeur of the dooms
We have imagined for the mighty dead; &c. &c.'—pp. 3,4.

Here it is clear that the word, and not the idea, *moon* produces the simple sheep and their shady *boon,* and that 'the *dooms* of the mighty dead' would never have intruded themselves but for the '*fair musk-rose blooms.*'

Again.

'For 'twas the morn: Apollo's upward fire
Made every eastern cloud a silvery pyre
Of brightness so unsullied, that therein
A melancholy spirit well might win
Oblivion, and melt out his essence fine
Into the winds: rain-scented eglantine
Gave temperate sweets to that well-wooing sun;
The lark was lost in him; cold springs had run
To warm their chilliest bubbles in the grass;
Man's voice was on the mountains; and the mass
Of nature's lives and wonders puls'd tenfold,
To feel this sun-rise and its glories old.'—p. 8.

Here Apollo's *fire* produces a *pyre,* a silvery pyre of clouds, *wherein* a spirit might *win* oblivion and melt his essence *fine,* and scented *eglantine* gives sweet to the *sun,* and cold springs had *run* into the *grass*, and then the pulse of the *mass* pulsed *tenfold* to feel the glories *old* of the new-born day, &c.

One example more.

'Be still the unimaginable lodge
For solitary thinkings; such as dodge
Conception to the very bourne of heaven,
Then leave the naked brain: be still the leaven,
That spreading in this dull and clodded earth
Gives it a touch ethereal—a new birth.'—p. 17.

Lodge, dodge—heaven, leaven—earth, birth; such, in six words, is the sum and substance of six lines.

We come now to the author's taste in versification. He

cannot indeed write a sentence, but perhaps he may be able to spin a line. Let us see. The following are specimens of his prosodial notions of our English heroic metre.

'Dear as the temple's self, so does the moon,
The passion poesy, glories infinite.'—p. 4.
'So plenteously all weed-hidden roots.'—p. 6.
'Of some strange history, potent to send.'—p. 18.
'Before the deep intoxication.'—p. 27.
'Her scarf into a fluttering pavilion.'—p. 33.
'The stubborn canvas for my voyage prepared——.'—p. 39.
' "Endymion! the cave is secreter
Than the isle of Delos. Echo hence shall stir
No sighs but sigh-warm kisses, or light noise
Of thy combing hand, the while it travelling cloys
And trembles through my labyrinthine hair." '—p. 48.

By this time our readers must be pretty well satisfied as to the meaning of his sentences and the structure of his lines: we now present them with some of the new words with which, in imitation of Mr. Leigh Hunt, he adorns our language.

We are told that 'turtles *passion* their voices.' (p. 15); that 'an arbour was *nested*,' (p. 23); and a lady's locks *'gordian'd* up,' (p. 32); and to supply the place of the nouns thus verbalized Mr. Keats, with great fecundity, spawns new ones; such as 'men-slugs and human *serpentry*,' (p. 41); the *'honey-feel* of bliss,' (p. 45); 'wives prepare *needments*,' (p. 13)—and so forth.

Then he has formed new verbs by the process of cutting off their natural tails, the adverbs, and affixing them to their foreheads; thus, 'the wine out-sparkled,' (p. 10); the 'multitude up-followed,' (p. 11); and 'night up-took,' (p. 29). 'The wind up-blows,' (p. 32); and the 'hours are down-sunken,' (p. 36).

But if he sinks some adverbs in the verbs he compensates the language with adverbs and adjectives which he separates from the parent stock. Thus, a lady 'whispers *pantingly* and close,' makes *'hushing* signs,' and steers her skiff into a *'ripply* cove,' (p. 23); a shower falls *'refreshfully*,' (p. 45); and a vulture has a *'spreaded* tail,' (p. 44).

Reynold's Reply to Croker in the *Examiner**

LITERARY NOTICES.

A manly and judicious letter, signed J. S. appeared in the *Morning Chronicle* the other day, respecting the article in the *Quarterly Review* on the *Endymion* of the young poet Mr. Keats. It is one of several public animadversions, which that half-witted, half-hearted Review has called indignantly forth on the occasion. "This is the hastily-written tribute," says the writer, "of a stranger, who ventures to predict that Mr. K. is capable of producing a poem that shall challenge the admiration of every reader of true taste and feeling; may, if he will give up his acquaintance with Mr. Leigh Hunt, and apostatise in his friendships, his principles, and his politics (if he have any), he may even command the approbation of the *Quarterly Review*."—We really believe so; but Mr. Keats is of a spirit which can afford to dispense with such approbation, and stand by his friend. We should have given the whole of this letter, but we have since met with another in the *Alfred Exeter* paper, which is more elaborate on the subject; and we have not room for both.

THE QUARTERLY REVIEW.—MR KEATS.

We have met with a singular instance, in the last number of the *Quarterly Review*, of that unfeeling arrogance, and cold ignorance, which so strangely marked the minds and hearts of Government sycophants and Government writers. The Poem of a young man of genius, which evinces more natural power than any other work of this day, is abused and cried down, in

---

* Unsigned review, *Examiner*, Oct. 11, 1818, 648-9.

terms which would disgrace any other pens than those used in the defence of an *Oliver* or a *Castles.* We have read the poetic romance of *Endymion* (the book in question) with no little delight; and could hardly believe that it was written by so young a man as the preface infers. Mr. Keats, the author of it, is a genius of the highest order; and no one but a Lottery Commissioner and a Government Pensioner, (both of which, Mr. William Gifford, the Editor of the *Quarterly Review,* is) could, with a false and remorseless pen, have striven to frustrate hopes and aims, so youthful and so high as this young Poet nurses. The Monthly Reviewers, it will be remembered, endeavoured, some few years back, to crush the rising heart of Kirk White; and indeed they in part generated that melancholy which ultimately destroyed him; but the world saw the cruelty, and, with one voice, hailed the genius which malignity would have repressed, and lifted it to fame. Reviewers are creatures that "stab men in the dark:"—young and enthusiastic spirits are their dearest prey. Our readers will not easily forget the brutality with which the Quarterly Reviewers, in a late number of their ministerial book, commented on the work of an intelligent and patriotic woman, whose ardour and independence happened to be high enough to make them her enemies. The language used by these Government critics, was lower than man would dare to utter to female ears; but Party knows no distinctions,—no proprieties,—and a woman is the best of prey for its malignity, because it is the gentlest and the most undefended. We certainly think that criticism might vent its petty passions on other subjects; that it might chase its objects from the vain, the dangerous, and the powerful, and not from the young and the unprotected.

> "It should strike hearts of age and care,
> And spare the youthful and the fair."

The cause of the unmerciful condemnation which has been passed on Mr. Keats, is pretty apparent to all who have watched the intrigues of literature, and the wily and unsparing contrivances of political parties. This young and powerful writer was noticed some little time back in the *Examiner,* and pointed out, by its Editor, as one who was likely to revive the early vigour of English poetry. Such a prediction was a fine but dangerous compliment to Mr. Keats: it exposed him instantly to the malice of the *Quarterly Review.* Certain it is, that hundreds of fashionable and flippant readers will henceforth set down this young poet as a pitiable and nonsensical writer, merely on the assertions of some single heartless critic, who has just energy enough to despise what is good, because it would militate against his pleasantry, if he were to praise it.

The genius of Mr. Keats is peculiarly classical; and, with the exception of a few faults, which are the natural followers of youth, his imaginations and his language have a spirit and an intensity which we should in vain look for in half the popular poets of the day. Lord Byron is a splendid and noble egotist: he visits classical shores; roams over romantic lands, and wanders through magnificent forests; courses the dark and restless waves of the sea, and rocks his spirit on the midnight lakes; but no spot is conveyed to our minds that is not peopled by the gloomy and ghastly feelings of one proud and solitary man. It is as if he and the world were the only two things which the air clothed. His lines are majestic vanities;—his poetry always is marked with a haughty selfishness;—he writes loftily, because he is the spirit of an ancient family;—he is liked by most of his readers, because he is a Lord. If a common man were to dare to be as moody, as contemptuous, and as misanthropical, the world would laugh at him. There must be a coronet marked on all his little pieces of poetical insolence, or the world would not countenance them. Mr. Keats has none of this egotism—this daring selfishness, which is a stain on the robe of poesy. His feelings are full, earnest, and original, as those of the older writers were and are; they are made for all time, not for the drawing-room and the moment. Mr. Keats always speaks of, and describes nature, with an awe and a humility, but with a deep and almost breathless affection.—He knows that Nature is better and older than he is, and he does not put himself on an equality with her. You do not see him when you see her. The moon, and the mountainous foliage of the woods, and the azure sky, and the ruined and magic temple; the rock, the desart, and the sea; the leaf of the forest, and the embossed foam of the most living ocean, are the spirits of his poetry; but he does not bring them in his own hand, or obtrude his person before you, when you are looking at them. Poetry is a thing of generalities—a wanderer amid persons and things—not a pauser over one thing, or with one person. The mind of Mr. Keats, like the minds of our older poets, goes round the universe in its speculations and its dreams. It does

not set itself a task. The manners of the world, the fictions and the wonders of other worlds, are its subjects: not the pleasures of hope, or the pleasures of memory. The true poet confine's his imagination to no one thing—his soul is an invisible ode to the passions.—He does not make a home for his mind in one land—its productions are an universal story, not an eastern tale. The fancies of Moore are exquisitely beautiful, as fancies, but they are always of one colour;—his feelings are pathetic, but they are "still harping on my daughter." The true pathetic is to be found in the reflections on things, not in the moods and miseries of one person. There is not one poet of the present day, that enjoys any popularity that will live; each writes for his booksellers and the ladies of fashion, and not for the voice of centuries. Time is a lover of old books, and he suffers few new ones to become old. Posterity is a difficult mark to hit; and few minds can send the arrow full home. Wordsworth might have safely cleared the rapids in the stream of time, but he lost himself by looking at his own image in the waters. Coleridge stands bewildered in the cross-road of fame;—his genius will commit suicide, and he buried in it. Southey is Poet Laureate, "so there is no heed in he taken of him." Campbell has relied on two stools, "*The Pleasures of Hope,*" and "*Gertrude of Wyoming*;" but he will come to the ground, after the fashion of the old proverb. The journey of fame is an endless one; and does Mr. Rogers think that pumps and silk stockings (which has genius wears) will last him the whole way? Poetry is the coyest creature that ever was wooed by man: she is something of the coquet in her; for she flirts with many, and seldom loves one.

Mr. Keats has certainly not perfected any thing yet; but he has the power, we think, within him, and it is in consequence of such an opinion that we have written these few hasty observations. If he should ever see this, he will not regret to find that all the country is not made up of Quarterly Reviewers. All that we wish is, that our readers would read the Poem, as we have done, before they assent to its condemnation—they will find passages of singular feeling, force, and pathos. We have the highest hopes of this young Poet. We are obscure men, it is true, and not gifted with perilous power of mind, and truth of judgment, which are possessed by Mr. Croker, Mr. Canning, Mr. Barrow, or Mr. Gifford, (all "honourable men," and writers in the *Quarterly Review.*) We live far from the world of letters,—out of the pale of fashionable criticism,—aloof from the atmosphere of a Court; but we are surrounded by a beautiful country, and love Poetry, which we read out of doors, as well as in. We think we see glimpses of a high mind in this young man, and surely the feeling is better that urges us to nourish its strength, than that which prompts the Quarterly Reviewer to crush it in its youth, and for ever. If however the mind of Mr. Keats be of the quality we think it to be of, it will not be cast down by this wanton and empty attack. Malice is a thing of the scorpion kind—it drives the sting into its own heart. The very passages which the *Quarterly Review* quotes as ridiculous, have in them the beauty that sent us to the Poem itself. We shall close these observations with a few extracts from the romance itself:—If our readers do not see the spirit and beauty in them to justify our remarks, we confess ourselves bad judges, and never more worthy to be trusted.

The following address to Sleep is full of repose and feeling:—

"O magic sleep! O comfortable bird,
That broodest o'er the troubled sea of the mind,
Till it is hush'd and smooth! O unconfined
Restraint! Imprisoned Liberty I Great key
To golden palaces, strange minstrelsy,
Fountains grotesque, new trees, bespangled caves,
Echoing grottoes, full of tumbling waves,
And moonlight!"

This is beautiful—but here is something finer:—

"——That men, who might have tower'd in the van
Of all the congregated world, to fan
And winnow from the coming step of time
All chaff of custom, wipe away all slime
Left by men slugs and human serpentry,
Have been content to let occasion die,
Whilst they did sleep in Love's Elysium.
And truly I would rather be struck dumb,
Than speak against this ardest listlessness:
For I have ever thought that it might bless
The world with benefits unknowingly;
As does the nightingale up-perched high,

And cloister'd among cool and bunched leaves,
She sings but to her love, nor e'er conceives
How tip-toe Night holds back her dark-grey hood."

The turn of this is truly Shakespearian, which Mr. Keats will feel to be the highest compliment we can pay him, if we know any thing of his mind. We cannot refrain from giving the following short passage, which appears to us scarcely to be surpassed in the whole range of English Poetry. It has all the naked and solitary vigour of old sculpture, with all the energy and life of old poetry:—

"———At this, with madden'd stare,
And lifted hands, and trembling lips, he stood,
Like old Deucalion mounted o'er the flood,
Or blind Orion hungry for the morn."

Again, we give some exquisitely classic lines, clear and reposing as a Grecian sky—soft and lovely as the waves of Ulyssus:—

"———Here is wine,
Alive with sparkles.—Never, I aver,
Since Ariadne was a vintager,
So cool a purple; taste those juicy pears,
Sent me by sad Vertumnus, when his fears
Were high about Pomona: here is cream,
Deepening to sickness from a snowy gleam;
Sweeter than that nurse Amalthea skimm'd
For the boy Jupiter."

This is the very fruit of poetry,—a melting repast for the imagination. We can only give one more extract—our limits are reached. Mr. Keats is speaking of the story of *Endymion* itself. Nothing can be more imaginative than what follows:—

"—————Ye who have yearn'd
With too much passion, will here stay and pity,
For the mere sake of truth; as 'tis a ditty
Not of these days, but long ago 'twas told
By a cavern'd wind unto a forest old;
And then the forest told it in a dream

> To a sleeping lake, whose cool and level gleam
> A Poet caught as he was journeying
> To Phoebus' shrine; and in it he did fling
> His weary limbs, bathing an hour's space,
> And after, straight in that inspired place
> He sang the story up into the air,
> Giving it universal freedom."

We have no more room for extracts. Does the author of such poetry as this deserve to be made the sport of so servile a dolt as a Quarterly Reviewer?—No. Two things have struck us on the persual of this singular poem. The first is, that Mr. Keats excels, in what Milton excelled—the power of putting a spirit of life and novelty into the Heathen Mythology. The second is, that in the structure of his verse, and the *sinewy* quality of his thoughts, Mr. Keats greatly resembles old Chapman, the nervous translator of Homer. His mind has "thews and limbs like to its ancestors." Mr. Gifford, who knows something of the old dramatists, ought to have paused before he sanctioned the abuse of a spirit kindred with them. If he could not feel, he ought to know better.

Patmore's Review in the *London Magazine**

That the periodical criticism of the present day, as criticism, enjoys but a slender portion of public respect,—except among mere bookbuyers and blue-stockings,—cannot be denied. It would be unjust not to confess that it has its uses. But, in

* *London Magazine*, April, 1820, 380-90. The most perceptive of the replies to the attacks of *Endymion.* Patmore recognizes the nature of dream-work in *Endymion,* suggests that a new concept of what constitutes a poem is needed, and asserts that the good and bad qualities of Keats's style "are inextricably linked together."

return, it has its reward. The public, and public critics, mutually serve and despise each other; and if both, for the most part, know that this is the case, the latter are too politic to complain of injustice, and the former too indolent to resent it. Each party is content to accept the evil with the good.

But a feeling much stronger than that of contempt has attached itself to this part of the public press, in consequence of certain attempts of modern criticism to blight and wither the maturity of genius; or—still worse—to change its youthful enthusiasm into despair, and thus tempt it to commit suicide; or—worst of all—to creep to its cradle, and strangle it in the first bloom and beauty of its childhood. To feel that all this has been attempted, and most of it effected, by modern criticism, we need only pronounce to ourselves the names of Chatterton and Kirke White among the dead, of Montgomery, and Keats, and Wordsworth among the living;—not to mention Byron, Shelley, Hunt, &c. It is only necessary to refer, in particular, to the first four of these names; for the others, with an equal share of poetic "ambition," have less of "the illness does attend it;"—less of its over-refined and morbid sensibility.

The miraculous boy, Chatterton, might have been alive, glorying in, and glorifying himself, his country, and his age, at this day, if he had not encountered a shallow-thoughted and cold-blooded critic: for though he was one of the true "children of the sun" of poetry, his more than human power was linked to more than human weakness. Poor Kirke White, too! different as they were in almost every thing—the one a star, the other a flower—yet both received their light and beauty from the same sun, and both participated in the same fate. To think that the paltry drudge of a bookseller should be permitted to trample in the dirt of a review such an amaranthine flower as this—worthy as it was, to have bloomed in the very Eden of Poetry!—And what had the brilliant, and witty, and successful creator of a new era in criticism to do with the plainitive and tender Montgomery?—If he was too busy or too happy to discover any music in sighs, or any beauty in tears, at least he might have been too philosophical, or too good-natured, to laugh at them. Suppose the poet did indulge a little too much in the "luxury of grief,"—if it was weakness, at least it was not hypocrisy; and there was small chance of its infecting either the critic or his readers—so that he exhibited little either of skill or courage in going out of his way to pick a quarrel with it. The poet, with all his fine powers, has scarcely yet recovered from the effects of that visitation; and the critic, with all his cleverness, never will.

It would lead us too far from our present purpose,—and indeed does not belong to it,—to do more than refer to the exploits of the same work against the early attempts of the two writers who at present share the poetic throne of the day. Whatever else they might want, these attacks had at least boldness; and they could do little mischief, for the objects of them were armed at all points against the assault. It is not to these latter, but to such as those on Kirke White and Montgomery, and a late one on the work which we are about to notice, that the periodical criticism of the day owes that resentment and indignation which is at present felt against it, by the few whose praise (in matters of literature) is not censure. To make criticism subservient to pecuniary or ambitious views is poor and paltry enough; but there is some natural motive, and therefore some excuse, for this: but to make it a means of depressing true genius, and defrauding it of its dearest reward—its fair fame—is unnaturally, because it is gratuitously, wicked. It is a wickedness, however, that might safely be left to work out its own punishment, but that its anonymous off-spring too frequently do their mischievous bidding for a time, and thus answer the end of their birth.

In thinking of these things we are tempted to express an opinion which perhaps it would be more prudent to keep to ourselves,—viz. that poetical criticism is, for the most part, a very superfluous and impertinent business; and is to be tolerated at all only when it is written in an unfeigned spirit of admiration and humility. We must therefore do ourselves the justice to disclaim, for once, any intention of writing a regular critique in the present instance. Criticism, like every thing else, is very well in its place; but, like every thing else, it does not always know where that is. Certainly a poet, properly so called, is beyond its jurisdiction;—for *good* and *bad*, when applied to poetry, are words without a meaning. One might as well talk of good or bad virtue. That which *is* poetry must be good. It may differ in kind and in degree, and therefore it may differ in value; but if it *be* poetry, it is a thing about which criticism has no concern, any more than it has with other of the highest productions of Fine Art. The sublimities of Michael Angelo are beyond the reach of its ken—the divine forms of Raphael were not made to be meddled with by is unhallowed fingers—the ineffable expressions of Corregio must not be sullied by its earthy breath. These things were given to the world for something better than to be written and talked about; and they have done their bidding hitherto, and will do it till they cease to exist. They have opened a perpetual spring of lofty thoughts and pure meditations; they have blended themselves with the very existence, and become a living principle in the hearts of mankind;—and they are, now, no more fit to be touched and tampered with than the stars of heaven—for like them

Levan di terra al cielo nostr' intelletto.

We will not shrink from applying these observations, prospectively, to the young poet whose work we are about to notice. Endymion, if it be not, technically speaking, a poem, is poetry itself. As a *promise,* we know of nothing like it, except some things of Chatterton. Of the few others that occur to us at the moment, the most remarkable are Pope's Pastorals, and his Essay on Criticism;—but these are proofs of an extraordinary precocity, not of genius, but of taste, as the word was understood in his day; and of a remarkably early acquaintance with all the existing common-places of poetry and criticism. It is true that Southey's Joan of Arc, and Campbell's Pleasures of Hope, were both produced before their authors were one-and-twenty. But Joan of Arc, though a fine poem, is diffuse, not from being rich, but from being diluted; and the Pleasures of Hope is a delightful work—but then it *is* a work—and one cannot help wishing it had been written at thirty instead of twenty.

Endymion is totally unlike all these, and all other poems. As we said before, it is not a *poem* at all. It is an ecstatic dream of poetry—a flush—a fever—a burning light—an involuntary outpouring of the spirit of poetry—that will not be controuled. Its movements are the starts and boundings of the young horse before it has felt the bitt—the first flights of the young bird, feeling and exulting in the powers with which it is gifted, but not yet acquainted with their use or their extent. It is the wanderings of the butterfly in the first hour of its birth; not as yet knowing one flower from another, but only that all *are* flowers. Its similitudes come crowding upon us from all delightful things. It is the May-day of poetry—the flush of blossoms and weeds that start up at the first voice of spring.

It is the sky-lark's hymn to the day-break, involuntarily gushing forth as he mounts upward to look for the fountain of that light which has awakened him. It is as if the muses had steeped their child in the waters of Castaly, and we beheld him emerging from them, with his eyes sparkling and his limbs quivering with the delicious intoxication, and the precious drops scattered from him into the air at every motion, glittering in the sunshine, and casting the colours of the rainbow on all things around.

Almost entirely unknown as this poem is to general readers, it will perhaps be better to reserve what we have further to say of its characteristics, till we have given some specimens of it. We should premise this, however, by saying, that our examples will probably exhibit almost as many faults as beauties. But the reader will have anticipated this from the nature of the opinion we have already given—at least if we have succeeded in expressing what we intended to express. In fact, there is scarcely a passage of any length in the whole work, which does not exhibit the most glaring faults—faults that in many instances amount almost to the ludicrous: yet positive and palpable as they are, it may be said of them generally, that they are as much collateral evidences of poetical power, as the beauties themselves are direct ones. If the poet had had time, or patience, or we will even say taste, to have weeded out these faults as they sprang up, he could not have possessed the power to create the beauties to which they are joined. If he had waited to make the first half dozen pages of his work faultless, the fever—the ferment of mind in which the whole was composed would have subsided for ever. Or if he had attempted to pick out those faults afterwards, the beauties must inevitably have gone with them—for they are inextricably linked together.

The title of Endymion will indicate the subject of it. It is, in one word, the story of the mutual loves of Endymion and the Moon,—including the trials and adventures which the youthful shepherd was destined to pass through, in order to prepare and fit him for the immortality to which he at least succeeds.

It is not part of our plan to follow the poet and his hero—for they go hand in hand together—through their adventures; for, as a tale, this work is nothing. There is no connecting interest to bind one part of it to another. Almost any two parts of it might be transposed, without disadvantage to either, or to the whole. We repeat, it is not a poem, but a dream of poetry;

and while many of its separate parts possess that vivid distinctness which frequently belongs to the separate parts of a dream, the impression it leaves as a whole is equally indistinct and confused.—The poet begins by noticing the delightful associations we are accustomed to attach to beautiful thoughts and objects, and continues,

—————therefore 'tis that I
Will trace the story of Endymion.
The very music of his name has gone
Into my being.

Then, after dallying a little with the host of beautiful images which are conjured up by that name, he exclaims

And now at once, adventuresome, I send
My hearld thought into a wilderness.

These two lines are very characteristic. It is the bold boy plunging for the first time into the stream, without knowing or caring whither it may carry him. The story, such as it is, commences with the description of a procession and festival, in honour of the god Pan. The following are parts of this description: [Quotes I.107-121; 135-152].

After these comes Endymion, the "Shepherd Prince."

A smile was on his countenance; he seem'd,
To common lookers on, like one who dream'd
Of idleness in groves Elysian:
But there were some who feelingly could scan
A lurking trouble in his nether lip,
And see that oftentimes the reins would
slip
Through his forgotten hands.

The following are parts of a hymn to Pan, sung by a chorus of shepherds. We direct the reader's attention to the imagery as well as the rhythm of these extracts in particular. They are, likewise, almost entirely free from the writer's characteristic faults. [Quotes I.232-46; 279-92].

After this hymn the sports begin, and—

————————They danc'd to weariness,
And then in quiet circles did they press
The hillock turf, and caught the latter end
Of some strange history, potent to send
A young mind from its bodily tenement.

The love-stricken Endymion cannot partake in the sports, but is led, by his sister Peona, to her own favourite bower, where

Soon was he quieted to slumbrous rest:
But, ere it crept upon him, he had prest
Peona's busy hand against his lips,
And still, a sleeping, held her finger-tips
In tender pressure. And as a willow keeps
A patient watch over the stream that creeps
Windingly by it, so the quiet maid
Held her in peace: so that a whispering
    blade
Of grass, a wailful gnat, a bee bustling
Down in the blue-bells, or a wren light
    rustling
Among sere leaves and twigs, might all be
    heard.

Nothing can be more exquisitely beautiful than this—nothing more lulling-sweet than the melody of it.—And let us here, once for all, direct the readers' attention to the rhythm of the various extracts we lay before them; and add that, upon the whole, it combines more freedom, sweetness, and variety than are to be found in that of any other long poem written in the same measure, without any exception whatever. In the course of more than four thousand lines it never cloys by sameness, and never flags. To judge of the comparative extent of this praise, turn at random to Pope's Homer, or even Dryden's Virgil, and read two or three pages. Sweetness and variety of music in the versification of a young writer, are among the most authentic evidences of poetical power. These qualities are peculiarly conspicuous in Shakespeare's early poems of Lucrece, and Venus and Adonis. It should be mentioned, however, that in the work before us, these qualities seem to result from—what shall we say?—a fine natural ear?—from any thing, however, rather than system—for the verse frequently runs riot, and loses itself in air. It is the music of the happy wild-bird in the woods—not of the poor caged piping-bullfinch.

The following description of the impressions Endymion receives from various external objects,—on awakening from an Elysian dream of love, and finding that it was *but* a dream,—is finely passionate and natural: [Quotes I.682-705] .

Peona succeeds in rousing her brother from the listless trance into which he has fallen, and he again feels the true dignity of his being, and its mysterious bridal with the external forms and influences of Nature. The following strikes us as being exceedingly fine, notwithstanding some obvious faults in the diction.—It is the very faith, the religion, of imaginative passion.

> ————————Hist, when the airy stress
> Of music's kiss impregnates the free winds,
> And with a sympathetic touch unbinds
> Eolian magic from their lucid wombs:
> Then old songs waken from enclouded
>   tombs;
> Old ditties sigh above their father's grave;
> Ghosts of melodious prophecyings rave
> Round every spot where trod Apollo's foot;
> Bronze clarions awake, and faintly bruit,
> Where long ago a giant battle was;
> And, from the turf, a lullaby doth pass
> In every place where infant Orpheus slept.
> Feel we these things?—that moment have
>   we stept
> Into a sort of oneness, and our state
> Is like a floating spirit's.

They who do not find poetry in this, may be assured that they will look for it in vain elsewhere.—At the end of the first book, Endymion confides the secret of his mysterious passion, and all the circumstances attending it, to his sister Peona; and at the beginning of the second book we find him wandering about, without end or aim,

> Through wilderness, and woods of mossed
>   oaks;
> Counting his woe-worn minutes, by the

strokes
Of the lone wood-cutter;

till at length he meets with a winged messenger, who seems commissioned from heaven to direct his steps; and who leads him

Through buried paths, where sleepy twilight
dreams
The summer time away. One track un-
seams
A wooded cleft, and, far away, the blue
Of ocean fades upon him; then, anew,
He sinks adown a solitary glen,
Where there was never sound of mortal
men,
Saving, perhaps, some snow-light cadences
Melting to silence, when upon the breeze
Some holy bark let forth an anthem sweet,
To cheer itself to Delphi.

"Snow-light cadences," &c. may be a little fantastical, perhaps; but it is very delicate and poetical, nevertheless. The passage in italics is also very still and lonely.—The following delightful little picture of cool quietude is placed in contrast to the restless fever of Endymion's thoughts, when his winged conductor leaves him:—

Hereat, she vanished from Endymion's
gaze,
Who brooded o'er the water in amaze:
The dashing fount poured on, and where
its pool
Lay, half asleep, in grass and rushes cool,
Quick waterflies and gnats were sporting
still,
And fish were dimpling, as if good nor ill
Had fallen out that hour.

After this he yields up his whole soul to the dominion of passion and imagination, and they at last burst forth with an ecstatic address to his unearthly mistress, the moon—though he does not yet know her as such. The latter part of this address follows: and amidst numerous faults, both of thought and diction, the reader will not fail to detect much beauty. In the picture which follows the close of this address there is great power, and even sublimity. [Quotes II.179-98].

At this moment a caverned voice is heard, bidding the young lover descend into the hollows of the earth; and adding

————He ne'er is crown'd
With immortality who fears to follow
Where airy voices lead.

From this time Endymion quits the surface of the earth, and passes through a multitude of strange adventures in "the sparry hollows of the world," and in the other mysterious regions of the air, the sea, and the sky—meeting, in the course of his journeyings, with Glacus and Sylla, Alpheus and Arethusa, Adonis, &c. part of whose stories are related. Till at length, having fulfilled the measure of his destinies, we find him once more on the earth, and near his own home; where, after an interview with his sister Peona, his immortal mistress appears to him under her proper form, and they ascend the sky together.

It will be seen that here is a rich fund of materials, fitted for almost every variety and degree of poetical power to work upon. And if the young builder before us has not erected from them a regular fabric, which will bear to be examined by a professional surveyor, with his square and rule and plumb-line,—he has at least raised a glittering and fantastic temple, where we may wander about, and delightedly lose ourselves while gazing on the exquisite pictures which every here and there hang on its sunbright walls—the statues and flowervases which ornament its painted niches—the delicious prospects opening upon us from its arabesque windows—and the sweet airs and romantic music which come about us when we mount upon its pleasant battlements. And it cannot be denied that the fabric is at least as well adapted to the airy and fanciful beings who dwell in it, as a regular Epic Palace—with its grand geometrical staircases, its long dreary galleries, its lofty state apartments, and it numerous *sleeping-rooms*—is to its kings and heroes.

The whole of the foregoing extracts are taken from the first and the beginning of the second book. We had marked numerous others through the rest of the work; but the little space that we have left for quotations must be given to a few of the fancies, images, and detached thoughts and similes—the pictures, statues, flowers, &c.—which form the mere ornaments of the building, and are scattered here and there, almost at random.

The little cabinet gems which follow may take their place in any collection. The first might have been cut out of a picture by Salvator:

Echoing grottos, full of tumbling waves
And moonlight. p. 25.

The next we can fancy to have formed a part of one of Claude's delicious skies. It is Venus ascending from the earth.

————At these words up flew
The impatient doves, up rose the floating
car,
Up went the hum celestial. High afar
The Latmian saw them 'minish into
nought.

The third reminds us of a sublime picture of the Deluge, by Poussin. It is a lover who loses his mistress, he knows not how, and afterwards, while swimming, finds her dead body floating in the sea.

Upon a dead thing's face my hand I laid;
I look'd—'twas Scylla———————
—————Cold, O cold indeed
Were her fair limbs, *and like a common
weed*
The sea-swell took her hair.

The fourth picture has all the voluptuous beauty of Titian:

Do not those curls of glossy jet surpass
For tenderness the arms so idly lain
Amongst them? Feelest not a kindred
pain,
To see such lovely eyes in swimming search
After some warm delight, *that seems to*

perch
Dovelike in the dim cell lying beyond
Their upper lids?

The following are a few of the wild flowers of Fancy that are scatter'd up and down.

When last the wintry gusts gave over strife
With the conquering sun of spring, and
left the skies
Warm and serene, *but yet with moistened*
eyes
In pity of the shatter'd infant buds—

A brook running between mossy stones

'Mong which it gurgled blythe adieus, to
mock
Its own sweet grief at parting.
The little flowers felt his pleasant sighs,
And stirr'd them faintly.

LOVER'S TALE.

———And then there ran
Two bubbling springs of talk from their
sweet lips.

The following are a few of the detached thoughts which float about like clouds, taking their form and colour from the position and the medium through which they are seen.

SUPPOSED EMPLOYMENTS OF DISEM–
BODIED SPIRITS.

—————To nightly call
Vesper, the beauty-crest of summer wea-
ther;
To summon all the downiest clouds together
For the sun's purple couch:———
To tint her pallid cheek with bloom, who
cons
Sweet poesy by moon-light.

A POET.

———One who through this middle
earth should pass
Most like a sojourning demi-god, *and leave*
His name upon the harp-string.

THE END OF UNREQUITED LOVE.

And then the ballad of his sad life closes
With sighs, and an alas!

LOVE.

———Awfully he stands,——
No sight can bear the lightning of his bow;
His quiver is mysterious, none can know
What themselves think of it.———
A scowl is sometimes on his brow, but who
Look full upon it feel anon the blue
Of his fair eyes run liquid through their
souls.

REMEMBRANCE OF PAST YEARS.

—————Is it then possible
To look so plainly through them? to dispel
A thousand years with backward glance
sublime?
To breathe away as 'twere all scummy
slime
From off a crystal pool, to see its deep,
And one's own image from the bottom
peep?

The following similes are as new as they are beautiful:

———his eyelids
Widened a little, as when Zephyr bids
A little breeze to creep between the fans
Of careless butterflies.

———As delicious wine doth, sparkling,
 dive
In nectar'd clouds and curls through water
 fair,
So from the arbour roof down swell'd an air
Odorous and enlivening.
 —————like taper-flame
Left sudden by a dallying breath of air,
He rose in silence.

One more cluster of beautiful thoughts, fancies, and images meeting together, and one example of a totally different style of composition,—and we have done with quotations. The first is part of an address to the Moon, by the poet in his own character: [Quotes III.42-71].

If there be such a thing as inspiration, breathed forth by the forms and influences of the external world, and echoed back again from the inner shrine of the poet's breast—this is it. The image of the wren, is, in its kind, not to be surpassed in the whole circle of poetry. We remember nothing equal to it, except Burns's morning picture, which is an exact companion to it, and probably suggested it.

Just when the lark,
'Twixt light and dark,
Awakens, by the daisy's side.

Our last extract shall be part of a song, supposed to be sung by an Indian maid, who has wandered far away from her own native streams: [Quotes IV.146-63; 182-7; 279-90].

This is, to be sure

 —————Silly sooth,
And dallies with the innocence of grief;

but it is very touching and pathetic, nevertheless. Perhaps we like it the better from its reminding us (we do not very well know why) of two little elegies that are especially favourites with us,—one by Chatterton, beginning "O sing unto my roundelay;"— and the other by Kirke White, "Edwy, Edwy, ope thine eye!" It was perhaps suggested by Fletcher's divine song to Melancholy, in the Passionate Madman.

We cannot refrain from asking, is it credible that the foregoing extracts are taken, almost at random, from a work in which a writer in the most popular—we will say *deservedly* the most popular—critical journal of the day, has been unable to discover any thing worthy to redeem it from mere contempt? Those who have the most respect for the Quarterly Review will feel most pain at seeing its pages disgraced by such an article as that to which we allude. Almost anywhere else it would have been harmless, and unworthy of particular notice; but *there* it cannot fail to gain a certain degree of credit from the company which it keeps. It would be foolish to doubt or to deny the extensive effect which such an article is likely to produce, appearing as it does in a work which is read by tens of thousands, nine-tenths of whom are not able to judge for themselves, and half of the other tenth will not take the trouble of doing so. Its chief mischief, however, is likely to take effect on the poet himself, whose work is the subject of it. Next to the necessity of pouring forth that which is within him, the strongest active principle in the mind of a young poet is the love of fame. Not fame weighed and meted out by the scales of strict justice. Not fame, properly so called. But *mere* fame—mere praise and distinction. He loves it for itself alone. During a certain period, this love exists almost in the form of an instinct in a poet's nature; and seems to be given him for the purpose of urging or leading him on to that "hereafter" which is to follow. If it is not the food and support of his poetical life, it is at least the *stimulus* without which that life would be but too apt to flag and faulter in its appointed course.

The same reasons which make it unnecessary to point out the peculiar faults of this work, make it difficult, if not impossible, to state its peculiar beauties as a whole, in any other than general terms. And, even so, we may exhaust all the common-places of criticism in talking about the writer's active and fertile imagination, his rich and lively fancy, his strong and acute sensibility, and so forth,—without advancing one step towards characterising the work which all these together have produced: because, though the writer possesses all these qualities in an eminent degree, his poetical character has not yet taken up any tangible or determinate ground. So that, though we know of no poetical work which differs from all others more than Endymion does, yet its distinguishing feature is perhaps nothing more than that exuberant spirit of youth,—that transport of imagination, fancy, and sensibility—which gushes forth from every part, in a glittering shower of words, and a confused and shadowy pomp of thoughts and images, creating and hurrying each other along like waves of the sea. And there is no egotism in all this, and no affectation. The poet offers himself up a willing sacrifice to the power which he serves: not fretting under, but exulting and glorying in his bondage. He plunges into the ocean of Poetry before he has learned to stem and grapple with the waves; but they "bound beneath him as a steed that knows its rider;" and will not let him sink. Still, however, while they bear him along triumphantly, it is, evidently, at *their* will and pleasure, not at his. He "rides on the whirlwind" safely; but he cannot yet "direct the storm."

We have spoken of this work as being richer in promise than any other that we are acquainted with, except those of Chatterton. It by no means follows that we confidently anticipate the fulfilment of that promise to its utmost extent. We are not without our fears that it may be like that flush of April blossoms which our fine soil almost always sends forth, but which our cloudy and uncertain skies as often prevent from arriving at maturity. Notwithstanding the many living poets that we possess, the times in which we live are essentially unpoetical; and powerful and resolute indeed must that spirit be, which, even in its youth, can escape their influence. When the transports of enthusiasm are gone by, it can hardly dare hope to do so. It must submit to let "the years bring on the inevitable yoke." This has been one strong inducement for us to notice the young writer before us; and we cannot conclude these slight and desultory remarks without entreating him not to be cast down or turned aside from the course which nature has marked out for him. He is and must be a poet—and he may be a great one. But let him never be tempted to disregard this first evidence of that power which at present rules over him—much less affect to do so: and least of all let him wish or attempt to make it any thing but what it is. Nothing can ever tame and polish this wild and wayward firstling, and make it fit to be introduced to "mixed company;" but let him not therefore be ashamed to cherish and claim it for his own. He may live to see himself surrounded by a flourishing family, endowed with all sorts of polite accomplishments, and able not only to make their own way in the world, but to further *his* fortunes too. But *this*—the first-born of his hopes—the child of his youth—whatever he may say or think to the contrary—must ever be the favourite. He may admire those which are to come, and pride himself upon them; but he will never love them as he has loved this; he will never again watch over the infancy and growth of another with such full and unmixed delight: for *this* was born while his muse was his mistress, and he her rapturous lover. He will marry her by and bye—or perhaps he has already—and then he may chance to lover her *better* than ever; but he will cease to be *her lover.*

BIBLIOGRAPHY OF REFERENCES CITED

Abrams, M. H. "The Correspondent Breeze: A Romantic Metaphor," in *English Romantic Poets.* New York: Oxford University Press, 1960, 37-54.

Abrams[2]. *The Mirror and the Lamp: Romantic Theory and the Critical Tradition.* New York: Norton, 1958.

Allen, Glen O. "The Fall of Endymion: A Study of Keats's Intellectual Growth." *Keats-Shelley Journal,* VI (1957), 37-57.

Allott, Miriam, ed. *The Poems of John Keats.* London: Longman, 1970.

Apuleius. *The Golden Ass.* Trans. Jack Lindsay, Bloomington: Indiana University Press, 1932.

Baldwin, Edward. *The Pantheon.* 2nd ed., London, 1809.

Bate, Walter Jackson. *John Keats.* Cambridge, Mass.: Harvard University Press, 1963.

Bate[2]. *The Stylistic Development of Keats.* New York: Humanities Press, 1958.

Berger, Harry, Jr. "Spenser's Gardens of Adonis: Force and Form in the Renaissance Imagination," *University of Toronto Quarterly,* XXX (1961), 128-49.

Beyer, Werner. *Keats and the Daemon King.* New York: Oxford University Press, 1947.

Blackstone, Bernard. *The Consecrated Urn: An Interpretation of Keats in Terms of Growth and Form.* London: Longmans, Green, 1959.

Blake, William. *The Poetry and Prose of William Blake.* Ed. David Erdman, Garden City: Doubleday, 1965.

Bloom, Harold. *Poetry and Repression: Revisionism from Blake to Stevens.* New Haven: Yale University Press, 1976.

Bloom[2]. *The Ringers of the Tower: Studies in Romantic Tradition.* Chicago: University of Chicago Press, 1971.

Bloom[3]. *The Visionary Company: A Reading of English Romantic Poetry.* Garden City: Doubleday, 1961.

Bloom[4]. *Yeats.* New York: Oxford University Press, 1970.

Bradley, A. C. "The Letters of Keats," in *Oxford Lectures on Poetry.* 1909; rpt. London: Macmillan, 1959, 209-44.

Bridges, Robert. "A Critical Introduction to Keats," in *Collected Essays.* London: Oxford University Press, IV, 1929, 85-93.

Brisman, Leslie. *Milton's Poetry of Choice and Its Romantic Heirs.* Ithaca, New York: Cornell University Press, 1973.

Brisman[2]. *Romantic Origins.* Ithaca, New York: Cornell University Press, 1978.

Brown, Leonard. "The Genesis, Growth, and Meaning of 'Endymion,' " *Studies in Philology.* XXX (1933), 618-53.

Browne, William. *Poems.* Ed. G. Goodwin, London: Lawrence and Bullen, I, 1894.

Bush, Douglas. *John Keats.* New York: Macmillan, 1966.

Bush[2]. "Keats and His Ideas," in *English Romantic Poets.* Ed. M. H. Abrams, New York: Oxford University Press, 1960, 326-39.

Bush[3]. *Mythology and the Romantic Tradition in English Poetry.* 1937; rpt. New York: Norton, 1969.

Bush[4]. ed. *Selected Poems and Letters of John Keats.* Boston: Houghton Mifflin, 1959.

Chatterjee, Bhabatosh. "Echoes of Cary's Dante in Endymion," *Notes and Queries.* 14 (Jan., 1967), 23.

Clarke, Charles Cowden. *Recollections of Writers.* 1878; rpt. Sussex: Centaur Press, 1969.

Coleridge, Samuel Taylor. *The Poems of Samuel Taylor Coleridge.* Ed. Ernest Hartley Coleridge, London: Oxford University Press, 1931.

Colvin, Sidney. *John Keats: His Life and Poetry, His Friends, Critics and After-fame.* New York: Scribners, 1925.

D'Avanzo, Mario. *Keats's Metaphors for the Poetic Imagination.* Durham, North Carolina: Duke University Press, 1967.

De Man, Paul. "Keats and Holderlin," *Comparative Literature.* VIII (winter, 1956), 28-45.

De Selincourt, Ernest. ed. *The Poems of John Keats.* New York: Dodd, Mead, 1905.

Dickstein, Morris. *Keats and His Poetry.* Chicago: University of Chicago Press, 1971.

Drayton, Michael. *The Works of Michael Drayton.* Ed. J. William Hebel, 4 vols., Oxford: Blackwell, 1931.

Eliade, Mircea. *Patterns in Comparative Religion.* New York: New American Library, 1963.

Ende, Stuart A. *Keats and the Sublime.* New Haven: Yale University Press, 1976.

Finney, Claude Lee. *The Evolution of Keats's Poetry.* Cambridge, Mass.: Harvard University Press, I, 1936.

Fletcher, Angus. *The Prophetic Moment: An Essay on Spenser.* Chicago: University of Chicago Press, 1971.

Fogle, Richard Harter. *The Imagery of Keats and Shelley: A Comparative Study.* Chapel Hill: University of North Carolina Press, 1949.

Ford, Newell F. "*Endymion*—A Neo-Platonic Allegory?" *Journal of English Literary History.* 14 (1947), 64-75.

Ford[2]. "The Meaning of 'Fellowship with Essence' in *Endymion*," PMLA. 62 (Dec., 1947), 1061-76.

Ford[3]. *The Prefigurative Imagination of John Keats.* London: Oxford University Press, 1951.

Frye, Northrop. *Anatomy of Criticism: Four Essays.* Princeton: Princeton University Press, 1957.

Frye[2]. "Charms and Riddles," in *Spiritus Mundi: Essays on Literature, Myth, and Society.* Bloomington: Indiana University Press, 1976, 123-47.

Frye[3]. *Fearful Symmetry: A Study of William Blake.* Princeton: Princeton University Press, 1947.

Frye[4]. *A Natural Perspective: The Development of Shakespearean Comedy and Romance.* New York: Harcourt, Brace and World, 1965.

Frye[5]. "New Directions from Old," in *Fables of Identity: Studies in Poetic Mythology.* New York: Harcourt, Brace and World, 1963, 52-68.

Frye[6]. *A Study of English Romanticism.* New York: Random House, 1968.

Garrod, H. W. *Keats.* Oxford: Clarendon Press, 1926.

Garrod[2]. ed. *The Poetical Works of John Keats.* 2nd ed. London: Oxford University Press, 1958.

Giovannini, G. "Keats' Elysium of Poets," *Modern Language Notes.* LXIII (1948), 19-25.

Gittings, Robert. *John Keats.* London: Heinemann, 1968.

Gittings[2]. "Keats and Chatterton," *Keats-Shelley Journal.* IV (winter, 1955), 48-54.

Godfrey, Clarisse. "*Endymion*," in *John Keats: A Reassessment.* Ed. Kenneth Muir, Liverpool: Liverpool University Press, 1958, 20-38.

Grundy, Joan. "Keats and the Elizabethans," in *John Keats: A Reassess-*

ment. Ed. Kenneth Muir, Liverpool: Liverpool University Press, 1958, 1-19.

Guy, E. G. "Keats's Use of 'Luxury': A Note on Meaning," *Keats-Shelley Journal.* XIII (winter, 1964), 87-94.

Hartman, Geoffrey H. *Beyond Formalism: Literary Essays 1958-1970.* New Haven: Yale University Press, 1970.

Hartman[2]. *The Fate of Reading and Other Essays.* Chicago: University of Chicago Press, 1975.

Hartman[3]. *Wordsworth's Poetry, 1787-1814.* New Haven: Yale University Press, 1964.

Jack, Ian. *Keats and the Mirror of Art.* London: Oxford University Press, 1967.

James, D. G. *Scepticism and Poetry: An Essay on the Poetic Imagination.* London: George Allen, 1937.

Jones, John. *John Keats's Dream of Truth.* New York: Barnes and Noble, 1969.

Knight, G. Wilson. "The Priest-like Task: An Essay on Keats," in *The Starlit Dome: Studies in the Poetry of Vision.* 1941; rpt. London: Oxford University Press, 1971, 258-307.

Le Comte, Edward S. *Endymion in England: The Literary History of a Greek Myth.* New York: King's Crown Press, 1944.

Lempriere, J. *A Classical Dictionary.* London: Routledge and Sons, 1812.

Lowell, Amy. *John Keats.* Boston: Houghton Mifflin, I, 1925.

Matthews, G. M. ed. *Keats, the Critical Heritage.* New York: Barnes and Noble, 1971.

Miller, Bruce E. "On the Meaning of Keats's *Endymion,*" *Keats-Shelley Journal.* XIV (winter, 1965), 33-54.

Milton, John. *The Poems of John Milton.* Ed. John Carey and Alastair

Fowler, New York: Norton, 1968.

Murry, John Middleton. *Keats.* Revision of *Studies in Keats,* 1930; New York: Noonday Press, 1962.

Murry[2]. *Keats and Shakespeare: A Study of Keats' Poetic Life from 1816 to 1820.* London: Oxford University Press, 1925.

Notcutt, H. Clement. *An Interpretation of Keats's Endymion.* 1919; rpt. New York: Haskell House, 1964.

Owen, F. M. *John Keats: A Study.* London: Paul, 1880.

Patterson, Charles I., Jr. *The Daemonic in the Poetry of John Keats.* Urbana: University of Illinois Press, 1970.

Perkins, David and Clarence Thorpe. "Keats," in *The English Romantic Poets: A Review of Research and Criticism.* Ed. Frank Jordan, 3rd ed., New York: *MLA*, 1972.

Perkins[2]. *The Quest for Permanence: The Symbolism of Wordsworth, Shelley, and Keats.* Cambridge, Mass.: Harvard University Press, 1959.

Pettet, E. C. *On the Poetry of Keats.* London: Cambridge University Press, 1957.

Porphyry. "The Cave of the Nymphs," in *Philosophical and Mathematical Commentaries of Proclus.* Ed. Thomas Taylor, London, II, 1789, 278-307.

Puttenham, George. *The Arte of English Poesie.* Reprod. of 1906 rpt., Kent, Ohio: Kent State University Press, 1970.

Reiman, Donald H. ed. *The Romantics Reviewed: Contemporary Reviews of British Romantic Writers.* New York: Garland, pt. C, I & II, 1972.

Ricks, Christopher. *Keats and Embarrassment.* London: Oxford University Press, 1974.

Rollins, Hyder Edward. ed. *The Keats Circle: Letters and Papers, 1816-1878.* 2 vols. Cambridge, Mass.: Harvard University Press, 1948.

Rollins[2]. ed. *The Letters of John Keats.* 2 vols. Cambridge, Mass.: Harvard University Press, 1958.

Saintsbury, George. *A History of English Prosody: From the Twelfth Century to the Present Day.* London: Macmillan, III, 1923.

Sandys, George. *Ovid's Metamorphosis Englished, Mythologiz'd, and Represented in Figures.* Oxford, 1632.

Shakespeare, William. *The Complete Works.* Ed. Alfred Herbage, Baltimore: Penguin, 1969.

Shelley, Percy Bysshe. *Poetical Works.* Ed. G. M. Matthews, London: Oxford University Press, 1970.

Spense, Joseph. *Polymetis.* London: R. Dodsley, 1747.

Spenser, Edmund. *Poetical Works.* Ed. J. C. Smith and E. de Selincourt, London: Oxford University Press, 1912.

Sperry, Stuart M. "The Allegory of *Endymion,*" *Studies in Romanticism.* II (1962), 38-53.

Sperry[2]. *Keats The Poet.* Princeton: Princeton University Press, 1973.

Spurgeon, Caroline F. E. *Keats's Shakespeare.* London: Oxford University Press, 1928.

Stillinger, Jack. *The Hoodwinking of Madeline and Other Essays on Keats.* Urbana: University of Illinois Press, 1971.

Stillinger[2]. ed. *The Poems of John Keats.* Cambridge, Mass.: Harvard University Press, 1978.

Swinburne, Algernon Charles. *Complete Works.* London: Heinemann, XIV, 1926, 295-302.

Thorpe, Clarence Dewitt. *The Mind of John Keats.* 1926; rpt., New York: Russell and Russell, 1964.

Trilling, Lionel. "The Fate of Pleasure," in *Romanticism Reconsidered.* Ed. Northrop Frye, New York: Columbia University Press, 1968, 73-106.

Trilling[2]. "The Poet as Hero: Keats in His Letters," in *The Opposing Self.* New York: Viking Press, 1955, 3-49.

Van Ghent, Dorothy. "Keats's Myth of the Hero," *Keats-Shelley Journal.* III (winter, 1954), 7-25.

Wasserman, Earl. *The Finer Tone: Keats's Major Poems.* Baltimore: John Hopkins Press, 1953.

Wigod, Jacob D. "The Meaning of *Endymion*," *PMLA*. 68 (1953), 779-90.

Wordsworth, William. *Poetical Works.* Ed. Thomas Hutchinson and E. de Selincourt, London: Oxford University Press, 1936.